THE
PERFORMANCE
MINDSET

THE
PERFORMANCE
MINDSET

7 STEPS TO SUCCESS IN SPORT AND LIFE

ANTHONY J. KLARICA

WILEY

First published in 2022 by John Wiley & Sons Australia, Ltd

42 McDougall St, Milton Qld 4064
Office also in Melbourne

Typeset in Palatino LT Std 11pt/15pt

© John Wiley & Sons Australia, Ltd 2022

The moral rights of the author have been asserted.

ISBN: 978-0-730-39468-6

A catalogue record for this
book is available from the
National Library of Australia

Cover design by Wiley
Cover Image: © Supersmario/Getty Images

Disclaimer

SKYFE8BB055-6E5A-4FD3-91D8-A030D58793B9_051222

CONTENTS

CONTENTS

ABOUT THE AUTHOR

Anthony J Klarica is passionate about people and their performance and wellbeing. He has been heavily involved in sport all his life, starting at a young age. He has competed in athletics, tennis, cricket, Australian rules football, triathlon, endurance events and many other sports from social to high level. He has also been a track and field coach and coached a running squad, The Nail, with athletes who achieved high performance levels and became lifelong friends.

Professionally, Anthony has worked for over 30 years as a psychologist, coach and high-performance manager in a wide variety of sports. He has worked with AFL teams, including Melbourne, Carlton as well as Hawthorn during their Grand Final three-peat, the AFL umpiring squad, a wide variety of motorsports including V8 Supercar drivers, road and off-road motorbike riders, tennis players and a wide variety of Olympic sport organisations and individual athletes. He has travelled extensively to work with individual athletes and teams at state and national events, world championships and Olympics. He has sat in coaches boxes and been on the interchange with players at football matches, attended Grand Slams and spent time in the pit lane to apply his trade. This has involved consulting and coaching in leadership, culture, wellbeing, performance and one-on-one counselling over many years, mainly through his Melbourne-based business, Elite Performance.

He is a lifelong learner with an undergraduate degree in education and master's degrees in psychology and business, and has attended many short courses and workshops along the way. He has consulted on and delivered many workshops and presentations in the education and corporate sectors as well as sport. This work was built on the foundation of being a teacher and psychologist in a variety of settings, including working as a psychologist in schools, in industrial rehabilitation and a hospital setting.

Through his extensive work in education, he also founded the Six-Star Wellbeing and Engagement Survey, which has been used by more than 45 000 students and teachers in primary and secondary schools across Australia and workers in corporate settings, and is now distributed by the Australian Council for Education Research (ACER).

Anthony still engages in a range of sports. He is an avid runner and trains regularly in the pool, at the gym and on the bike.

The Performance Mindset is a summation of his education, passion for learning and experience participating and working in many sports and other fields.

ACKNOWLEDGEMENTS

The Performance Mindset would never have been written without the encouragement and inspiration of my fantastic support team. I have benefited immeasurably from informal inspiration too, including from people who aren't even aware of the motivation and energy they provided. This extends to the many athletes, coaches, teams and general clients I have worked and been associated with over a career spanning more than 30 years. You are all a big part of this project and I thank you.

Closer to home, I thank my parents for their support, and the ongoing day-to-day support of my wife Johanna and our children Alister, Annabelle and Penelope who made this project possible.

Words of encouragement from friends never go astray. They created the energy I needed to start this book and keep going to the finish line. There are too many to mention here, but Philip Whelan and Craig Millar in particular have assisted more than they know. Helen Pitt, Merv Jackson and Greg Murphy have also been a great help and support. Thank you to Phil Whelan and Darren Gray for providing informed feedback on the manuscript, to Jedd Dow for assisting with referencing, and to Darren McMurtrie for working on the statistics and data. It was a team effort. Thank you.

Without a publisher this project would not have eventuated. To Lucy Raymond, Leigh McLennan and the team at John Wiley & Sons, thank you for taking on the project and guiding me through it.

I am exceedingly grateful to the amazing athletes and coaches who willingly gave their time and accepted invitations to be interviewed for the book. Their stories, insights and reflections not only confirmed the importance of a performance mindset, but also provided me with a source of inspiration. I am not sure I have done justice to their stories but I cannot thank them enough. Each of their stories is itself worthy of a book and several have authored or had books written about them. They are:

Youcef Abdi (athletics)

David Andersen (basketball)

Dean Boxall (swimming)

Jacqui Cooper (aerial skiing)

Scott Draper (tennis and golf)

Tayla Harris (Australian rules football)

Mat Hayman (cycling)

Sam Mitchell (Australian rules football)

Brigitte Muir (mountaineering)

Sasa Ognenovski (soccer)

Nicole Pratt (tennis)

Michael Ritter (motorsport)

Storm Sanders (tennis)

Garth Tander (motorsport)

Rohan Taylor (swimming)

Liz Watson (netball)

Jamie Whincup (motorsport)

PREFACE

Australia is a sport-loving nation. Our opportunities to be actively involved in sport are abundant. Beyond participation, many people follow and support their favourite athletes, teams or sport with great passion. For our nation's size, Olympic and other international sporting performances are impressive, especially considering the range of professional sports codes women and men participate in.

The Performance Mindset evolved from my experience over 30 years of working with many sports and individual athletes in Australia. In that time, interest in the mental space of sport has grown significantly. Antiquated views that saw athletes simply as either 'weak' or 'strong' have been overtaken by a greater understanding of what is involved in maximising performance. A common perception is that talent and hard work are the only, or at least the key, prerequisites for high performance in sport. There is, however, another vital ingredient — *mindset*.

From my experience, I know that while talent and hard work are extremely relevant, they are not the foundation of performance. What underpins an athlete's performance is their mindset. As well as contributing to work rate, mindset is the key to unlocking any talent a person may possess.

In this book I explore a range of factors that influence mindset, including:

- environmental (socio-cultural and contextual influences on people, including access to resources, support, opportunities, and the culture of a squad, team, organisation or even a nation)

- social (how people interact and deal with their environment, situations and others, as well as how they use resources, including the role of coaches and supports)

- personal (how people think, feel and behave).

Naturally, the above overlap and interact. Importantly, I emphasise that mindset skills can be *learned*. They can be learned in many ways, beginning with a willingness to embrace mindset concepts. This learning is both intuitive and the result of overt focus and coaching. My goal is that *performance mindset skills* be learned from deliberate engagement in some of the processes I examine in this book.

The introduction puts forward a case for mental skills being the foundation of performance. Each of the seven 'steps' that follow explores a specific mindset topic: motivation, resilience, focus, leadership, culture, wellbeing and performance. I believe these topics are central to and contribute fundamentally to a mindset that enables maximum performance.

To gain insight into these important areas, I interviewed a wide range of amazing performers and athletes, as well as outstanding coaches, who willingly shared stories and experiences from their own journeys. Some of these stories are referred to across several chapters; others are presented in stand-alone features.

To balance these real-life examples, I have drawn on empirical research from the field of psychology and collected information from publications, documentaries and even social media. Additionally, I have offered some of my own thoughts, models, strategies, program examples, checklists and activities from my work in performance and other fields. At the end of each step I have included a 'build' section that lists practical strategies.

Ideas around performance clearly extend beyond sport. I see a performance mindset as applicable to many fields beyond sport and as relevant for anyone interested in improving their performance. Athletes, coaches, parents, teachers or people working in or just interested in sport may enjoy and benefit from the pages ahead. I hope people in other fields interested in performance may also profit from what is presented. While the concepts examined through the book are interrelated, each step may be read as a stand-alone topic.

One of the fascinating aspects of performance and human behaviour is how powerful the mind is. Also interesting is how individual a path to higher performance can be. This book sets out to inspire and upskill readers to develop their own performance mindset. Whether or not you agree with the ideas and philosophies put forward, I hope you gain some benefit and enjoyment from reading *The Performance Mindset*.

INTRODUCTION

MADE NOT BORN

Yes, you need a certain level of talent or innate skill, coordination and physical aptitude that are, at least in part, a product of your genetic code to become an athlete, but not as much as you might think. You also need to work relentlessly, investing hours, weeks, months and years, to realise any talent. But mindset is the key that unlocks talent, allowing you to remain engaged and committed to any practice to maximise this talent. Without a finely tuned mindset, the work doesn't happen. It also enables performance when it counts. Mindset is the cornerstone because it both contributes to doing the work and, once the work is done, helps to realise the talent and work. It's also important to understand that a performance mindset can be learned.

Laying a mindset foundation

Many environmental, social and personal factors contribute to mindset. It is about how a person thinks, feels and behaves in a wide range of situations, as well as how environmental and social situations are managed. Mindset also influences behaviour, sustaining motivation and focus, being resilient, decision making in and out of a sport, and managing personal wellbeing and relationships. A *performance mindset* is about having an attitude and toolkit of mental performance skills to help development and then perform at competitions. These skills are relevant not only in sport, but in spheres such as study, work and other activities. Here I want to explain why mindset is the foundation of performance. The chapters, or steps, that follow discuss how to build your performance mindset.

In most sports, a foundation of skill development, practice and conditioning is best laid in early years, which typically coincide with teenage life and early adulthood. Attitude and mental skills formed at this stage complement physical development and contribute to future performance. Mindset *after* an initial general technical and physical foundation is laid is vital, yet often overlooked. It helps to sustain motivation, deal with transition phases and capitalise on any initial work done. This is important because in sport, as in many fields in life, there are constant changes and new challenges. Being a high-performing junior with elite talent is *not* a ticket to being a successful athlete in an open career. Don't be demoralised if you're not at the top of the ladder when you are 16, 18 or even 20. A commitment to building and sustaining a performance mindset is the biggest contributing factor for further development and performance.

Early success does not guarantee future success

Tennis is a global sport that draws an estimated 60 to 85 million players. There are about 160 000 coaches and almost half a million tennis courts around the world. A wide range of factors other than talent contribute to becoming a top 50 tennis player. For many weeks of the year, junior tournaments brim with young players hoping to forge a career in the big time. Four times a year, 32 of the best juniors qualify to play in the junior Grand Slam tournaments around the world: the Australian Open in Melbourne, the French Open at Roland Garros in Paris, Wimbledon in London or the US Open played at Flushing Meadows in New York.

Reviewing 10 years of junior Grand Slam finalists from 2001 to 2010 is fascinating. The top two from any of these tournaments are rated as among the top junior players in the world at that time. From this achievement and standing, one would expect that on average they would go on to become at least top 50 players in the world at any stage in their career in open tennis. But that's not the case.

Of all the junior male Grand Slam finalists from 2001 to 2010, the average career-high ranking was 126 (not including two players who did not achieve a ranking inside 1000). Of all the junior female Grand Slam finalists from 2001 to 2010 the average career-high ranking was 65. This data includes the players who did go on to become world number one. (In my review of the careers of 10 years of junior Grand Slam finalists I have not included 2011 onwards. This was to make data more valid by taking into account that players who played in a junior Grand Slam final after 2010 may have still not reached their peak ranking.) You would imagine that such data would sway the total pool to more players reaching at least a top 50 rank at some stage in their career. But it doesn't — so why not?

Keep in mind that a junior Grand Slam finalist is likely to attract greater support and encouragement from their national tennis federations or sponsors through funding, coaching or other means. This support would likely contribute to an increased opportunity to transition from a top junior to top 50 in an open career.

Naturally the answer to why more junior stars do not progress as high as one would expect is complex, and every sport has its own nuances. Some juniors win based on early physical maturity. In tennis this is negated somewhat by the relative importance of the skill component. Tennis players also travel for many weeks of the year to accumulate points and earn prize money as income.

This is often with limited support or financial security, particularly for players outside the top 150 in the world. Injury and access to resources, including coaching, also impact possible progression. And as players transition from junior to open tennis, their competitors tend to be older, physically more developed and more experienced. This indicates that opponents in a one-on-one battle could have the advantage of 10 years' training, conditioning, maturity and mental skill development. Athletes in many sports transition from being top of the tree as a junior to a drop in results or selection when they join open ranks. Winning can be tough and they can face stretches with few victories, compared with their junior competition experience. Having been to junior Grand Slams around the world, I can vouch that some seriously good players are reaching finals. With some of the challenges mentioned, however, it is apparent that a performance mindset is necessary to convert a successful junior career to an open one.

It takes a particular mental fortitude to persist with the lifestyle of an athlete and, with the prospect of an insecure future, to chase their goal of becoming a top 50 or top 100 player in the world, let alone reaching the top 10 or number one. Mindset becomes a determining factor to capitalising on the initial foundation laid. Dealing with losing on the open tour, being patient when progress is slow, and sustaining motivation, commitment and work rate are all challenging. And they all involve mindset. I've found this a very common story — and not just in world-class tennis.

The mindset to keep going

A challenge to developing a high-performing open athlete is appreciating how individual the journey is. It is not a linear progression. Athletes, like everyone pursuing an endeavour, have different personal characteristics and backgrounds, and come from different geographical regions with varying support bases. Support, opportunities and even luck all play a role in the roller-coaster path of sporting progression. Recognising and appreciating that each athlete's journey is unique and that there are many paths to achieving goals can aid persistence and development.

Ashleigh Barty, the world number one female tennis player in 2021, is an example of how challenges need to be overcome to keep going in sport. After winning Junior Wimbledon in 2011 and making the finals of open Grand Slam doubles events in 2013, Barty took a break from her sport in 2015. It was a bold move that many athletes would struggle to make. She stopped playing tennis and played cricket. However, after time away and likely with a fresh mindset, she returned to tennis in 2016 aged 20. Even then it wasn't smooth sailing. She lost in the qualifying rounds of Wimbledon in 2016 and in 2017 lost in the first round.

To facilitate Ash's return to tennis from cricket, she moved to a new base in Melbourne and began an individualised program. In her transition, she was supported and coached by the highly regarded Jason Stoltenberg, himself a former Wimbledon men's singles semifinalist. Ash then began working with her current coach, Craig Tyzzer, who was also very experienced. Her new schedule was flexible and her support network were patient and encouraging. The relationship between Craig and Ash went from strength to strength. These factors contributed to her being able to capitalise on her original foundation of work. After three years back on tour she climbed to the top of the sporting mountain and won the French Open in 2019, Wimbledon in 2021 and her home Australian Open in 2022. We'll never know what might have happened had she not taken the break and the path back that she did.

Attitude nurtures talent

Ash's doubles partner at the 2021 Tokyo Olympic Games, Storm Sanders, experienced a very different path to realising her goal of representing Australia. Storm was not a junior slam winner. Of the four junior slams she did play, including two in Australia, she had a best result of third round. Due to a limited number of junior tournaments her best junior ranking was 55. Storm grew up about an hour from Perth playing a variety of sports, including soccer, gymnastics and surfing, as well as different sports at school. 'I never got selected for a state team, as I was only about the fourth or fifth best in Western Australia. I didn't win things or get sponsorship as a junior,' she reflected when I interviewed her.

'I honestly don't believe I have that much raw talent,' Storm said. 'My talent is to stick to everything I do and commit, day in day out. It ended up helping me because I realised I had to go about it my own way. For three years I set my alarm and regularly got up at 5 am, caught the train an hour into Perth to practise in the morning, then back home to get to school, and repeat in the afternoon. If my parents drove me, it still took 45 minutes each way. I recognise now I was behind in my tennis development, especially because I didn't play as many tournaments as others due to my circumstances. As a result of this I developed more mental skills than my peers at that time. I think it enabled me to have a career and a lot of the other people ahead of me then have now stopped.'

Storm's attitude ultimately assisted her career progression. 'I remember going for a hit with a junior male player during the Hopman Cup in Perth when I was 15. It was super-hot, but we kept working through the session. Because of the timing, a few courts down former player and now coach Nicole Pratt was working with Australian player Alicia Molik. She must have noticed us because she came over to speak to me when they finished. She was impressed with how I went about it. There was no coach there. I was running my own session, being independent. She said she was so impressed with my attitude that she would like to help me. I got invited to go to Melbourne for a week to hit and the following year I was invited to an academy there and moved to Melbourne. I had just finished year 11 in Perth, but once in Melbourne I made sure I finished year 12.'

The transition wasn't smooth. After several challenges, including injuries that forced her out of the game for almost a year, and with no ranking in 2018, Storm is now ranked about 120 in the world in singles and 30 in doubles. She has built her game back on the foundation of doubles and in 2021 made the Wimbledon doubles semifinal and US Open doubles quarter-finals, and represented Australia at the Olympics and the Federation Cup (now the Billie Jean King Cup). She began competing in singles again in 2020, effectively starting her singles career in her mid-twenties. It's a career that wasn't built on talent, but on mindset. Ash Barty's and Storm Sanders' stories also reflect the variety of pathways that a sporting career can take. They can be unpredictable, with twists and turns and different talent bases. Using supports, patience and a determined resolve were key mindsets for both athletes that enabled them to advance.

You grow in the direction of your focus

Take another example, this time from a team sport. Sam Mitchell is a retired Australian rules football player who was appointed coach for 2022 of the team he'd had most success with—the Hawthorn Football Club. Hawthorn played in four consecutive Australian Football League (AFL) Grand Finals, winning three in a row from 2013 to 2015. This feat deserves special recognition due to the equalisation policies of player and staff salary caps and drafting policy that the AFL introduced in the late eighties. Since equalisation, 14 teams have won premierships while only two have won three consecutively, which makes the Hawks' achievement even more impressive.

In this winning team, Sam won the AFL Brownlow Medal in 2012. The Brownlow is arguably the game's most prestigious individual honour. It is awarded to the 'best and fairest' player in the entire competition in any given season. By the time he retired in 2017, Sam was the third highest total vote scorer in the history of the medal. He had won four premierships, played the third most games in Hawthorn's history and won five club champion awards.

In addition, Sam captained the club from 2008 to 2010, with '08 yielding a premiership.

What's interesting is that Sam was overlooked altogether in the 2000 draft, then was selected in 2001 with draft pick 36. So, in the year of his draft, he was overlooked by every club in the AFL before he was selected in the third round with Hawthorn's fifth pick.

One strength Sam had was his capacity to kick with either left or right foot. He wasn't especially tall or quick. His endurance wasn't necessarily the greatest either. But he had a reputation for his skill and decision making. His proficiency on both sides of his body was so evident that commentators often remarked on the difficulty of distinguishing which his 'natural' side was. When I interviewed him late in 2021, Sam said, 'We had no sporting background in our family at all. Dad actually bought some books about football to learn the game. When I was quite young, Dad had a person working with him, Bill, who had some experience and skill in football, and he said it would be good to alternate one left-foot kick and one right-foot kick when I went for a kick.' Sam took it as gospel. He adopted the principle, and it stuck. 'I still find it natural to alternate left–right and it actually felt weird right through my career if I had a few kicks on one side of my body before using the other side. It was a learned skill.' Bill's unsolicited advice many years before Sam was drafted helped make him the champion footballer he became. It was a spark that developed one of his key football skills. And his commitment to practice developed this weapon for him.

Regarding talent, Sam said, 'Some genetic factors help, but I think the ratio of importance of talent to development is about 10:90. Skill development hasn't got a lot to do with talent. I believe that if you have long-term commitment, focus and desire, year after year, your development will be strong. Sometimes starting with a lot of talent doesn't help because you become reliant on current skills and don't have to work as hard. You grow in the direction of your focus.'

Is talent overrated?

One interesting insight that arises from Sam's experience is how difficult it is to identify talent or how perceived talent, even at 18, may or may not be realised. Considering the resources, including the experience and expertise of recruiting teams in many sports, identifying future performers remains a challenge. Recruiters and talent scouts need to consider how a future athlete will approach their career once they are drafted as much as or even more than what they have already delivered. Attitude and mindset will determine whether any talent is fully realised and whether they are able to continue to develop.

If we investigate one angle reflecting the challenges, let's look more closely at the Brownlow Medal. Taking into account 19 Brownlows between 1996 and 2021, the average draft selection for the winner was pick 26. (To determine this average, I excluded father/son and zone draft selections as these factors influence where they were selected. Prior to 1996 the draft was not as relevant as today, and players were recruited through zones and other avenues.)

I know some will regard pick 26 as a reasonably high selection. Many diverse factors can also contribute to a prospective winner's chances, such as injury or availability to play, or the team they were selected to and teammates who might draw votes away. It is evident, however, that some of the highest awarded players in the history of the AFL were not recognised at that level at the time of being drafted. Athletes such as Sam Mitchell made themselves into the players they became — through mindset.

That mindset contributed to Sam's left foot–right foot regime, which was one reflection of his determination to achieve his goal of becoming an AFL player. It is even arguable that considering the players who have won the Brownlow as a top 10 draft selection, the feat was achieved on the back of mindset, which enabled them to capitalise on their talent after they were drafted, rather than depending on talent alone. The average number of years that this group had been playing when they won the award is just over seven. This indicates that the length of time to learn and grow is likely a better predictor of a Brownlow winner than draft selection.

Ash, Storm, Sam and the other athletes featured in this book drew on a wide and varied talent base. Even for talented athletes, the path is not straightforward. A forward trajectory is governed by mindset, which in turn contributes to a capacity to learn and grow, as well as do the work required.

> Interesting reading on the topic of talent includes *The Talent Code* by Daniel Coyle, *The Sports Gene* by David Epstein and *Talent Is Overrated* by Geoff Colvin.

Assessing mindset variables

An oft-cited story, due to his stellar career in the American National Football League (NFL), is that of Tom Brady. Brady was drafted at pick 199 in 2000. At the time of writing, he had won more championships as a player than some NFL clubs have won in their entire history. What is less well known about his story is the investment he made as a junior in a football coach with a wealth of experience, Tom Martinez. In his book *The Talent Code*, Daniel Coyle describes how Brady carries in his wallet a list of technique tips learned from the veteran coach and that he has an ongoing relationship with his long-time mentor.[1] In the *Brady 6* documentary, former NFL head coach Steve Mariucci comments on Brady being overlooked by clubs and his low draft pick: 'We didn't open up his chest and look at his heart … and resiliency, and all the things that are making him great now.'[2]

While not identified at his draft as the player he would become, Brady had already invested in a range of ways other than his physical development while a junior that paid him back. Recognising this, Ian O'Connor, reporting for ESPN.com in 2016, wrote an article headlined: 'Tom Brady's greatest talent is his desire to be great.'[3] It's clear that more than talent contributed to his accomplishments.

I have had an insider's view of the AFL draft process, as well as selections of athletes in other sports. Over some 20 years I have been contracted by different AFL clubs and sports to participate in the interview process that supports coaches and recruiters in the selection of athletes. Over that time I have seen the emphasis on personal attributes and qualities grow significantly. Areas that recruiters now consider more than they used to include (in no particular order):

- capacity to learn and grow
- determination and drive
- independence
- capacity as a team member
- competitive spirit
- cultural fit
- general game-day mental skills
- resilience
- wellbeing
- decision making on and off the field
- training attitude and commitment
- coachability.

The growth in consideration of psychological variables in athlete selection processes reflects the increased recognition of the importance of mindset. This consideration also helps support the wellbeing and development of players once selected. In sports, there is more awareness of the support a player may need before they begin. In the recruiting process, references from junior coaches and key support staff are checked. Of course, physical data and testing, injury history, specific sporting IQ, how they play the game and vital information on sport performance history are important and meticulously scrutinised. However, a multitude of other factors have been increasingly recognised as important when assessing whether a player will be able to utilise, and grow from, any talent shown.

One challenge in the selection process of any athlete in any sport is that while physical prowess can easily be tested and compared (it's simple to test how fast an athlete can run or how high they can jump), psychological variables are much harder to determine and rank. They are not as visible, they vary significantly and they are impacted by many factors, which makes mindset much more difficult to identify, compare and project. That many athletes are selected while still developing physically and emotionally adds further complexity. A person at 16 or 18 is often very different from the person they become in their late twenties.

Through the process of considering mindset variables, it is apparent that observed talent is only one variable in future performance. That's why Sam Mitchell and Tom Brady slipped through the top order of the draft net, only for time to reveal their true ability. If they had not been selected at those late picks, their sporting talent might not have been realised. I wonder what they would be doing now if they had been overlooked in their respective drafts.

On this topic, Alex Hutchinson, author of *Endure: mind, body and the curiously elastic limits of human performance*,[4] observes that 'even relying on the best science available, you're inevitably going to pick duds — and perhaps more significantly, miss some athletes with potential to develop into world beaters'.[5]

Research insights

A 2004 study examined 'primary' and 'secondary' influences on sport expertise:

- Primary influences include genetics, training and psychological factors.
- Secondary influences include socio-cultural and contextual elements.[6]

Research insights

Research suggests that coaches and sport psychology staff working with younger athletes should consider targeting specific mindset skill development including personal wellbeing and self-reliance to enhance sport development in juniors. Skills required to assist young athletes transition from youth squads to elite performers in rugby include:

- enjoyment
- responsibility
- adaptability
- squad spirit
- being a self-aware learner.[7]

Enjoyment matters

Consider what keeps a person highly engaged long enough to maximise the foundation of physical conditioning and skill they have laid in their sport. You cannot become an athlete without dedicated hours of purposeful training and time-on-task. If an athlete over time is not enjoying what they are doing, it is unlikely they will train often and hard enough, or with enough engagement and intent, to realise their talent. This applies to all ages but is particularly relevant for younger athletes during their development or transition years from junior to open sport. There are many competing interests for young people so enjoying what they do from an early age is paramount. It is also relevant to more mature athletes, because the level of competition in most arenas is competitive enough that once practice, attitude or mindset slides, performance will give, regardless of talent, even for experienced performers.

In Search of Greatness, an insightful sports documentary by Gabe Polsky released in 2018, features a host of sporting legends including basketballer Michael Jordan, Brazilian soccer star Pelé, Canadian

NHL ice-hockey star Wayne Gretzky, tennis player Serena Williams and San Francisco 49ers NFL player Jerry Rice, often cited as the best wide receiver there ever was. Interviews with each of the athletes provide telling insights into their development and performance.[8]

Rice insists he didn't feel he had any genetic advantage and was not the most talented receiver, size- or speed-wise, but 'I knew I had football speed'. His mother wasn't a fan of the game, thinking it too rough. Acknowledging his challenges, however, he explained that 'what enabled [my] performance was that I worked on certain qualities that I was lacking to make up for my deficiencies'.

Gretsky also recognised early that 'speed and power was not going to get me to the next level. My wisdom and vision on the ice [got me to the next level]'. Such was his enjoyment of the game of ice-hockey that from an early age, as he watched games, he would trace the line of the puck on a sketch he had made of the ice-rink. He also practised regularly on his own. 'No-one told me to do it,' he added.

For both Rice and Gretsky, enjoyment of their sport was integral to their development. This enjoyment drove them to practise alone or play active unstructured games with friends, related or unrelated to their sport. It also developed creativity in how they saw the game and contributed to feeding a strong intrinsic passion to improve.

I have found this passion in many athletes I have worked with over the years. The reasons for their enjoyment varies, from being outdoors to expressing themselves physically, being in a team environment, trying to master a skill or trying to achieve something. A key, consistent factor is that enjoyment is in some way related to their chosen sport, which drives their engagement and time-on-task. For this reason, I ask athletes I work with to identify and list what they enjoy and to regularly revisit and update their notes.

How much practice?

Over the past decade much has been written about the '10 000 hours rule', which posits that 10 000 hours of practice is required to become expert in any field, such as sport, music, medical practice or teaching. The notion that 10 000 hours of practice will guarantee expertise was popularised by Malcolm Gladwell in his 2011 book *Outliers*.[9] Although this 'rule' is often cited, it is an oversimplification that has been taken far too literally. Early discussion on 10 000 hours of practice was generated by Anders Ericsson and colleagues when reviewing contributing factors to musical expertise.[10] They found that by the age of 20 'expert' pianists had accumulated approximately 10 000 hours of practice, compared with a total of about 2000 hours for amateur pianists.

In Ericsson's 2016 book *Peak: secrets from the new science of expertise* (co-authored by Robert Pool), he observes that 'unfortunately, the 10 000 rule — which is the only thing that many people today know about the effects of practice — is wrong in several ways'.[11] Among the reasons he identifies are that the amount of practice to become expert 'varies from field to field' and that 'not every type of practice leads to improved ability'. He also says that 'anyone can improve, but it requires the right approach'.

In sport, the reality is that 10 000 hours of dedicated, deliberate practice is unlikely to be accumulated by late teenage years or age 20. Research also confirms that in many sports athletes achieve national representation or professional contracts with less than 10 000 hours of dedicated practice. Even for those with high volumes of practice, it is not the differentiating factor. Mindset will contribute to practice and make best use of the time invested.

Transferring accumulated hours of training into competition environments is something I have seen many athletes struggle with. Large volumes of training can also lead to mental fatigue and burnout, creating additional pressure that negatively impacts both people and performance. One of the more common referrals to performance psychology practices is to help athletes replicate training levels in competition. Mindset is the bridge linking training and performance.

Research insights

A meta-analysis of a large number of studies concluded that deliberate practice accounted for about 18 per cent of sport performance overall. In elite-level performers, deliberate practice accounted for only 1 per cent of variance in performance. Performers who reached a high level of skill did not tend to start their sport earlier than lower skill athletes.

In addition to deliberate practice, the study noted that other experiences may contribute to individual differences in performance. These include competition experience, play activities and possible participation in multiple sports during certain stages of development. Later specialisation may also reduce the incidence of injuries and psychological burnout. Specific psychological variables that could account for performance differences beyond deliberate practice include attention control, confidence, propensity to experience performance anxiety and aversion to negative outcomes.[12]

Many different paths

It is evident, then, that there are many different paths to becoming an elite athlete. An important 2016 paper suggested that in contrast to Ericsson's deliberate practice framework, in which linear sporting progression through time spent in practice is inferred, successful athletes follow complex, non-linear, individualised routes to the top of their sport.[13] They must adapt to anticipated and unanticipated developmental opportunities, setbacks and a range of transitions as they progress. The authors also noted that athletes who achieve a high level are differentiated by positive, proactive coping and a learning approach to challenges.

As alluded to, I have witnessed many individual paths to competitive arenas. I've worked with athletes who were early starters and progressed through the ranks, those who have had interruptions and late starters. What has enabled them to achieve their sporting goals has been a commitment driven by passion, outstanding support and an investment in mindset to deal with and learn from the challenges experienced on their journey. These are some of the factors that have enabled continued progression towards goals.

Matthew Syed, in his book *Bounce: the myth of talent and the power of practice*, emphasises how the power of practice, environment and mindset helped him become a British table tennis champion and Olympian.[14] He recounts that a combination of circumstances contributed to his laying a foundation of many hours of playing table tennis, but that mindset was a key ingredient to his progression. He also admits that he had powerful advantages not available to hundreds of thousands of other youngsters. 'What is certain,' he writes, 'is that if a big enough group of youngsters had been given a table at eight years of age, had a brilliant older brother to practice with, had been trained by one of the best coaches in the country (who coached nearby), had joined the only 24 hours club in the country, and practiced for thousands of hours by their early teens, I would not have been number one in England.'

When Matthew was 19, one of the greatest players in table tennis history, Chen Xinhua, from China, moved to England and became his coach. Matthew's new practice regime bore no relation to what he had seen or experienced previously, or even imagined. This 'quirk of fate', as he describes it, contributed to his ongoing development and fuelled his passion to strive harder.

Sometimes luck plays a role in sporting success. Meeting the right person at the right time may be all that is needed. Not working with a particular coach can be attributed to bad luck as much as bad choices. Working with a coach who has faith and is supportive can be due to luck or choice. It's a fine line between the two. Picking up an injury that limits opportunity can be just bad luck rather than bad management. A talent scout watching a game or event that happens to produce a standout performance is the kind of good luck that can go a long way to launching a sporting career.

These studies and stories emphasise that there is no single path to development. Playing a variety of sports at an early age to build engagement and enjoyment, maximising motivation and early development of mindset, is likely more important than is typically appreciated.

Patience and persistence

Aerial skiing is a complex sport. It is also one of the more challenging sports for Australians to excel in, given how much the climate limits opportunities for time-on-task in the snow (although water jumps play a big part in specific aerial training). Our geography likely contributes more to our international performance in swimming than in skiing, compared with, say, Switzerland, where the conditions are reversed. It's not about talent, but opportunity. In addition, minimal attention and few role models in the sport limits potential extrinsic motivation to become involved or excel in winter sports compared with other sports. So for Jacqui Cooper to become one of Australia's greatest Olympians and the first Australian woman to make five Olympic Games was a feat par excellence.

When I spoke to Jacqui about her journey she told me, 'If you had to rate my talent it would have been zero out of 100. And that wasn't just my opinion — the coaches and administrators agreed!' Such was her reputation that, in 1999, after being freshly crowned world champion and world number one, she was asked by a coach to speak to a group of young female athletes and give them some inspiration. Upon introduction, one of the girls in the group politely enquired if she could ask a question. 'Sure,' Jacqui replied, thinking it would be about one of her achievements. Rather, the query was 'Are you the acrobatic moron?' The junior was Lydia Lassila, who became a training partner and teammate and progressed to win gold ahead of Jacqui 11 years later at the 2010 Winter Olympics. 'We still laugh about it today,' Jacqui said.

'You can have talented people, but in my sport, if they don't have a capacity to take some risk, they won't achieve,' she explained. 'I was a risk taker. I also loved acrobatics. And I did work hard.' Growing up, she recalls, she had no training as a gymnast and didn't focus on any specific sport. She tried different things but wasn't necessarily good at anything. 'Mum and Dad were busy, with me being a triplet, so weekend sport didn't happen much. We didn't even have a trampoline. What I did have was lots of energy — Dad used to call me an energy ball — and whenever I could I would go to a friend's house or the trampoline centre to play,' she said.

Then, in 1989, Jacqui met Geoff Lipshut, the current CEO of the Australian Winter Institute and the chef de mission for the 2022 Winter Olympics in Beijing. 'He's a blend of Mr Myagi from *The Karate Kid* and Yoda from *Star Wars*,' Jacqui recalled. 'He literally saw me jumping on a trampoline that was next to the road when he was driving past. He was in the area to visit another athlete. The next day he met my parents, and that started my journey in aerial skiing. I was 16 years old. He put forward a 10-year plan, and 10 years later he was there when the plan was achieved.'

Lipshut also nurtured the development and careers of Kristie Marshall, Alisa Camplin and Lydia Lassila, who all competed for Australia. Lassila was in a transition program for people leaving gymnastics who might be interested in aerial skiing. He happened to be at the Royal Melbourne Show one day and saw Alisa Camplin playing on a trampoline. Again he asked her parents if she might be interested in aerial skiing. Camplin went on to win an Olympic gold ahead of Jacqui at the 2006 Winter Olympics. If not for those lucky encounters, I wonder if Jacqui or Alisa would have gone on to become the athletes they did.

'I was able to do only about 40 hours per year at the snow, so the first two years were slow growth with skiing. I got encouragement from others to keep going. I didn't back myself at all. What I did have was a place to direct my energy. It took me five years before I could land a jump.' After she left school, Jacqui went to Colorado to pursue her development. 'At the start I couldn't keep up with any of the athletes, so I skied with holiday makers and was even getting tips from them.'

Each of these aerial skiers followed a unique path that wasn't based solely on physical talent. They started out with a degree of talent and different experiences, but mindset enabled their persistence. Jacqui broke no junior records and was not a high achiever in any sport. She played multiple sports as a junior, but drew on an intrinsic passion, patience and energy, as well as the support and encouragement of others.

Early bolters and late bloomers

One of the many sports I have worked in over the years is swimming. Swimming clubs and squads include a wide mix of athletes with diverse motivations, from general fitness to social connections and Olympic aspirations. During adolescence, when many of their peers enjoy sleeping in, swimming squads begin training before school when it's still dark. After school, it's often back to the pool.

In early adulthood they receive no, or minimal, financial reward for their efforts, though it can consume much of their time, energy and emotional resources. Pool training is often complemented by gym and various other strength and conditioning sessions. For years on end parents, as their personal drivers and supports, wake before dawn to act as chauffeur to and from training sessions. I have seen early bolters win national championships and fade away when their priorities change or because of injury. Meanwhile late bloomers can rise from the foundation of their training to peak at national championships and gain selection to state or national teams in late adolescence or early adulthood.

It is an issue I often discuss with junior athletes and parents: being good as a junior is very different from becoming or lasting as a senior or open athlete. Integrating mindset education into junior programs becomes important, not only to assist transition, but also to ensure that athletes leaving a sport have positive experiences to remember and reflect on for life. Going on to become a national representative is not for everyone.

Research insights

Research has found that being a finalist at World Junior Swimming Championships did not predict success at open world championships. Only 17 per cent of athletes were finalists at both juniors and opens; 83 per cent of open finalists were not represented at the junior finals. The factor that was found to have a positive impact on open performance was number of years at world championships.[15]

Based on my own experience, the finding that over 80 per cent of open swimming finalists were not represented at junior championship finals did not surprise me. Variation in physical growth during adolescence is only one variable that contributes to performance at all junior competitions, not just swimming. The impact of school and the development of different variables such as skills and fitness at different stages of growth can also impact both development and performance at junior levels. Support and encouragement to continue with a sport are also key factors.

Even with well-developed programs in Australia in a range of sports, the transition to senior performance is not easy. The tennis and swimming data from the world stage presented are only two examples of this. How sports best support young people who choose either to leave or to stay in a sport beyond junior years becomes a critical factor. Certainly many sports need to improve in this space.

Reasons for leaving

It is worth considering why promising athletes, young or otherwise, leave a sport. Many reasons to leave are situational or personal;

however, mindset challenges may also contribute. I have seen athletes leave their sport for a wide range of reasons, including:

- competing demands such as education and schooling
- conflicting social interests
- lack of or stress about finances
- perceived or actual lack of support
- challenging family or personal circumstances
- injuries
- lack of confidence about performing at higher levels
- difficulty with transition from junior to senior sport
- lack of access to programs
- negative experiences
- lack or loss of enjoyment
- low or diminished peer relationships in the sport
- dejection from not being selected into talent pathways or programs
- personal or behavioural challenges that arise from maintaining a sporting lifestyle and feeling they are 'missing out' compared to non-sport peers
- perceived lack of success or not valuing performance in the sport
- choosing and preferring to spend time doing something else.

Certainly, there's nothing wrong with leaving a sport to pursue other interests. It is a choice many people happily make. However, two questions should be considered. First, are they leaving their sport with positive, enduring experiences, relationships and memories? Secondly, if they were managed differently, or were introduced to mindset education, might they have chosen to remain in the sport for further enjoyment or to realise further potential? Both questions should be considered by people in sport development roles. Working with athletes on these questions aids a smooth transition away from sport, if that is the choice they make, rather than leaving them with regrets. Not being selected for a squad or team may be another reason athletes leave a sport. The key is that they can appreciate, recognise and take away positive experiences and can benefit from having been involved.

Tough transition

In my experience of working with athletes in both individual and team sports, dealing with transition is a challenge to sustaining performance, as well as to staying in a sport. Transition is associated with new demands, including developing new relationships with coaches and support staff, new competitors or new teammates, and adjusting to different cultures in different squads, programs and teams. These can be confronting for young people as well as experienced athletes.

One aspect of transition is the shift to becoming more 'serious' as athletes progress through different levels. This seriousness includes a greater emphasis on strategy and plans, compared with simpler plans that enable greater emphasis on technique, relaxation, effort and enjoyment. Higher levels of critique and more complex feedback can also impact athletes transitioning into new, more advanced or different teams or environments. They are often associated with greater demands, both emotional and on their time, as well as higher expectations. Transition must be managed well if a person wants to become a serious athlete, and this means managing mindset.

Research insights

A recent study concluded that the performance of 15-year-olds did not correlate with becoming a professional road cyclist. From age 17 onwards, performance started to predict future success. A top 10 performance in under 17 and under 19 was associated with a 3 to 5 per cent and 6 per cent higher chance of reaching elite level as an adult. Transition to a new competition category was a variable found to negatively impact performance of future 'non-achievers'.[16]

McDonald's to Olympics

Canadian high jumper Nicole Forrester competed at the 2008 Beijing Olympic Games. Her athletic career began after a chance meeting with track coach Dave Hunt, who dropped into McDonald's while Forrester was working there as a 17-year-old. Nicole grew up in a small town of about 800 people, where her focus was on study and physical activities, rather than specialising in a sport. After speaking with her while being served and noting her interest and high-jump physique, Hunt referred her to the high-jump coach Carl Georgevski at the University of Toronto.

Nicole has attributed her 'quick progression in the high jump to the various sports I played growing up … Had I specialized in my sport at an earlier age, I doubt I would have lasted for as long as I did or had the same level of success'.[17] Three years after meeting Georgevski she represented Canada at the 1997 World University Games in Italy. However, it took a further 11 years of commitment before she reached her goal of being an Olympic athlete in 2008. In 2010 she won gold at the Commonwealth Games in India. Her account reinforces the major role played by mindset in enabling her to transition from McDonald's to the Olympics. It also reminds us that the training of a junior athlete need not all be specialised.

Nicole later completed a PhD in Sport Psychology with a dissertation titled 'Good to great in elite athletes: towards an understanding of why some athletes make the leap and others do not'.[18] Nicole has commented that 'becoming an Olympian requires a mixture of important ingredients that may vary according to the sport and the individual athlete. Ultimately for many, the path is navigated through deliberate play and the involvement in various sports, developed through a commitment of deliberate practice, reinforced by support, resources, motivation and effort'.

Maintaining discipline

So many variables behind the scenes need to be managed to enable an athlete to shine. Maintaining focus and discipline, and performing in unusual and challenging circumstances with minimal support are common components of the sporting journey that the public doesn't see. To achieve sporting ambitions, an incredible resolve and intrinsic drive are necessary staples from an early age.

Nicole's first competition was at the World University Games in Sicily in 1997. I attended the Games with the Australian team as a psychologist. Before departure for Italy, the team assembled at a hotel beside Sydney airport, where athletes and staff sat through formalities and listened to well-wishing guest speakers. It was here I heard one of the shortest and best speeches at any official ceremony that I've attended. I don't recall who the speaker was, but the substance of the speech was burned into my memory. It went along these lines: 'Congratulations for making your national team. Keep in mind that if you perform well, you may not even be noted in the one-line sports results section at the back of the newspaper. However, if you make one personal mistake you will be on the front page of every newspaper in Australia.'

It was a sobering lesson. An elite sportsperson must not only perform, but also uphold behavioural standards when representing a squad, team, state or country. It is another ingredient that must be managed to assist development and performance. To become or to remain an elite athlete requires both training discipline and personal and behavioural discipline. It reflects the necessity to deal with scrutiny on performance and non-performance areas.

At the Games, the accommodation was in a hotel complex guarded by armed military. There were not enough beds when the team arrived, and buses and other transport to training and events were constantly late. On top of that, several athletes and staff became unwell and were restricted to their small rooms. Many competitors had to work with unfamiliar coaches and support staff. For most athletes the trip was either fully or partly self-funded. There were other challenges that were generally to be expected for such a large international sporting competition, including disorganised training spaces or facilities, traffic getting to and from venues, and language barriers. None of this is to say that it was not a tremendous experience. It was a fantastic trip, and a privilege to work with a great team. I mean only to illustrate the kinds of demands made on athletes striving to apply their craft at many sporting competitions, even before the competition begins.

Environments that help performance

Consider another sport — motorsport. Motorbike and car racing are as physically and mentally challenging as any sport. The mechanical componentry needs to be operating optimally, as does the athlete. In Australia, the V8 Supercars Championship is one of the most fiercely contested of all motorsports globally. At the most famous race on the calendar, the two-driver Bathurst 1000, the difference in the qualifying session in 2021 from first place pole sitter at 2.03.89 minutes to 15th on the grid was under one second. That is a mere 0.8 per cent difference. Such statistics make Jamie Whincup, the record-holding driver of seven championships, four Bathurst race victories and 123 race wins spanning a career of 19 years from 2002 to 2021, even more intriguing. Is he talented? Yes. Does he work hard? Yes. Does he think he has achieved such dizzy success from talent and hard work alone? No. In fact, Whincup almost missed the opportunity that led to his winning ways.

After progressing through junior development ranks in a category known as Formula Ford, Whincup debuted at a young age in V8 Supercars and earned a contract in 2003 with a team committed to supporting emerging drivers. In his first full season he finished 27th and lost his drive. Unable to secure another contract in 2004, he sat out the main season but accepted an offer as a co-driver at the endurance races. He was fortunate to be able to race after injuring his shoulder while skiing. He had a retirement in the first endurance event and a ninth at Bathurst. It was not enough to interest any teams to give him another contract for 2005. Doubts overshadowed any offers.

At the last minute Jamie and his supports convinced a team run by Kevin Murphy, father of Bathurst champion Greg, to reluctantly give him a contract. This was his ticket back into the championship. Through his time away from full-time driving, however, Jamie had continued working on his conditioning and mindset, which he had been doing since Formula Ford days. Following a season of renewed energy, he finished the championship in 16th place. Although his results were not outstanding, his positivity, determination and willingness to grow saw his performances improve across the season. It was enough to get him an offer from another team, this time with some security. The emerging Red Bull Racing team had a seat vacancy and recognised Whincup as the incumbent. He never looked back.

'For me the brain is a muscle and, in some regards, the most important one in the body,' he said when I interviewed him about the early stages of his career. 'It blows me away that some sports still have minimal work that goes into strengthening the mind. Of course you need talent and work, but whoever performs mentally has the upper hand. In motorsport I feel it is especially important. Bathurst is six and a half hours, so it's a mental endurance game in and out of the car. Beyond that it is the whole week leading up to the race as well. I'm glad I developed mental skills in my younger years. I continued to work on them right through my career.'

What is less well known about Whincup is the time he spent as a junior at Sonic Motorsport. Sonic is a hugely successful organisation, with numerous championship trophies from drivers they have developed. Whincup cut his teeth in Formula Ford with Mick Ritter, the team owner at Sonic. Sonic has effectively been a production line for future champions. In addition to Whincup,

Will Davison, David Reynolds and Nick Percat have all gone on to win Bathurst and be highly regarded drivers in the competition. All passed through Sonic in their junior days. Mick estimates that 15 to 20 drivers from his junior program have gone on to V8 Supercar or Bathurst drives.

Mick was ahead of his time in Australian motorsport. While working in Europe as a young mechanic on race cars in the mid 1990s he realised there was a lack of 'overall professionalism' in juniors in Australia, compared with what he was seeing there. So he introduced a mental and physical skills training program to his developing drivers. 'Talent is relevant,' he told me, 'but it's overrated. Some of the most natural drivers I've seen over 30 years have *not* gone on to have successful careers in the sport due to relying on their talent and not working enough in all the areas necessary.'

In his opinion, 'The most important thing to build a successful career on is hunger and desire. That's because there's so much to do in so many areas to become professional. And that includes mental and physical work.'

Mick also integrated mindset into his own thinking and work. 'I realised I had so much to learn as well. The key was embracing people who specialise in a high-performance mindset, then we all work together. I had to stay open-minded, and the work we did helped me to talk to drivers in different ways about different things. Getting all the people involved and on the same page was a big deal. The drivers also developed a capacity to identify different areas to work on and to build means of dealing with a wide variety of different situations as they happen.

'Helping the athletes understand themselves and how they can get the most out of themselves was also a big deal. All of this helped them to take ownership of their performance, and champions embrace that,' he added. 'What separates them at the upper echelon, where talent is more equal, is that performers then draw on all that mindset work they have done and refine it over a period of time as part of looking to constantly improve.' That's what Whincup did.

Ritter isn't alone in contributing to an environment that enables people like Whincup to flourish. There are many other such programs that help nurture talent and reinforce work rate and performance mindset, including the one Geoff Lipshut established to nurture Jacqui Cooper and other aerial skiers.

Talent doesn't coach you

Of course, some people will never thrive as athletes for purely physical reasons. And some sports, by virtue of their composition, make selection challenging based on physiological factors. But in most sports talent alone is not enough to forge a career or achieve goals and ambitions. At times, talent can even be counterproductive for high performance, as it seduces an athlete into thinking that all will be well because of their proven talent. But talent is not enough. Even talent and work rate are not enough.

Without the motivation to participate in hours, days, months and years of dedicated, engaged time-on-task, talent in sport is unlikely to be realised. A performance mindset helps sustain this motivation, manage personal and emotional challenges, overcome competing interests and demands, and utilise supports to realise talent.

Sally Pearson, Australian hurdler and 2008 Beijing Olympic Gold medallist, affirmed this view in a comment she posted on LinkedIn in 2021. She noted how annoyed she would get when it was implied that her success was attributed not to her hard work, but to the talent she was born with. Her talent, she argued, wasn't what encouraged her to train to get better, or what coached her.[19]

Keep in mind that this discussion extends well beyond the few athletes who are household names. Mindset skills are relevant for fringe athletes deciding how much energy to invest and how to improve. They are relevant for athletes hidden in lower ranks, who enjoy only limited game time, and for team members moving in and out of a squad. Of course, a performance mindset is also applicable beyond sport — whether you're in a classroom, at work or striving for personal development. Building a performance mindset while engaged in any trade or task will help people to perform and flourish.

This notion reflects the power of the human spirit. It was preached by Percy Cerutty, a great character in Australian sport in the fifties and sixties who coached Herb Elliott. As a runner, Herb was unbeaten over the mile and the 1500 metres. His victory in the 1500 metres at the Rome Olympics in 1960 is still widely regarded as one of the great performances by an Australian athlete.

In one of his six books, *Athletics: how to become a champion*, from 1960, Cerutty spoke about the power of the human spirit. 'I do admit freely, frankly and fully that we are not all born equal in graces, brains or ability, but I *do* affirm that no power exists, human or superhuman, that opposes the genuine aspirations and sincere attempts of any personality to advance itself ... I affirm that our destiny *is* in our own hands [although] no one but a fool would deny that we do find difficulties, set-back, frustrations, even inevitabilities at times, and by the dozens — hundreds.'[20]

When I met and interviewed Herb in 1992, he spoke about his belief in the importance of mindset. 'The basic ingredients for success haven't changed in 50 000 years,' he told me. 'They are the spirit, soul, body and mind.' And, he added, 'If I could pick one thing that is vital to be successful internationally, it's mental toughness. The wonderful thing about it is that you're not born with it. You can train it into yourself.'[21]

Summary

The first step towards embracing and deliberately working on mindset skills is appreciating that talent and hard work are important, but are realised and maximised only with a performance mindset. Here is a model I advocate when thinking about achieving anything.

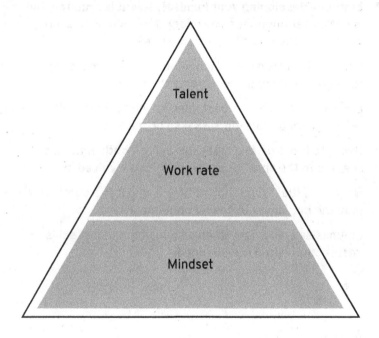

Talent is not the foundation, or even the middle layer. A performance mindset is the foundation. Without a performance mindset there can be no progress because there is no beginning or continuing. The following chapters explore some methods of building your performance mindset.

BUILD ON YOUR TALENT

- Embrace developing your mindset. Talent is required, but is not as paramount as one might think. Mindset is more important and contributes to work rate.

- Respect balanced development in the early years of sport. Recognise individual development journeys.

- Embrace the idea that becoming an elite athlete takes a long time — years of time-on-task — so be patient.

- Begin to focus on mindset skills early — both general and specific to the sport or pastime you are involved in.

- Once an initial foundation of time is given to a sport, view it as only the beginning to enable ongoing growth.

- Emphasise enjoyment when developing mindset skills to ensure motivation is embedded.

STEP 1

HARNESS YOUR MOTIVATION

Motivation is a cornerstone of most advancement and achievement. Becoming and staying motivated, however, is often a very complex process, especially over a long period compared with a short burst of time. Motivation is also arguably one of the most discussed aspects of human behaviour, spanning school learning environments, relationships, work, health, even thrill seeking. Behind the scenes of a sporting endeavour, motivation is required to stay determined and to overcome multiple challenges that are often not apparent when a score or hit is made, a catch taken or a race time achieved.

A person who can understand and manage their motivation is on the way to maximising their experience in sporting or other endeavours. This is because motivation influences behaviour.

The seven summits

Brigitte Muir was awarded an Order of Australia medal for good reason. Not only was she the first Australian woman to conquer Mount Everest, but she was also the first Australian, male or female,

1

to summit the highest mountain peak on each of the seven conti-
nents. This project was over a decade in the making, but the idea that
became a goal to make an assault on the seven summits was born in
1984. 'It was a way to see the world,' Brigitte said with a smile when
she spoke with me from her western Victorian base where she now
lives. In 1997, following three unsuccessful attempts on Everest, she
achieved her dream. It was a feat of mental endurance, perseverance
and motivation as much as, or more than, it was physical.

Brigitte recounted where her drive was ignited. 'I grew up
around factories in a Belgian town and the best way to get out of it
was through books,' she said. 'I read all the Tintin stories, about the
boy reporter who travelled around the world having adventures.
That ignited my adventurous spirit. I also had a turning point in
a French class at school when the teacher said, "We must live our
dreams, not dream our lives." Once you think like that enough, it
has a habit of becoming reality.'

The next link that spurred her journey was a trip to the local fair
with a friend when she was 16 years old, where she spotted a flyer
about caving: 'I thought I'd like to do that, and it took three weeks
of convincing my mum that I should go. Eventually she did let me,
and it started from there. I already felt there was no limit to what
someone could do. Or imagination was the only limit, and for me
that was fed by what I read and the people I was with.'

Brigitte also spoke about her 'curiosity and hunger for learning'.
Such an attitude fed her drive. Other factors that fuelled her
motivation included having a mentor, whom she talks about fondly
and remains in contact with to this day. 'The culture in the Himalaya
also inspired me and gave me that little bit of extra motivation,' she
added. 'When I set my mountain climbing goals, I also had to build
a team. I did that from people I had met along the way. As we went
forward, they showed belief in me, which helped.' Her motivation
was fed by a wide range of influences.

'Once I set the long-term goal of climbing the seven peaks, it
also became a full-time job of finding sponsors to fund the dream.

It became an obsession, and I was very single-minded. But I loved what I was doing. And I had emotional and mental support.' In 1997, after realising her dream, her passion for the Himalayan people and culture remained. To this day she regularly visits and supports a local community there, funding women's literacy and other projects. It adds meaning to what she has done and continues to do.

When speaking with Brigitte, it is evident that she has lost none of the spark that was ignited by the Tintin stories and her French teacher. Now, though she has her own adventures to share and reflect on, her motivation for life remains as strong as ever.

Action ignites motivation

Motivation doesn't have to be on a grand scale to begin with. Any small action can enhance motivation and lead to something more. Put another way, a person's own actions can build, reinforce and increase motivation. When working with casual fitness enthusiasts who want to achieve a personal goal of running in a fun run or reaching a health target from a low base, I encourage them to start small. For example, a consistent five- or ten-minute jog-walk will enhance motivation.

Regularly doing something will help because consistency builds habits. Habits in turn reduce the demand for extrinsic and intrinsic energy to help action become more automatic. To assist this process and reinforce habits, managing as many variables as possible to get going is a great strategy. To build your running, for example, leave running shoes at the front door, organise to meet a friend on the run, and choose a time of day when it will be easiest to get going. Build in accountability structures to support your efforts. Over time it becomes easier to find the shoes and go on your own, at any time of day. Using as many external variables as possible to build internal drive can be very helpful.

If it's not possible to manage and manipulate the environment, use any spark to ignite action. Consider the benefits of taking action. Even in high-performance environments, motivation will not necessarily be high all the time. When it wavers, continuing to focus on small things can become self-fulfilling. Drawing on established supports and environmental influences balances and sustains internal energy. Even in team sports, motivation varies between individuals. For some, motivation on one particular day may be driven by the enjoyment of being with the group. For others, it may be a session in which they want to master a craft or challenge themselves. For others it may be the lure of a contract or selection.

Percy Cerutty emphasised the importance of 'doing' in his book *Athletics: how to become a champion*: 'I am an apostle of the *now*, the everlasting *present*. Do today *all* that you *reasonably* can — in your training, your affairs. Do not attempt to see the *end* of the road. Keep your "ends" or goals in mind, but direct your brains to the solving and satisfactorily *doing* of all that your hands or feet find to do today ... it is true that imagination is an essential quality, but not when it stops at just imagining ourselves as great athletes or persons, and entirely lacks the next step — *action* — the getting up and doing — in the rain, in the heat, in the cold, in the dark!'[1]

I can imagine Percy preaching this philosophy to Herb and his other athletes at their Portsea training base. It reinforces the point that action — big or small — can feed motivation and lead to bigger things.

Intrinsic and extrinsic drivers

Motivation laid bare can be viewed as 'intrinsic' or 'extrinsic'. Intrinsic is commonly understood as motivation from within or internally driven. In contrast, extrinsic motivation is derived from externally driven factors and forces outside oneself. Intrinsic drivers include personal satisfaction, enjoyment, mastering a skill, personal accomplishments and fulfilment. Extrinsic drivers include achieving a place or time, a contract, an award, a ranking, money or status, or striving for a goal or standard for someone other than oneself. Extrinsic motivators also include other people encouraging, pushing and prodding. I have always recommended to people that they find their internal drivers and maximise any external ones to sustain motivation.

Consider how motivation is impacted by extrinsic forces, such as time or media scrutiny, as an event gets closer. The last six months, six weeks or six days prior to an Olympic trial are different motivators compared with three years before the event. For a team, the start or middle of the season is different from the last game of a season that needs to be won to secure a finals position. The change in circumstances based on the event, time and other factors reflects how different factors influence motivation. Deadlines can help to enhance motivation but they are useless if not enough motivation has contributed to solid work leading to the deadline, especially in high-performance sport. Sometimes there is a need to create artificial deadlines to help motivation. Keeping an eye on the bigger picture can help. External commentary can also influence motivation, either positively or negatively, no matter how irrelevant some opinions are.

Doing something for the sheer joy of it or because you are convinced it's the right thing to do are simple examples of intrinsic drivers. A desire to test yourself is another. Running a marathon because it's something you've always wanted to do is another example of an intrinsic driver. The key point is that managing intrinsic and extrinsic motivation is a necessity and skill.

As already noted, elite performers are not solely intrinsically motivated. It's a myth that they are. Multiple motives are likely to exist. Environmental, social and personal factors can all influence intrinsic or extrinsic motivation. For this reason, I often view the maintenance of motivation as a skill that can be optimised by self-knowledge and self-management. How and when does your inner desire glow or fade? What factors around you help to maintain the glow and manage a fade? Athletes, coaches and support teams who know the answers to these questions are best placed to sustain motivation. The key is to know oneself. In a squad or team, the key is also to know each other.

To feed their motivation, at times athletes may focus on a point to prove. This could be real or artificially created. A widely cited example is basketball legend Michael Jordan. His Hall of Fame speech in 2009 reflects how multiple motivators, both internal and external, contributed to his drive. It's worth listening to this on the Official Hoophall site, if you haven't already. After rapturous applause, Jordan begins the speech in an emotional way. He says that 'people added wood to that [competitive] fire ... there is Leroy Smith, now you guys think that's a myth ... when I got cut he made the [varsity] team ... when he made the team and I didn't, I wanted to prove not just to Leroy Smith, not just to myself, but to the coach who actually picked Leroy over me, I wanted to make sure you understood, you made a mistake dude'. These remarks illustrate how Jordan was not just skilled at basketball — he was highly skilled at managing his drive.

Research insights

Researchers interviewed five male and five female elite track and field athletes about motivation. They had finished in the top 10 of Olympics or world championships. When it came to motivation, it was found that the athletes a) were highly driven by personal goals and achievement, b) had strong self-belief and c) made track and field central to their lives. They also had multiple intrinsic and extrinsic drivers.

The variety of motivators included excitement, enjoyment, love of competing and connection with fellow athletes.

Additional motivators included money, social recognition and seeing their sport as a job.

The transition and link between intrinsic and extrinsic variables and social conditions were all seen to be important to sustain motivation across the lifespan of a high-performance career.[2]

This study confirms that motivation is very personal: what motivates one person may not motivate another. How receptive a person is to different motivators is also relevant. Different motivators at different stages of the lifespan of an athlete are also likely to exist, so adapting to and using different motivators as a sporting career progresses is relevant. However, having something to strive for consciously and deliberately is important to igniting action and sustaining motivation.

Multiple motivators

Many athletes report that when they have struggled to sustain intrinsic motivation they have drawn upon extrinsic motivation from a person or group of people supporting their journey and encouraging them. These could be coaches, family members, friends, other athletes or support people. This is one reason why support networks are important. Extrinsic motivators can help limit the drain on intrinsic drive. Indeed, to return to Michael Jordan, extrinsic drivers help fuel the fire along the journey.

This is noteworthy as it reflects the importance of identifying multiple motivators to sustain energy. It is helpful to look beyond winning or getting drafted or achieving a certain place, time or distance to simply fuelling motivation. Having a single focal point is important, but other motivators are also helpful to sustain energy, especially as achievement in any endeavour, including sport, has many hurdles and takes a long time.

Herb Elliott provided insight into this line of thinking in an interview with Brian Lenton: '... I wanted to be a better human being. That was my number one thing ... at training you'd be exhausted, but you knew that was a moment of weakness challenging you. So, if you were going to grow, your motivation had to be more than just winning or getting money.'[3]

While this was a clear intrinsic drive, there is little doubt that Herb also had a very strong extrinsic drive as his focal point — to win the Olympic gold in Tokyo in 1960. In his book with Alan Trengrove, *The Golden Mile*, he described his thoughts the day before his 1500 metre race in Rome.[4] 'Tomorrow is the day. The day I marked down as *my* day four years ago.' He added, 'when the Australian flag was hoisted ... the pride that filled my heart was for my country, not myself. The tears welled up and I realised I'd been fooling myself. I am an Australian and I'd been running for my country no matter how strongly cold reason told me I'd been running for myself.' Clearly, multiple motivators drove Herb to his victory.

Tennis player turned coach Nicole Pratt, who walked across a few courts in Perth to speak to a young Storm Sanders, hailed from sugarcane farming country one hour from the north Queensland town of Mackay. It was a far cry from representing Australia in the Federation Cup (now the Billie Jean King Cup) and the Olympic Games, the grass courts of Wimbledon, or reaching the top 50 tennis players in the world. As a teenager Nicole could not have imagined she would have a sporting career that would take her around the world and last almost 20 years. It was built on a reputation as a 'fox terrier, nipping at opponents' heels', she reflected when I interviewed her.

'My motivation was to try to be the best version of myself I could be. I wanted to turn over any stone to be better. It started with my family. Growing up I was instilled with a sense of hard work and pride. I used to work in the sugarcane fields and walk in front of the tractor my dad drove. My job was to pick up rocks to avoid damage to the machinery. Seeing all the rocks in the back of a truck gave me a sense of accomplishment. From another perspective, planting and growing sugarcane helped me to learn that growth is built on hard work. Being a professional athlete requires discipline and monotony. I realised you need character to embrace the small things that matter on a day-to-day basis that others might see as boring. That mindset helped me sustain my motivation.'

When Storm Sanders reflected on her motivation, she told me, 'Not having many extrinsic motivators early on kept me planning and trying to find ways to improve. Because I was behind others through my junior years, I realised I was on my own journey. I didn't get caught up with comparing myself to others, who seemed to have amazing opportunities. If I had had a lot of extrinsic motivation early on, I'm not sure how it would have influenced me. I don't think my intrinsic motivation would have been as good.'

These stories reinforce the importance of multiple intrinsic and extrinsic drivers in life and sport. In my work I have sat with many athletes consolidating and building their motivation. What I have found is that over time, motivation will change. In these conversations, high-performing athletes constantly identified multiple motivators to maintain high-quality training while working towards their goals.

Competence, autonomy and relatedness

'Self-determination theory' (SDT) offers a broad framework for understanding factors that help or hinder intrinsic or extrinsic motivation and psychological wellness. Developed by psychologists Richard Ryan and Edward Deci, SDT has been used to help understand and grow motivation in education and work as well as in sport.[5] They emphasise that the basic psychological needs of *competence*, *autonomy* and *relatedness* are critically important to maximising motivation:

- Competence reflects a level of proficiency. It's about feeling like you have attained a level of skill or strengths in what you do and can keep growing.

- Autonomy involves a sense of choice and endorsement. It's about being empowered and involved in what you are doing.

- Relatedness is based on a sense of connection and belonging. It's about positive relationships.

Research has suggested that these factors enhance task perseverance and wellbeing, and reduce stress, anxiety and self-criticism.

For individuals, coaches and sporting organisations, I recommend reinforcing competence by embracing self-referenced standards and growth with other evaluation methods, as well as by monitoring personal development.

Autonomy can be facilitated by involving athletes in decision making related to aspects of their overall direction, training and performance plans. Being consulted or acknowledged is empowering.

Relatedness can be established through building connections, relationships and a sense of belonging. It makes a big difference for an athlete to feel like others care about them as a person, not just an athlete. To feel a part of something, rather than simply making up the numbers, also strengthens feelings of relatedness.

Engagement

Engagement is about a person's relationship with and investment in what they are doing. In sport, as well as other fields, higher engagement has been associated with positive health, learning and performance outcomes. I often ask athletes how their relationship with their sport is going. At first it seems an odd question. However, it encourages consideration about why their sport is important to them and why they devote so much energy to it. It also considers reflection on what you get back from sport, as well as what you give, which can be motivating. There are many benefits people derive from being involved in sport, beyond winning. These should be identified.

Research insights

A 2015 study described engaged athletes as experiencing enduring positive states of mind, including perceptions of confidence, vigour, enjoyment and dedication.

Elite Swedish junior downhill skiers who felt autonomous were more likely to be intrinsically motivated and to feel more engaged in their sport.

The researchers determined that 'elite athletes may require engagement in order to overcome challenges inherent in high-performing sport (e.g. travel, intensive training, injury and media demands) and to foster sustained involvement'.[6]

Exploring *why you do what you do* can be a valuable starting point to a conversation about engagement and motivation. Being aware of these variables helps athletes reflect on and develop personal management skills, as well as understand the influence of their environment on motivation and wellbeing. It also encourages reflection on how they interact and influence the environment they are in so they are able to see themselves as participants, rather than simply recipients, in an environment.

Choices and sacrifices

Balancing 'choices' and 'sacrifices' is relevant for many athletes. At times sacrifice is essential when pursuing a goal. Time away from family and friends, time spent training, early mornings, evenings, weekends, social gatherings may all be important sacrifices. Depending on the sport, sacrifices might include postponing further education or earning an income.

I believe that feeling as though you are making constant and high-level sacrifices is draining and eventually demotivating. Australian runner Debbie Flintoff-King, who won gold in the 400 metres hurdles at the 1988 Seoul Olympics, sees missing out on things not as sacrifices but as choices. In the book *Winning Attitudes* she shares her view that 'your life fits around your sport. Your sport is your life. In my case I would eat, sleep, breathe athletics. I guess I was lucky in this respect in that I had my husband Phil to help me do all this. If I'd had a boyfriend or husband who wasn't interested in it, it would have been extremely hard to do. Phil always told me that what I was missing out on were not sacrifices, they were my choices — which is so true. You make your own choice to do this, and if you've made the choice, then do it 100%.'[7]

Garth Tander is one of the most successful V8 Supercar drivers in Australia, being credited with the second–most race starts (641 at the end of 2021) in the history of the sport. He has been a championship winner and is a four-time Bathurst winner. He still competes, but only as an endurance driver teammate. In this role he stood on top of the podium at Bathurst as recently as 2020 with Shane van Gisbergen. During my interview with Garth he explained, 'When I was about 15 or 16 years old, I enjoyed going out with friends and socialising, but there was a specific moment on a Saturday night before a party that I had a decision to make. I remember not going to the party because I was worried about how it would affect me the next day, and I didn't want to get caught in a bad social cycle. I made a choice. Once a professional athlete, there were times I felt like I was making sacrifices. If I had a 80 km bike ride to do and was in bed early, instead of doing something else, I used to think it was a sacrifice, but as my career progressed, I realised, it wasn't really a sacrifice – it was what I wanted to do'.

In line with the earlier discussion on autonomy, encouraging and empowering people to make choices can increase motivation and longevity. It can also help people enjoy what they are doing. As a simple example, think of running in the rain for a fun runner. They may initially see it as unpleasant, but the experience can become enjoyable once they reflect on all the reasons they are choosing to do it. Even if it isn't fully enjoyable, recognising that it serves a goal provides motivation to do it. Mind you, running in the rain can be great fun.

Dave Andersen, former basketball player in the NBA and four-time Australian Olympic Boomers team member, described how he missed 16 consecutive Australian summers to maintain his international professional career. 'I called it the eternal winter,' he said when I spoke with him back at his Melbourne base. 'Sure, there was missing Christmas, but we worked around it. I never saw it as anything other than what I did to stay at the highest level — playing in the USA and Europe. It ended up extending my career. When I was younger it was easy, but once I had a family and we all travelled around the world to different countries, I had to make a conscious decision to stay on that path. It wasn't easy, not seeing family and friends back in Australia. It was a choice *and* a sacrifice. Many people find it hard to make that choice and sacrifice, but being prepared to make those choices and sacrifices helped me.'

No one is superhuman

Sasa Ognenovski is not well known outside soccer circles in Australia, but he is renowned within them. He forged a professional career that took him from working as a carpenter to travelling all over the world, determined to 'make the most of every opportunity to get another contract'. He debuted for the Australian Socceroos at age 31 and played 22 matches in the green and gold, 'giving everything' on each occasion. When I spoke with him he had just started as a part-time coach at Melbourne Victory, casting his experienced eye over their upcoming youth.

'I was not the most talented at all,' he admitted. 'I knew others were faster or stronger and technically better, but I had a driven mindset. My goal was to be better than others mindset-wise and never to break mentally at crucial moments. That's what allowed me to achieve more than others who were more talented. I was willing to push more and do more than others. From when I was young I always told myself *no one is superhuman*. My opponent might be a better footballer but with my mentality I thought I could beat anyone. I focused on my strengths and treated every game as a battle.'

Even after he was selected for the national team, Sasa would do an extra 30 minutes of his own drills after training sessions. 'I remember being in Japan with the national team and kicking left foot–right foot against a wall for 30 minutes. I did it because I was driven and wanted to be the best I could. That enabled me to look back at the end of my career and say I did all I could to be the best I could.'

He left school at 15 to become a carpenter, but was always focused on pursuing and forging a professional sport career. 'I didn't have a mentor or a lot of support, so I made sure I pushed myself. That helped me and I made sure I was prepared to do whatever it took, regardless of finances or where in the world an opportunity arose.'

Sasa's story illustrates the importance and power of sustaining an inner drive over a long period of time. It also reinforces the importance of being very clear about your goal, even if your path is not clear or is, at times, rocky.

Goal setting

When introducing goal-setting sessions with individuals and teams, I often draw from Percy Cerutty's advice on 'doing', quoted at the beginning of this step. It gives notion to the simplest mode of goals. Have an overall outcome goal — where you want to get to or what you want to achieve — and link it to process goals, the actions required to achieve the outcome. From such a starting point, there are multiple variations available for individuals and teams to set their goals.

Many aspiring Olympians set their goals four, eight or twelve years ahead of time. Such long-term goals require a map to ensure the athletes stay on track. There could be many mini-goals along the way, small milestones to tick off as they progress. Depending on the environment, the goals and actions may be open-ended or framed within specific categories. Pre-season, in-season, physical, mental, technical or personal are some categories I have suggested athletes think about. Long, medium or short term, specific, measurable and realistic are also frequently discussed in relation to goals.

Individual, small-group or whole-team goals can also be considered. Coaches, wellbeing, and conditioning staff can and should be involved in these processes. For individuals, too often planning isn't recorded, shared or reviewed. It's not compulsory, of course, but science has demonstrated that these strategies work, and that goal setting is one of the most essential ingredients of motivation and performance.

THE ART OF GOAL SETTING

At times, goal setting can be viewed, particularly by more experienced athletes, as boring or trivial. That is where the art of goal setting comes in. Establishing and using goals is itself a skill. How and when they are formulated, who is involved, and where they are kept or displayed, as well as how often they are reviewed, are some of the factors that help bring them to life. Creativity can help goal building through simple activities, such as use of colour, quotes and images. Adding a category to goals, such as something new to learn or someone to help, is a simple way to add another dimension to goals. There are many ways to make goal setting engaging.

Managed poorly, goals can be a distraction or, worse, deflating but used well, goals guide thinking and energy. It's important that goals are adopted by athletes at all levels, and by people who are highly motivated as well as others with more limited motivation.

Once goals have been established, follow-up activities are essential. As a simple activity I have often created worksheets to identify and reflect on what *helps* or *hinders* progress towards goals. It's a strategy that provides insight into what is influencing advancement towards achieving or not achieving the goal. It is also a way of providing feedback. The process or actions identified to help achieve the goal can be reviewed at this time. At times the goal itself needs to be modified to keep it alive and active, rather than meaningless and unproductive.

A while after Sam Mitchell embraced the idea of alternating right and left foot when practising his kicking skills, another piece of unsolicited advice stuck. 'I had a coach early on in my career who said "always aim high" and that was reflected in my goals. I had two sets of goals. One that was public and one that was private. My goal setting also evolved as I evolved as a person,' he reflected. The coach's tip set Sam on a goal-setting path that, while it took different forms across his career, remained a key aspect of his growth. 'Early in my career it was about winning awards and was very data driven — and about kicks, marks and handballs. Later in my career I didn't need the numbers, and it was more about a balanced life.

'In my thinking and in my heart goal setting guided every action. The desire to improve and get better was strong. I was always trying to better myself. The goal setting of wanting to win or achieve was a stepping-stone, but the bigger picture of this was becoming the player I wanted to be. Goal setting was the driving force behind that progression. When I got drafted, in my head I was the 44th [last] player on the list and Shane Crawford was the first. If I wanted to be the first, whatever he did, I needed to do more to bridge the gap. It seemed rational to me. How I thought about it helped me with goal setting.'

I understood just what Sam was talking about. In 1996, Hawthorn was the first AFL club I worked with. I had been an under 19 player there in the eighties, so when I went back as a psychologist I had the chance to work with some of my old teammates. Shane Crawford was then in the early days of his career. Such was his motivation that in the evenings when others had ventured home, at times he would do tough extra training sessions to push to new physical standards, which was one of his goals.

OWNING GOALS

In 1985, Edwin Locke and Gary Latham wrote one of the more popular and widely recognised papers on goal setting in sport.[8] They found that specific, difficult goals lead to better performance than vague or easy goals, and that short-term goals can facilitate the achievement of long-term goals. Goals affect performance by impacting effort, persistence and direction of effort, as well as motivating strategy development. They also noted the importance of feedback and that goals must be accepted by the athlete if they are to affect performance. I often refer to this as the athlete 'owning' the goals. At times I have encouraged signatures on goal sheets.

Locke and Latham recommended setting goals for practice or training, and for different physical elements, such as strength or stamina. In their early work they also identified what they considered to be five important principles of goals: clarity, challenge, acceptance, feedback and complexity.

'I use a lot of goal setting,' Storm Sanders told me. 'They are more process related. They include how I want to go about my tennis, as well as everything outside of tennis. They include things like ensuring I have and use good routines and I have and keep a good team around me. When I was injured and unable to play, I created different goals to keep me going.'

When discussing goal setting with athletes and coaches, one benefit I describe is enhancing confidence. If something is achieved on the back of a goal, rather than without the premise of a goal, a person will feel a greater sense of accomplishment and empowerment from feeling in control of their destiny. They feel more responsible for the outcome because it was their goal.

Some people resist goal setting out of a fear of failure. Avoiding goals can be a self-protection mechanism. It can also be an indicator of diluted focus or lack of clarity and commitment. Avoiding goal setting for fear that they might not be achieved can place limits on development and fully realising potential. I suggest confronting the fear.

Understanding and appreciating individuality in goal setting can help. For some people it may be more effective when done infrequently or intermittently, while others will benefit most from constant engagement in goal setting. Know what works best for you and own your goals.

Once goals are established, one challenge is working out when to take responsibility for achieving or not achieving them. Many coaches and support staff working with athletes, including me, wrestle with this challenge. Again it relates to the art of utilising goals. Rather than viewing not achieving goals as a failure, identify it as a learning opportunity. Were the goals too ambitious? Why weren't the goals achieved? Was personal or performance progress made, even if the goal wasn't achieved? What opportunity can arise from the learning? Whether or not the goal was achieved, the experience should assist personal and performance growth, which is part of the reason for setting goals in the first place.

Creating goals and plans effectively and appropriately does not correlate with over-analysis. Goals aim to minimise 'just playing' or 'going through the motions'. Goals and plans managed effectively enable an athlete to direct energy to what is important and required. They do not have to be scrutinised every day or every moment. They don't have to be big and constantly in front of mind. Coaches and support people can be stakeholders in the plan, allowing and enabling athletes to channel energy and execute the plan. Ideally goals become the motivator, rather than just a reflection of motivation.

CREATIVE GOALS — '34 BY 34'

By 2006, 33-year-old Nicole Pratt had developed solid experience on the tennis tour. She achieved a career-high ranking of 35 in the world in 2002. Her journey to that level had swung between elation in representing Australia at the Olympic Games and the Federation Cup and frustration when plagued by injury. Now her ranking had dropped outside the top 100 for the first time in seven years. 'Through my career I was diligent at reviewing and planning what I wanted to achieve in the short, medium and long term,' she told me. 'The Olympics every four years was a carrot that helped me focus on smaller goals. I would write down my goals, break them into blocks and discuss them with my coach. They included what tournaments I wanted to play and what the travel schedule looked like. I always considered what would put me in the best position to perform and where I would be happy.' But with a ranking slide in 2006, there was no automatic entry to the main draws of Grand Slams, and to get into those tournaments she had to progress through qualifying.

'I lost in qualifying at the French Open and it *really* hurt,' she recalled. 'I could have hung up my racquet. Wimbledon was the next big tournament, and I hadn't typically done well there on grass. I also felt the expectation as an Australian to perform at Wimbledon and it was 10 years since I had had to qualify there. I decided to set a goal of getting back to a career high by the Olympics in 2008. I came up with the goal to be ranked 34 by the time I was 34 — "34 by 34" was ambitious, but it focused me.

'On the back of that refocus, I ended up having my career-best result at Wimbledon. After getting through qualifying, I got to the third round. There is no doubt I had elevated the tournament to having a higher level of meaning for me. By 2008 I got back to 35, one ranking shy of my goal leading to the Olympics. Unfortunately I ended up getting an injury, and I realised my career was over. I fell a few months short of my final goal, which was to get to Beijing in 2008,' Nicole explained. Although just missing out on the 2008 Olympics, the goal set after the French Open led to new highs and set a path for her to get back to an almost career-high ranking, inside the world's top 40. The performance was built on a carefully thought through plan and mindset. Without that approach, her racquet might have been hung up sooner. Nicole's story illustrates how goal setting and flexibility can play a role in setting outcome and process goals at different times. It also reflects the importance of creativity when setting goals.

Benchmarking

Swimmer Ariarne 'Arnie' Titmus achieved a dream at the Tokyo Olympics when she defeated Katie Ledecky to win both the 200 and 400 metres freestyle finals. The effort, magnitude and significance of the result were a product of her determination. They were also reflected in her coach Dean Boxall's emotion post-race. The rivalry with Ledecky was built up well before the competition. The two athletes had previously faced off at the world championships in 2019. Such was the anticipation for the Olympics that a US film crew flew out to Queensland to document Arnie's preparation.

'In 2016 it was not even reasonable to consider that Arnie would defeat Katie or set that as a goal,' Dean told me a few months after Tokyo. 'Arnie had a very good blade, but it needed to be sharpened. Her mindset was very good, but in 2016 she was still a novice. Arnie is also not as talented as Katie,' he added. 'Katie has a ruthless attention to detail and loves the pursuit of excellence. I discussed that with Arnie for two reasons: to help her improve her mindset and to recognise that she needed to work hard. Arnie's talent was her capacity for work. Her most important ingredient was her mindset.

'In May 2016 Arnie was 8 seconds off Katie in the 200, 16 seconds off her in the 400 and a huge 38 seconds off her in the 800. If I'd set a goal for her to beat Katie then, I would have felt like a fraud, a fake. There's *no way* I could have said it,' he insisted. 'What I did try to do was set a benchmark. That's what I put to Arnie then. If you want to improve, here's the standard. There are only a few genuine trailblazers in most sports, and Katie was one of them.

'It was only after some small wins and small gains that I thought I could sell the dream. That was after the Pan Pacific competition in 2018. After that we discussed that maybe she could medal. Those small wins and gains fed the story.'

Dean's strategy of timing the discussion speaks to the art of coaching and goals. When and how to discuss them is a big part of that. It wasn't an outcome. The early focus was based purely on standards and mindset. Using Katie as a benchmark to fuel Ariarne's motivation and focus was another.

Benchmarking is a strategy that can be and has been used in many sports and pursuits. Identifying someone in a similar field who sets the performance or personal standard can provide both an example of what to do and motivation. The skill is in ensuring that the focus comes back to the individual and that they don't feel overwhelmed. Striving for a time, or looking to work on a standard that could lead to a particular time, is another strategy. The four-minute mile and two-hour marathon are two examples. A rival or benchmark can make this challenge more real for many, though.

Benchmarking can be readily applied to team sports too, even when benchmark players may never be direct competitors. Cricket and football are two obvious examples where players can look to an athlete in their position to use as motivational fuel. A small forward in Australian rules football, for example, can identify a small forward in the competition they can relate to and strive to be like, or to defeat. In a way it is an artificial competition, because the two will never actually compete directly against each other. A batter can monitor a rival's statistics, using them as a personal challenge. This provides an opportunity for learning, as well as a challenge when statistics or processes of performance are reviewed. It creates an extra layer, in addition to the obvious ones of beating a direct opponent, winning a game or meeting their own standards to focus on. It can also be applied when an athlete is the best in a country and only competes against their rivals once every one, two or four years. They can be on the other side of the world but still offer inspiration. Benchmarking can also fuel the drive of athletes in different squads. Such rivalries can elevate world standards. In addition to Arnie and Katie Ledecky, runners Sebastian Coe and Steve Ovett, swimmers Kieran Perkins and Daniel Kowalski, and cyclists Anna Meares and Victoria Pendleton come to mind.

Some athletes enjoy and embrace this approach, while others are reluctant. Many industries strive to use positive comparisons and benchmarks for progress. Examples are schools comparing data in a range of areas, or businesses comparing themselves with other businesses. The key is to manage the process effectively to fuel, rather than detract, from motivation. Dean Boxall did this with Arnie to perfection in the lead-up to and at the 2021 Olympics.

Expectation and motivation

Expectation can be a self-fulfilling prophecy and drive motivation. In sport, when a coach or significant individual develops an expectation about an athlete, it can help them to elevate their efforts to meet that expectation. This may be based on a wide range of true or biased opinions. These expectations influence how a coach, or others, will work with an athlete, including their attention, communication and time given, as well as their interaction style. As a result of this expectation, an athlete behaves in a way that reinforces it. Motivation can be heightened, self-belief enriched and goals enhanced. Overall effort can increase as a result of the expectation. This behaviour by the athlete, in turn, reinforces the coach's expectation, and so the cycle continues. Over time motivation is enhanced and both parties increase their effort.

In this way, expectation is a kind of *multiplier effect*. As Geoff Colvin explains in *Talent Is Overrated*, the multiplier effect refers to a very small advantage that can spark a series of events that produce far larger advantages.[9] For example, a multiplier effect may begin when, for any reason, a person is given an opportunity, such as being selected for a specific training squad or environment. That experience can expose the athlete to higher levels of training and support, which enables them to improve more rapidly. This too can fuel motivation.

The opportunity may not necessarily be a training squad. It may be increased knowledge about a pathway or what needs to be done. It may simply elevate motivation. Many people start out motivated without knowledge. A lack of knowledge and guidance can stall development and reduce motivation. Poor direction can also diminish an experience and motivation. As I've discussed with many athletes, you can be given good advice or bad advice — the challenge is to know the difference. Taking good advice can set your direction for advancement.

With a positive multiplier effect the improvement reinforces or multiplies motivation, opportunities, growth — and, ultimately, performance. Sure, the athlete must maximise the opportunity provided. The balance is that opportunities provided to athletes, while extremely appealing, need to be managed so as not to drain them emotionally or physically. This applies particularly to junior athletes in development pathways. Understanding and knowing the athlete as a person, not just as a performer, helps to ensure that the opportunities provided are motivating over time and not inadvertently demotivating.

Our understanding of expectation effects can be traced back to a popular, and at times debated, research study published in 1968 under the title *Pygmalion in the Classroom*.[10] Robert Rosenthal, a professor of social psychology at Harvard University, teamed up with Lenore Jacobson, who at the time was an elementary school principal in San Francisco. In the study of 320 students over a full calendar year, teachers were informed that, based on the results of a previous test, certain children could be 'growth spurters'. In fact, no such test was conducted and students were randomly assigned to different groups.

Rosenthal and Jacobson reported that the results 'provide further evidence that one person's expectations of another's behaviour may come to serve as a self-fulfilling prophecy. When teachers expected that certain children would show greater intellectual development, those children did show greater intellectual development'.

In my experience in sport, expectation theory operates in more than one direction. Low expectations can lead to reduced motivation and opportunities for that athlete. High expectations of athletes can lead to increased motivation and development opportunities. One example is when experienced athletes transition to new clubs or squads, and they flourish. A refreshed mindset and new expectations of the athlete play a big part in bringing about this uplift in performance, as does the athlete's fresh approach to the new environment.

Rewards and positive feedback

Effectively, positive reinforcement rewards desired behaviour, with the aim of increasing the likelihood of the behaviour being repeated. These rewards could be verbal or tangible, such as prizes or awards, but feelings of satisfaction can also serve as intrinsic rewards. For example, positive encouragement, feedback or praise can keep athletes in a state of high intensity or help them increase or correct technical skills. A simple 'well done', clap or fist pump from the sidelines can serve as a positive reinforcer. Many people find this motivating. Individual athlete styles need to be considered, however.

Athletes may specifically request coaches and others respond verbally and behaviourally in a certain way to assist them, particularly during competition. This may include encouragement or even speaking less. It can be a trap to overuse verbal feedback. At times, silence can be equally effective. It allows head space for key points to be absorbed.

Verbal feedback just for the sake of it, or that is not genuine, can be counterproductive. Some athletes prefer a simple corrective discussion so they can get on with it. How the message is delivered can be as important, if not more important, than what is said, but when positive reinforcement is used authentically and appropriately, it can be reassuring and motivating.

Ways to enhance verbal feedback include linking it with the specific behaviour and including feedback on specific instructions, such as technical elements of a skill. Using vision of the desired or successful behaviour is another positive reinforcement technique. Many coaches use a phone or tablet to record successful movement patterns or repeat efforts to reflect positive energy, for example. Alternatively, a squad or team may recognise standards or behaviours a group is striving for. The reward may also be as simple as recognition and acknowledgement in peer or group meetings. This not only serves as reinforcement for the individual, but consolidates for the group what is valued.

Some coaches avoid giving positive reinforcement for fear it will reduce motivation or effort and risk complacency. I have also heard stories from athletes fearing going to meetings that review game performances where an overly negative reel of behaviours is highlighted. While it is meant to be educational, the experience can be deflating and actually drain motivation, particularly when this is a constant theme. Offsetting corrective feedback with positive reinforcement is a balancing act in sport, and especially in motivation. Naturally corrective feedback is necessary, but balance assists it to lead to improve behaviour and performance as well as sustain enjoyment and engagement.

Self-positivity and celebration

Ideally athletes themselves can provide their own positive reinforcement to feed their motivation. This can be enhanced when coaches and others with whom an athlete has a positive relationship use language such as 'Give yourself a pat on the back for that effort' or 'Be proud of the way you approached that solid block of repetitions and worked through until the end'. This can be followed up with a question such as 'What specifically do you think you did well in the session?' In effect, this kind of language can help transfer the ownership of positive reinforcement to the athlete and enhance intrinsic motivation. It encourages an athlete to congratulate themselves or celebrate an achievement, whether small or big.

Celebrations are an underutilised form of positive reinforcement. They can add fun and enjoyment, but of course they can't be hollow or false. Recognising when and what to celebrate can also help maintain wellbeing. Celebrations don't need to be reserved for dizzy achievements such as breaking records and winning major events, or they are likely to be too infrequent. I often recommend that athletes record 'daily positives', even for short periods of time, to encourage them to recognise and celebrate what they are doing well. This serves to counterbalance harsh self-criticism that can gradually and unwittingly wear people down. Celebrating even small experiences is a quality that many athletes have recognised as necessary to maintain motivation and wellbeing.

Embracing endeavour, rather than overly focusing on outcome, is a way to find positives and sustain motivation. It relates to outcome *and* process. Embracing endeavour encompasses the whole experience of striving for something. Recognising opportunities that arise from an experience, including relationships formed and the enjoyment of the journey, is part of this. Identifying what is enjoyable plays a significant part in sustaining motivation and wellbeing. This is another activity that I regularly conduct with athletes at all levels, as mentioned in 'Made not born'. I'll ask them what they find enjoyable about their journey and experience of being involved in the sport. What has been one (or more) of the enjoyable experiences for them? This may be from junior days, training or open competition and may or may not relate to performance. It is an idea worth exploring, because it also helps to open many athletes' minds to the daily positives of activity.

Motivational dynamics

Motivational dynamics is a concept introduced by education researchers E.A. Skinner and J.R. Pitzer.[11] Like some other models used in sport, it has foundations in education but has been investigated with athletes, with interesting results. The model suggests that peers have a significant positive or negative influence on engagement in addition to coping and resilience. This has applications for both team and individual sports, particularly because even within groups of individual athletes there is a team environment.

I have seen many athletes become disengaged because they've felt unsupported by or disconnected from peers in both sporting and educational environments. I have found that this often extends beyond peers to coaches and teachers, who play an important role not only in forming relationships but also in mediating and managing the relationships of the group. Many coaches underestimate how important group dynamics are for an individual's motivation. By the same token, many athletes underestimate the importance of forming friendships with people they train with or compete against. Other squad members are too readily seen as rivals, and athletes become protective and guard against building relationships.

Research insights

Researchers who surveyed 351 adolescent athletes in the United Kingdom found that how athletes dealt with peer influence impacted their engagement. The authors noted that 'the influence of peers appears to be strong and can affect an athlete positively or negatively, so coaches and sport psychologists should be aware of the influence'.[12]

Environment and culture

As I'll go on to discuss in step 5 on culture, the *environment* and *culture* are key extrinsic drivers. In some squads or teams, the culture can be dispiriting or even toxic. A positive and healthy environment and culture, however, can be extremely fulfilling, rewarding and motivating. Athletes want to be involved in such an environment; it becomes a motivation for staying in the sport and striving to grow and perform well. Enthusiasm and energy for training can be enhanced by a positive environment. In-turn, positive environments drive and elevate performance.

For many athletes, managing their environment is not easy. Often athletes cannot choose the environment they are in, but an awareness that they can contribute to the environment and the impact it has on them can help them to feel more in control and to manage or deal with the situation better.

Even the most intrinsically driven person can be negatively impacted by their environment. Interests and values that conflict with those of others or the organisation, unhealthy internal competition, low stimulation from training, peer and coach relationships and leadership are factors that influence the environment. Left too long, a demotivating environment can eventually drain intrinsic motivation. On the other hand, establishing and maintaining an environment that emphasises mastering new skills and new levels of performance more than outcome can positively impact motivation. This is discussed further in step 5 on culture.

Task and ego

A mastery focus considers that energy is directed towards one's own efforts, standards and performances, rather than those of others. Athletes with this motivation compete against themselves and their own standards as much as, if not more than, an opponent. It shifts how energy is directed and what is evaluated.

Much work has been done by psychologists and researchers on *achievement goal theory*, which was first conceptualised by motivational psychologist John Nicholls in the late 1980s. This model suggests that self-referenced evaluations and standards, such as personal improvement and learning, create a link to success from a focus on the task and high effort. Alternatively, an ego orientation leads to normative evaluations and standards that emphasise winning or position.

Research insights

Many researchers have investigated this model in relation to athletes. A 2004 study found that task-oriented athletes principally emphasise mastering skills in their sport, along with improvement or growth, and are interested in the game or activity for its own sake. Ego-oriented athletes, on the other hand, emphasise status, or a predominantly normative referenced approach, meaning they reference standards based on others, rather than on themselves and their own development.[13]

A study from 2000 found that elite players were more task oriented and less ego oriented than sub-elite participants.[14] A later study from 2016 suggested that task-oriented athletes more readily link success with effort than ego-oriented athletes.[15]

It is important to recognise that, at times, either a task or ego focus will serve to assist motivation, but understanding the role each plays assists overall. As mentioned earlier, knowing when and how to utilise multiple motivators including task or ego motivation, can assist athletes greatly.

Managing motivational challenges

All athletes experience challenges to their motivation. Factors that negatively impact motivation include injury, lack of support, loss of confidence that goals can be achieved, and new and competing interests. Lack of patience and understanding of what may be needed to achieve a sporting goal can also have an impact, as can non-selection, lack of opportunity, lack of financial support or even bureaucracy or other real or perceived barriers.

Emotional fatigue can also be demotivating. Over time it can be mentally and physically draining to maintain a certain lifestyle. Some will find striving to perform at training and in competition, constant scrutiny, travelling and living a regulated lifestyle can become too challenging or unfulfilling. Being an athlete is not always exciting, glamorous or fun.

Taking breaks and stepping back from training and competition are as important as key training blocks and sessions. The lifestyle of being a high-performing athlete spans 365 days a year, but that doesn't mean training has to. Blocks of time to stay physically and mentally fresh are important to maintain wellbeing and reduce the accumulation of challenges. Ideally these are planned to maximise energy, although that is not always possible. At times I have said the most important training day is the day off.

Anyone who has worked with teams and individuals understands the role of rest. Don't underestimate the importance of down time. Good decisions about when and how much down time an athlete enjoys or requires can help sustain their energy and motivation, and their relationship with their sport. Some athletes are by nature extremely rigorous and serious, while others are more laid back and casual. One person may need extra time off training, while others may need an extra session. One person may need to spend some time with their family and away from training, while another person may simply need a short break. Knowing and respecting difference and individuality helps prevent challenges from mounting. Failure to acknowledge individualism can also be demotivating. Naturally, this conforms with recognising the balance of quality and quantity of work required by the athlete to achieve their goals and maintain standards.

At times, a person may choose not to pursue a sporting endeavour. It's a personal choice of course and there are many reasons to leave a sport, as discussed earlier. These include a change in life direction or a lack of desire to pursue a goal, race or competition. Loss of motivation over time or too many competing challenges should be listened to, rather than ignored. It doesn't mean failure. It means it may be time to reassess and make changes, or to take the lessons learned into the next stage of their life. Personal circumstances or simply timing can influence a decision to step back from a sport. In these instances, athletes need to give themselves permission to do so in a positive way rather than with regrets, keeping in mind that during this decision-making and transition phase they can be more vulnerable. Supports are important at these times. This is discussed further in step 6 on wellbeing.

Passion, meaning and purpose

What are you truly passionate about? What does it mean to pursue or achieve something? These are questions I often ask athletes at all levels. Identifying and clarifying the purpose, passion and meaning of doing something can provide lasting fuel for intrinsic drive. *Why do you do what you do?* is another way to look at it.

I was at the Olympic track and field trials in 2012 in Melbourne, working and watching the events. As a matter of interest, I had a keen eye on Youcef Abdi in the steeplechase. As he crossed the line in first to secure his spot on the Olympic team, he knelt down and kissed the track. Having followed his story from afar I appreciated the significance of that moment.

When I interviewed Youcef he explained that he began running with his older brother in a tiny village in Algeria. 'My brother did athletics at school and my dad wanted me to accompany him on some runs in the holidays because it wasn't safe to run alone. There was a lot of terrorist activity in Algeria at the time,' he explained. 'The 1992 Olympics were on TV about that time, and that also inspired me. My dad said if I wanted to be a runner it was another reason I should run with my brother.' Over time his motivation and training earned him a position on Algeria's national junior team.

Youcef first visited Sydney as a competitor at the World Junior Athletics Championships in 1996. His team officials missed the entry deadline for his 1500 metres event, so they entered him in the 800 metres instead. 'It wasn't my event and I finished fourth in the heats.'

On Youcef's return from Sydney to Algeria, another paperwork mess-up meant Youcef was called up to do his military training instead of continuing his athletics training. 'My dream was to go to the Olympics, not to fight terrorists. I had 24 hours to decide what to do.' With his visa for Australia still valid, he decided his only option was to escape Algeria and return to Sydney. 'My parents were very worried and concerned, as I was only 18 at the time. It was difficult for them to let me go to the other side of the world, where I didn't know a single person or speak the language. But I was very motivated and determined, and they realised they couldn't stop me.

'When I landed, I didn't know where to go so I asked a taxi to take me to the Ibis Hotel at Darling Harbour because that was the only place I knew, from the World Juniors. I almost fainted when I saw the price for one night because it was a high percentage of all the money I had. The next night I went to a youth hostel but my money was running out fast, so I also slept on the beach some nights. I was lucky it was November and the weather was warm.'

Eventually Youcef met an Algerian and then secured a job at Marrickville Metro, collecting trolleys. 'Some days I worked from 8 am to 10 pm to get by. It was a good job because I didn't need to communicate!' As his English improved and he began to feel more comfortable he got a job at a factory. About nine months later he started to do some training again. 'I slowly made some friends and then joined a training squad. Despite all the barriers, I knew my greatest asset was my motivation to get to the Olympics. I felt no matter what, I had to work towards that goal.'

By 2000 Youcef was running well. He also received his Australian citizenship, which enabled him to chase his dream. At the Olympic trials he missed the qualifying mark by 0.2 seconds. He won another trial race, but ultimately, 'I didn't get selected and watched the games from my couch'.

Undeterred, he pushed on and qualified for the 2002 Manchester Commonwealth Games, finishing third. Representing Australia for the first time was a proud moment. Then in 2004 he qualified for the Athens Olympics, but a discretionary selection method meant he wasn't chosen. 'It was a turning point,' he recalled. 'I was drained physically and mentally. I stopped athletics because I didn't see a future or feel supported. It lasted a month, but then a voice inside my head said, "keep trying". I was 28 years old, and I realised I needed a fresh start. I had never jumped a hurdle in my life but I decided to switch to the 3000 metre steeplechase.

'There were two reasons why I chose that event. The first reason was because 5000 metres was too far for me. The second reason was that the steeplechase reflected my life. It was flat, with barrier after barrier that had to be jumped. If I had all these barriers to get over, it was up to me if I wanted to keep going or stop. The event reflected how I was living in real life.'

And his choice paid dividends. After two years of specific steeple training he qualified for the 2008 Beijing Olympics. 'My heart almost stopped when I got selected. I was the last person to be added to the whole Olympic team so I had begun to think, here we go again. It was a huge relief.'

By 2012 the selection policy had changed, so anyone who had a qualifying time and finished first was automatically selected. 'That's why I kissed the ground,' he explained. 'It meant an non-discretionary automatic selection.'

'The whole time I kept thinking the reason I left Algeria was to achieve a goal. I had wondered what the reason was for leaving my family and friends. But chasing the goal also gave me a purpose. It gave me a life lesson, and it made my life. In addition to my athletics goal, my other dream was to have a better life. I wanted to live in a country where you can have a life. My athletics gave me life. A life where you can safely walk to the shops. Some of my friends back in Algeria don't have a life. They are living but they don't have a life.'

Youcef faced many obstacles. But time and again his motivation, his sense of being driven by a higher purpose, helped him to overcome them. A higher purpose may be short term or have longer-lasting impact. It may be for oneself, others or something quite independent. Finding purpose in what one is doing typically embraces the idea that an experience has a meaning beyond simply winning. It reflects why participation is so important; it adds motivational layers.

Higher purpose or meaning can be driven by associating value with representing a community, representing a culture, a team, a family or a nation. Many athletes have described to me the importance of representing or standing for something and how it fuelled their motivation. Dedicating a performance to a family member or the passing of a loved one can certainly create such meaning. I have worked with many athletes who have dedicated a game or a single performance to such a personal experience. You may have seen an athlete pointing skyward, reflecting their dedication at these times.

For some people, identifying and staying in touch with the meaning or purpose of why they are doing what they are can sustain their energy for years across a sporting career, or even a lifetime. Ultimately, whether or not the goal is achieved is of less relevance to its meaning. The journey itself matters. Even if Youcef had not achieved his goal of being an Olympic athlete, his commitment created a new life for him. 'That's what was really priceless,' he said.

Summary

Sustaining motivation over long periods of time is both very individual and complex. Knowing yourself and managing multiple internal and external drivers are key to managing motivation. Your personal background and circumstances, your experiences within the sporting environment, and what your participation in the sport means to you are only some of the contributing factors influencing your motivation.

Harnessed effectively, motivation is an essential and powerful tool. Once athletes become aware of the factors that influence their motivation and how they can sustain higher levels of motivation for longer, they will find it easier to enjoy the experience of being involved in their sport. It also fuels commitment and higher standards.

BUILD YOUR MOTIVATION

- Keep focusing on what you can do, putting energy into action to help ignite motivation.

- Manage and maximise multiple intrinsic and extrinsic drivers.

- Consider competence, autonomy and relatedness: think about what you are good at, how you can contribute and who you can connect with.

- Manage, record, share and review goals. Consider the wide variety of goals you can set, and be creative when developing them.

- Build and maintain positive relationships with coaches, teammates and supports.

- Celebrate what you do along the way. Don't wait for the big achievements. Consider keeping a record of daily positives.

- Recognise the impact of environment and culture on your motivation.

- Recognise and balance mastery or task and ego motivators.

- Proactively recognise and deal with challenges.

- Find passion, meaning and purpose in what you are doing.

- Look beyond winning for motivation. An awareness that multiple motivators are in play enables you to recognise achievements and growth on your own journey. This can also help performance.

STEP 2

BOOST YOUR RESILIENCE

Mat Hayman could be described as a journeyman in road cycling. His professional career in one of the most physically challenging sports lasted almost 20 years. He rode for high-profile teams such as Rabobank, Team Sky and Orica–Green Edge and competed in the Tour de France four times. Mat also won gold in the road cycling at the 2006 Melbourne Commonwealth Games. Through most of his career he was typically a 'domestique': a support rider who rides tactically for the benefit of the team. He also became a one-day race specialist. Mat experienced many ups and downs through his career. Along the way, he learned how to deal with these challenges, and the lessons learned had to be applied again and again.

Mat's career-best achievement came when he least expected it. It was in his favourite one-day classic, the gruelling Paris–Roubaix. In 2016, the 15th time he competed in the race, he crossed the line in first place by less than a second. The Paris–Roubaix is held over 250 kilometres of French countryside, with more than 50 kilometres of the race on old cobblestone farm tracks. In the insightful documentary *All for One*, which chronicles the formation and journey of the Australian cycling team, Orica Green-Edge, as well as Mat's own personal story, legendary race commentator Phil Liggett described the Paris–Roubaix as 'one that everybody hates to ride, but everybody wants to win'.[1]

Mat's mantra: Always keep riding

When I interviewed Mat about his career he reflected, 'My first races at the Paris–Roubaix were far from successful. In 2008 I was stone last. My job was to support my teammates and I just wanted to help them and get to the finish line. It would have been easy to give up, but it would have hurt more, in the long run, to stop.' He recalled how, after those early results, 'my relationship with the race blossomed'. That relationship, with encouragement and support from an older Belgian teammate, Marc Wauters, who he looked up to, proved to have a lasting and telling impact. 'Like me, he was not a traditional winner. He was a worker, an unsung hero, but instrumental to the team. He used to say to me, "always keep riding".' It became Mat's mantra.

After years of persistence, in 2016, and now an experienced elder statesman of the team, Mat had put together a solid pre-season. In the intervening years he had had varying results, from 8th in 2012 to 76th in 2015. Then unfortunately — or fortunately, as it turned out — six weeks before the 2016 event, Mat crashed in a lead-up race, fracturing the radial head of his elbow. The doctors told him his Paris–Roubaix was over and he returned to his family at their base in Belgium, arm in cast. 'I was disappointed but looked at the silver lining of getting home and spending some time with my five-year-old son,' he said. 'I also thought, let's get on the wind trainer and see what I can do. So when I got home, I started doing sessions on the wind trainer in the garage. I had no real goal or certainty at the time.'

Five weeks later, cast removed, Mat met up with the team again and, in a last-minute decision, secured the final position in the team selection. 'From my unusual lead-up I had no expectations.'

In the race, however, after about five and a half hours, with 15 or 20 kilometres to go, he was in a breakaway group of five. 'I realised it could be my best performance. Then I over-corrected on a corner and got dropped from the group. My first reaction was *Why me?* I had a total letdown and fell in a real slump. *Why did I dare to get my hopes up?* was another thought that came into my mind. Then, in a moment, I decided to change that thought to *If I don't go now and do absolutely everything I can, I'll never forgive myself.* I thought, *left leg, right leg, keep going,* and started chasing the group down.

'When I caught the pack, I had the opposite feeling — it was an absolute morale booster. I had a new lease of life. I realised after that if I hadn't had that error and that moment, I might not have won. It impacted how I thought and behaved and the choice I made for the remainder of the race,' he recalled with a smile. The final sprint to the finish line resulted in a narrow victory. It was followed by emotions of disbelief then elation. 'I can't believe it,' he said on finishing. 'This is my favourite race. It's a race I dream of every year. This year I didn't even dare to dream!'

Mat's story highlights the roller-coaster of emotions that can occur in the lead-up to and during an event. It also reinforces the importance of a resilient mindset, manifested in this instance it was how he coped with the initial injury, how he trained back at his base in Belgium, how he dealt with almost not being selected, and then the race itself. His resilient mindset was built long before his victory. It was forged through his wide range of experiences, his passion for the event, support from his team, a willingness to keep having a go, and his self-talk around that mantra: 'always keep riding'.

Aim to be resilient

The only guarantee in sport is that there is no guarantee. All athletes experience losses, disappointments and setbacks. They are more common than observers will be aware of and are a part of any athlete's journey. Indeed, these experiences are part of life.

How challenges are perceived, interpreted and managed is what resilience is about. For athletes, resilience is an essential ingredient of advancement, and becoming resilient should always be a goal. Consciously learning and working towards being more resilient should be embraced, because you can be sure it will be called upon.

I view resilience as being able to deal with adversity, to bounce back from challenges, big or small, and to keep going, regardless of the circumstances. Resilience is determined by how a person thinks as well as what they do in a wide variety of circumstances. They may not be able to do much to change a situation, but should nonetheless aim to remain steadfast and positive. Sometimes they may manage to manufacture no more than a hint of resolve, *but they still take positive action*. Resilience shapes how a person thinks and what they do. Some people will even seek challenges and thrive on them.

A person may need to be resilient in order to deal with thoughts or fears that others might view as insignificant. Worry, anxiety and fear can take over. Resilience is often required in these situations.

> Resilience is 'the role of mental processes and behaviour in promoting personal assets and protecting an individual from the potential negative effect of stressors'.[2]

In my work I have learned to respect a person's experience from their viewpoint. One thing that working with people's mindsets teaches you is not to judge. The same circumstances will be experienced differently by different people. Many factors influence whether a person views an event as a challenge as well as how they cope. These may include whether or not they are prepared, their expectations, their experience in a particular environment or the importance of events in the context of the bigger picture. A person's self-image and their emotional state at the time of an event can also influence how they interpret and manage a situation. Resilience is also built from creating opportunities for experiencing success, not only overcoming challenges.

Being clear on what resilience looks like in a range of circumstances can be powerful. It primes the mind. I invite athletes to reflect on when they have been resilient. What helped and how were they able to be resilient? I introduce activities and use worksheets to keep records of these resilient experiences and the strategies used. This shifts the focus from the challenge to the thoughts and actions that enabled forward momentum. It's amazing how resilience stories can be embedded in a person's narrative. It helps shift the enduring story from the challenge to the recovery or management of the situation.

For example, when working with athletes with two or more knee reconstructions, I look at the recovery as well as the injury. With a change of emphasis, the focus of the story can shift from the injury to the recovery. Many people have more resilience capacity than they realise. Sport certainly provides an opportunity to grow resilience.

Break it down into smaller parts

There's little doubt that resilience is important across a sporting journey just as it is across a lifespan. Challenges will always arise. How well prepared a person is, and how they respond to them, contributes to their experience in pursuing the goal and to the eventual outcome. Resilience is indispensable in a broad range of different circumstances, as may be seen in figure 2.1 (overleaf).

Different aspects to navigate within each component are outlined in table 2.1 (overleaf).

The explanatory list in table 2.1 is not exhaustive, and there are other details that could be included in each category. This model considers resilience 'in the moment' or during an event, compared with managing overall performance including before or after the event and week to week. It also considers life in general and sporting life.

I created this model to break resilience down into smaller components that athletes can more easily identify and manage. Of course, categories overlap, and how one is managed influences and impacts on others within the model. Helping athletes to focus on different categories if something is not going well means strategies and mindsets can be applied to deal with different, smaller situations. The model also helps people to recognise that resilience isn't fixed. It can vary from situation to situation and from time to time. It also helps people to recognise that if there is a challenge in one area, it doesn't mean everything is bad.

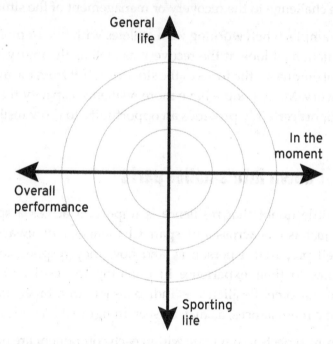

Figure 2.1: Resilience compass

This model of resilience is equally useful in sport or other real-life experiences. The categories for *sporting life, in the moment* and *overall performance* can be interchanged with any other endeavour — at work or school or for any other task or project. Importantly, resilience can be taught and developed. There is no doubt that accumulated experience in dealing with challenges assists with this. The challenge with experience is that she teaches the lesson after the event, which, though inevitable, is not always desirable.

What's important is that the experience is used for personal and performance progress.

Table 2.1: a resilience model

In the moment	In front or behind during a competition
	Win or lose a contest
	Scores for or against
	Facing defeat or victory
Overall performance	Performance within a season or competition blocks
	General week-to-week training including, development of mindset, skill or conditioning
	Form slumps or winning streaks
General life	Relationships
	Family
	Living arrangements
	Study and work outside sport
	Finances
Sporting life	Contracts
	Development and progression
	Relationships with peers, competitors and coaches
	General demands including, travel and time
	Balance
	Sport politics
	Selection, injury, illness
	Media

Ride the roller-coaster with multiple resilience strategies

Seeing the roller-coaster of experiences as part of sport can certainly help an athlete confront and manage challenges as they arise. Acknowledging that challenges exist and anticipating them can help athletes cope with them when they occur, as can acknowledging that when striving to achieve something, a wide range of challenges and emotions are inevitable. The more you strive for anything, the more likely it is that you'll come up against challenges. This doesn't mean you like the ups and downs, but you are more prepared for them. Applying this mindset to a challenge helps you embrace challenges with a management mindset of 'make the most of this time' by (a) recognising it as temporary (when that's the case), (b) recognising that lessons learned from a challenge can contribute to improvements and (c) looking forward to when circumstances are easier. Embracing the roller-coaster as ultimately contributing to progress is another way to look at challenges.

One big challenge Brigitte Muir had to overcome to achieve her goal of climbing the seven summits was fundraising. As with many sports, climbing mountains is not a cheap pursuit. 'As well as trying to get sponsors to fund my goal, I got jobs to raise money to climb mountains,' she told me. 'I did all sorts of work, including grape picking and painting.' But raising money was far from her only challenge.

In 1993, when Brigitte made her first attempt on Everest, the weather was just too bad. 'That's the nature of it,' she commented pragmatically. On returning in 1995, she was with her then–husband Jon, who was a fit and healthy person but got sick on the mountain. 'I had no choice. I had to get him back down.' On a second attempt that year she got (perilously) closer. 'I was at the back of a group on a steep section of the ascent. We got to just over 8500 metres (with less than 300 metres of climbing to the summit) and my headlight went out. It was dark. Pitch black. I couldn't see in front of me or behind. I made the big mistake of not saying anything straight away, so I was stuck. From experience I knew I had to wait and not try to go anywhere in the dark. I couldn't go up or down. I sat still and ended up waiting for three hours until I could see. By the time I had visibility it was too late to ascend and I was way too cold to go up anyway, so I made my own way back down to the last camp.' The group summitted and for a long time had not even noticed she was missing.

'After those experiences, I needed to work on my morale and reassure those supporting my quest. I decided I needed to climb an easier 8000 metre peak with no oxygen and no Sherpas or guides. It was necessary because I hadn't climbed above 8000 metres on a mountain yet.' Achieving that goal gave her the injection of confidence she needed, and she returned to Everest again in 1996. It was a tragic year on the mountain. Over the season, 11 people died trying to reach the summit. Her trip became a rescue mission rather than a summit attempt, as planned.

Finally in 1997, determined to complete her task, she returned once again. It was still not without drama. During the ascent, the expedition leader became unwell at base camp. Tragically, he died in his sleep. On the mountain, the weather also wasn't looking good, but a window opened. 'We left for our summit attempt at about 1 am. We stood on top of the world at 10.30 am.' But on the way down she faced another challenge. 'I got pulmonary oedema. It was so difficult to breathe I couldn't sleep. I had to stay awake for 65 hours to get down.' There were challenges around every corner, including getting back down safely, but she finally achieved her goal.

Brigitte's story demonstrates her capacity to deal with expected and unexpected challenges in each of the areas described in the model in figure 2.1. The strategies she used included keeping her challenges in context, staying determined to achieve the goal, learning from past experience, using supports and being patient. Through her resilience, Brigitte not only climbed the seven summits, but achieved her supplementary goal of seeing the world on her way.

Research insights

Eight male and four female Olympic champions from a range of sports were interviewed about their experiences of dealing with pressure across their careers.[3] The researchers found that 'numerous psychological factors relating to a positive personality, motivation, confidence, focus and perceived social support protect the world's best athletes from the potential negative effect of stressors'.

(continued)

They noted that 'high achievers actively seek to engage with challenging situations that present opportunities for them to raise their performance levels'. They also suggested that high performers at this level appear to engage with 'metacognitive' processes that involve reflecting on one's initial reaction to stressors.

Metacognition relates to an awareness of and, ultimately, control over one's thinking. I sometimes refer to metacognition as thinking about how you are thinking, which is relevant because not everything you think is true. The research highlighted indicated that high performers reflect on how they think about and interpret a situation, which helps them to reframe and deal with challenges. Thinking about how and why you are thinking something can be very empowering. Metacognition also helps a person to know and understand themselves, including how they approach different situations and the strategies they can use. That's one reason why I get people to reflect on how and why they handled certain situations a particular way.

Resilience grows with an open mind

Garth Tander has an impressive record in V8 Supercars, but he experienced many ups and downs across his career. 'The early part of my career wasn't straightforward,' he told me.

In 1997, Garth finished the Australian Formula Ford Championship in first place overall. It was a solid performance but it had exhausted his budget. With no options to compete in any categories in 1998, he was uncertain of where or if an opportunity would arise. His best option was to take up a role as a junior mechanic with the team he drove for. 'I had no budget and gave up being a race car driver. I thought I was done, with no money and no opportunity,' he admitted. Then, when Steven Richards, who was driving for Gary Rogers Motorsport, unexpectedly left after three rounds to take up an opportunity as a test driver for Nissan in

England, an opening emerged. Richards' opportunity was Tander's good fortune, as he excitedly took a call from Gary Rogers offering him a drive.

'I finished the 1997 season in August and had not been in a car since when I got the call in March. It was only an event-by-event offer until the end of the year. It felt like every opportunity was an audition and I tried way too hard,' Garth said. 'I made lots of mistakes but luckily the team stood by me and gave me another year. It was a one-year contract and the stability helped me feel more comfortable, which enabled me to make better decisions in the car when racing. From there I got a three-year deal, but it was shaky at the start.' Bumps in the road weren't over yet.

After a good start to his new contract the team was struggling, and Tander's performances again began to drop away. 'The sport had become more competitive and I had to keep up high performances. I started trying too hard again, overdrove and made way too many mistakes. I ended up taking a calculated risk and agreed with the team to finish my contract. I was 24 years old by then and realised I had to find a new team and a new mindset.

'Early in my career I didn't know what resilience was and how it could benefit me. I tried too hard to impress instead of letting the process of gaining experience help me grow. When we were struggling as a team, I really needed to develop resilience.

'For me, resilience is about looking in the mirror and saying I did everything I could and I helped the team do what they could to perform. In motorsport, it's not enough to say you did everything you could, without considering whether you assisted others. Resilience is not just about performance and technical execution. It's about doing your role as a cog in the wheel for the team. I learned that I needed to be open minded and look beyond the timesheet to determine if I was being resilient.'

As these stories illustrate, athletes who bring a resilient and learning mindset to challenges are better equipped to navigate the obstacles they confront on their sporting journey. With an open mindset, resilience grows over time.

A learning approach to building resilience

In 2016, a research study on resilience found that a combination of *psychological characteristics, social support* and *learning factors* assisted athletes to navigate their way through challenges.[4] The project involved 20 athletes between age 20 and 29 competing internationally in sports such as athletics, archery, mountain bike riding and hockey. Challenges in the study related to sport-specific experiences such as illness or injury, and not personal life trauma.

The researchers found that the challenges were negotiated through skills that were brought to, rather than generated by, such experiences. The research also concluded that, when effectively managed, events that require a resilient mindset can ultimately increase focus and motivation. The athletes used a range of strategies:

- Within the *psychological characteristics*, motivation was a key to stimulating and driving recovery. Increased focus on a specific goal and a reflective attribution style that attributed success to controllable factors and failure to uncontrollable factors was identified in the athletes. This attribution helped to maintain self-esteem and motivation. (More on attribution style shortly.)

- In relation to *social support*, the athletes described the value of identifying and knowing when to utilise social supports.

- *Learning factors* that assisted the athletes included drawing on and applying learning from previous experiences and enabling a 'big picture' approach to their situation.

How athletes deal with challenges was also investigated in a study by experienced psychologist Dave Collins and colleagues titled 'Super champions, champions and almosts: important commonalities on the rocky road'. This research, also referred to in the introduction, comprised interviews with 54 athletes from team and individual sports including soccer, rugby, athletics and rowing.[5] 'Super champions' had accrued a minimum of 50 appearances for their national team while 'champions' represented their country but had fewer than five international caps. 'Almosts' had achieved at youth level but had played only at second-level national league in their sport.

The researchers found that super champions were more proactive in dealing with challenges and differed from champions in how they conceptualised, thought about and actioned their experiences. They appeared to arrive at a challenge with an established attitude, rather than the reactive response adopted by the almosts. They also had a 'learn from it' approach to their challenges, while the lower achievers were characterised by external attributions and often seemed almost surprised by failure.

The authors noted that most of the challenges experienced were sport related, such as injury, non-selection or deselection, rather than personal issues. Interestingly, they also theorised that the proactive strategies used by higher achievers might begin to develop in teenage years, even before they got started on the 'rocky road'. They found no evidence to support a necessary role for major trauma in the development of resilience. The studies indicated that high performers use a variety of skills to enable them to be resilient. Learning from experience was a central theme.

In my experience, healthy sporting environments facilitate proactive coaching of resilience. Teenage years are not a time when these characteristics are necessarily developed naturally; rather, they are developed from deliberate or inadvertent lessons. Such skills should be part of an ongoing education for any athlete or young person right through their sporting career or life journey.

'I wasn't born with resilience,' remarked champion aerial skier Jacqui Cooper. 'I was probably weak as an individual at 16 years old.

I didn't back myself then. At 16 you don't really know anything about yourself. When Geoff Lipshut said, "I think you can be great", I felt like there was a shining light. I couldn't see the dream that he could see, but that was what I hung onto. His belief in me. From there I learned to be adaptive and resilient. I have no doubt resilience can be learned. I didn't want to forget challenges and move on. I wanted to remember them so I could applaud myself when I improved. I wanted to take this learning and put it in my resilience bank so I could use it to handle future challenges. I learned to take my failures with me, to try to avoid making the same mistakes. It was from my failures that I learned the most. A podium is great, but it only lasts three minutes, and I didn't learn as much. By the end of my career I was so robust nothing could throw me off!'

As mentioned, athletes face constant challenges — from niggling injuries to managing different relationships in a sport to fears and experiences of underperformance, even at a training session. Each of these experiences brings learning opportunities and are times to be resilient. Accepting these experiences as part of a sporting journey and viewing them as lessons and growth opportunities helps prepare athletes for dealing with them — not *if* they occur, but *when* they occur. That's what Jacqui did and it helped her performance and to prolong her career.

Keep going: injuries, disappointments and setbacks

By the time of the 2002 Salt Lake Winter Olympics, Jacqui had become a three-time world champion and earned the right to be the gold medal favourite leading into the aerial event. She had practised her sport for 13 years and in that time she had finished 16th at her debut Olympics in 1994. In 1998 she had crashed out of the event. Now, as world number one, it was her turn to shine. Her resilience had grown, but it was about to be tested. One day before the Games a training accident shattered her knee. She had a tibia plateau fracture, ruptured her ACL, damaged cartilage and destroyed her knee capsule. 'Since I was 16, I had never missed an event, so it was surreal to be sitting in the stands watching the event that people thought I was going to win. Four knee operations in the following 12 months rendered her unable to ski for two and a half years.

'Everyone was feeling for me,' she said. 'After the injury, Geoff came to talk to me and said, "No one will blame you for leaving the sport. But if you do want to come back, you'll need to come back different, to reinvent yourself. You'll need to relearn everything and come back even better." I realised I needed to move on from being an "acrobatic moron" and risk-taker to being a technician.' It took four years, but by 2006 she was back to world number one. 'That conversation with Geoff invigorated me. I set about reinventing my skiing.' Before returning to Australia, she stayed on at Salt Lake as long as she could, watching the semifinals. Waking up after surgery back in Australia, she saw that her younger teammate Alisa Camplin had gone on to win the gold. She had never won a major event before. 'I was so happy. I was happy Australia won a gold and it took a lot of pressure off the sport after all the support we'd been given.' Gratitude was Jacqui's overriding emotion going into her journey of rehabilitation and recovery. Her resilience had grown to a level where she was able to think beyond her own challenges to appreciate the achievements of others.

In 1999, at the age of 18, basketballer Dave Andersen left Australia for his first professional contract in Europe with the Italian squad, Team Bologna. It took him only a few years to become entrenched as one of the best imports in Europe. By 2004 he had been a central figure in winning two championships, as well as claiming a most valuable player in the finals series. He was quickly sought by CSKA, Moscow, in their bid for a title in the EuroLeague, a competition held each year between the best teams in Europe. After Dave's arrival at CSKA, the team proceeded to win four straight championships. The NBA was also beckoning. That would fulfil a career dream. Then, in 2007, at a big match in Spain against FC Barcelona, a freak accident left him with a snapped tibia and fibula near the ankle. His tendons and ligaments were also badly damaged.

'It was Australia Day too,' he recalled. 'People said it was a career-ending injury. I flew back to Moscow with it untreated, and my leg blew up like a balloon. It was a pretty painful flight. Once there, I took on board my treatment options and decided to have surgery back in Australia, which meant flying back home with the breaks. I had a great medical team in Melbourne who I had confidence in, so their advice helped me cope. I knew that resilience had to be a big focus for me then.

'I think resilience is the most important mindset for an athlete or anyone,' Dave told me. 'It extends beyond injuries. You need to keep working hard even when you don't feel like it. To stay resilient in general I also learnt to adjust my goals, which kept me looking forward. I carry a resilience card in my wallet — it's still there, even though I've retired!' It took about 10 months of rehab to recover, but after working with his support team and being clear and determined to pursue the NBA dream, Dave returned to Europe in 2008, this time playing for FC Barcelona, a European sporting powerhouse and, ironically, the team he was playing against when he was injured. From there the call finally came. It was from the Houston Rockets in the NBA. All his perseverance and resilience had paid off. He was US bound.

Jacqui's and Dave's stories are just two examples of what many athletes experience on their sporting journey. In each case, their motivation, focus on longer-term goals, use of supports and a mindset that saw their setbacks as growth opportunities enabled them to pick themselves up and get going again. While the specific instances described relate to injuries, they are only examples of the approach to dealing with any challenge.

Other than injury, disappointments can take many forms. Not having a personal best (PB) for an extended period of time is one. Non-selection in a squad or team is another. Not attaining a level of desired performance or achieving a desired outcome are also experiences that many athletes discuss as challenging and at times bitterly disappointing. Each of these scenarios requires a resilient mindset. Learning, staying patient, identifying positives and staying determined are only some strategies to manage these situations. Understanding the context of the performance is another, including how an opponent performed on the day.

Some might view Sasa Ognenovski's soccer journey as defined by disappointment after disappointment. He sees it differently. 'Because I didn't have a traditional pathway, I saw my path as one of keeping going and never giving in to rejection. I told myself to keep believing in what I could do. I saw all of the experiences I had as opening my mind to what I needed to do. That developed my resilience to the point where I wasn't scared to try anything.

'When I was playing in the National Soccer League (the local league in Australia) I paid for my own airfares and accommodation to go and trial with teams in Turkey, Croatia, Belgium and China. I didn't get selected by any of them. Then I got a call to trial for a Greek team and I paid for my fare to get back to Europe for that trial. I had 250 euros in my pocket and the public transport of a train, bus and taxi to get to the mountain training base cost me 248 euros. It ended up being worth it. It felt like a breakthrough when I was finally offered a four-year contract. I started the first season well, but unfortunately the club went bankrupt and I didn't get a cent. I came home broke. The timing meant the signing cut-off date for rosters in Australia had passed, so I went back on the tools as a carpenter and played in a local lower division.'

Through perseverance his agent got him a trial with the Brisbane Roar in the A-league. 'When I started training there I had a siege mentality, thinking I'm here now and I will do everything I can.' He got a two-year contract. Now 29 years old, he had three children and the family moved to Brisbane. 'That's when I felt like I'd made it,' he said. From there, his decade-long journey of persistence began to reap rewards. From Brisbane, Sasa was contracted to Adelaide, then a team in South Korea, where he became captain and won man of the match in the Champions League, as well as Asian player of the year. It was then that he caught the attention of the Australian national team selectors and got the invite to play his first game for Australia against Egypt in Cairo, aged 31. 'I felt vindicated,' he recalled. 'To be in the top 11 players in my country was an honour. It felt like all the work and training and all the trips around the world meant something more.'

Sasa's view of each disappointment as a learning opportunity helped him to grow, as did his willingness to spend all the money he had to get to trials. His readiness to travel around the world, even with his young family, also demonstrated his determination. His career was built on the back of a determined and resilient mindset. Sasa summed it up like this: 'Without being challenged, you can't be elite at anything.'

Learning to lose

Learning to lose is an important skill that helps build resilience. No one enjoys losing, but everyone loses at some stage. Effective management of losing helps people to grow, keep going and work towards their goals. At times the losses can be ongoing. In reality, every win takes an athlete or team one step closer to a loss and every loss takes them one step closer to a win. In some sports, winning doesn't happen very often. Embracing the journey and the positive experiences beyond outcome is vital. Adjusting goals is also important.

A missed goal, a poor start, feeling unwell or sore, a lost contest, missing a final, podium or point against an opponent — all these situations demand that the athlete get up and get going again. Quickly. How well the athlete responds to such setbacks can influence the outcome of a performance. How they use the time between these moments to get going again is crucial. A sporting performance can be defined by a moment. It can be a fine line between winning and losing.

Rafael Nadal's performance at the Roland Garros French Open is one of the most commanding international sporting performances by an individual over the past century. On the clay court surface, he has won a record 13 tournaments in 15 attempts since his first victory in 2005. It's a staggering record. To win a Grand Slam tournament means winning seven matches from a draw of 128 of the best tennis players in the world. By the end of the fortnight, when the champion is crowned, 127 male and 127 female players will have experienced a loss. Only one female and one male player won't have tasted match defeat.

Along the way, even the tournament winners will have endured many mini-challenges and defeats — in points, games and sets. How they respond to each mini-defeat influences the next point, the next game and the next set. Ultimately, how the roller-coaster ride of winning and losing is managed can decide the match and tournament outcome.

A review of every point in Nadal's 91 matches won in his tournament victories at the French Open up to and including 2020 indicates he has played a total of 16 234 points. Of those, he has won 9407 points and lost 6827. In percentage terms, it can be expressed as 58 per cent of points won against 42 per cent lost. It's unlikely that you would associate these figures with one of the world's most dominant sporting performances. Nonetheless it illustrates that even Nadal cannot afford to drop his head after losing a point. Indeed, resilience from point to point is surely one of his greatest skills. Yes, it also matters which key points are won, but resilience on points lost contributes to enabling a certain mindset on the 'big' points. This was never more evident than in his epic five set come-from-behind 2022 Australian Open win, where he lost 189 points in the match and won 182.

Resilience, as noted, can be taught. Both mindset coaching and physical training can help teach repeat efforts, repeat surges and recovery from a lapse or mini-loss. It is something Nadal has learned. One year in Brisbane, in the lead-up to the Brisbane International tournament, I gave a lecture along with Toni Nadal, Rafa's uncle and long-term coach. In his presentation he recounted how he coached

Rafa even as a junior to go again, keep hitting through every ball, regardless of the outcome of the shot before. He taught Rafa not to worry about errors. In *Rafa: My Story*, Nadal describes his mantra: 'Every single moment counts ... what I battle hardest to do in a tennis match is to quiet the voices in my head, to shut everything out of my mind but the contest itself and concentrate every atom of my being on the point I am playing. If I made a mistake on a previous point, forget it; should a thought of victory suggest itself, crush it.' It's not surprising he also outlines that 'The key to this game resides in the mind, and if the mind is clear and strong, you can overcome any obstacle, including pain. Mind can triumph over matter.' Regarding his uncle he says, 'Tony conditioned me from childhood that every match is going to be an uphill battle.'[6] From his commentary it is evident why Nadal treats the error, or shot before, once past, as simply a learning opportunity — it is just as he was taught as a junior. The coach of a world champion had instilled a learning approach. It's not surprising that Nadal has achieved what he has.

Life challenges

As much as we might try to protect people from significant life challenges, no one, not even elite athletes, can be isolated from the realities of life. During every sporting career, ordinary life still happens. Athletes, like anyone else, experience a full range of life events, including the difficult and even the tragic, such as terminal illness or sudden death of a family member, a car accident or another confronting event. Dealing with personal challenges, such as addiction or poor decision making, requires resilience. At times these experiences will stall a sporting career. For athletes in the media spotlight, sometimes these problems are publicly known; at other times they aren't.

In 1998, tennis player Scott Draper was in Paris, competing at the French Open. 'I was with my wife Kellie, who had cystic fibrosis,' he related when I interviewed him. 'The night before my first-round match she was in a lot of pain with what turned out to be a twisted bowel. We had to get to a hospital. It was midnight before we saw a doctor and she went in for emergency surgery and didn't wake until about 7.30 am. Thankfully she was okay, but I hadn't slept at all. I had to decide whether to play my match, scheduled for 11 am. Kellie had a great attitude and wanted me to play. "Muddy" Waters helped me make my mind up to play, and Mark Woodforde was kind enough to go to the hospital and sit with Kellie. So I went back to the hotel to get my gear and eventually arrived at the court at 11.05. I almost got forfeited. No warm-up. Tony Roach was courtside and gestured to ask what was going on.

I was a carer as well as a professional athlete, so I already had perspective, but that added another layer,' Scott said. 'Because of Kellie's positive attitude, my motivation was sky-high to win for her. It was a match I didn't want to lose. I ended up winning in straight sets. I rushed back to the hospital straight after to tell her the result. But it caught up with me later and I lost the second-round match. It meant I dropped out of the top 100 for the first time in three years. From that experience and what Kellie was going through. I was able to look at the bigger picture.

'At times I used to struggle with motivation because I was tired from dealing with bigger things than sport. I had a reputation for being inconsistent. I used to focus on doing what I could, in my circumstances, and that's what I judged myself on.

'I used to think about my high percentage play and commit to that. Assessing myself on that plan, rather than on the result, helped me stay resilient. Investing 100 per cent irrespective of the outcome gave me peace. That was different from when I was growing up and used to make excuses and didn't take ownership.

'Knowing my *why* helped me build my resilience and bounce back repeatedly. It helped me move forward. I haven't been a look-back person, unless it was to learn from something specific.'

Scott's story illustrates how life challenges can and sometimes do impact a sporting career. In these circumstances, it may be necessary to adjust how an athlete is operating as well as how they assess themselves. They don't have to be resilient all the time. It's okay and normal to dip and experience a range of emotions, and to be upset, disappointed or to struggle in certain contexts. Recognising that every journey is unique and includes a wide range of emotions can help resilience.

Explanatory style

In the Collins study mentioned earlier in the chapter, reflective attribution style was referred to as a strategy athletes use to build resilience. Let's delve a bit deeper into that strategy.

Attribution style, also referred to as explanatory style, relates to the way people explain events to themselves. Typically, explanatory style is broken into three components: *internal–external, stable–unstable* and *global–specific*.

An internal–external style relates to whether a person attributes an event to their own actions or to external factors. Stable–unstable relates to whether a person thinks the event is a one-off or will likely be sustained. Global–specific relates to whether the event is seen as impacting all aspects of their life, or just part of it.

How a person explains events reflects and impacts resilience. A positive or negative explanatory style has been associated with being optimistic or pessimistic. Importantly, explanatory style can be taught and learned.

The American psychologist Martin Seligman, often cited as the founder of the positive psychology movement, has been heavily involved in the development of this thinking, though the concept of positive psychology can be detected in many disciplines over centuries. In essence, positive psychology incorporates maximising subjective wellbeing for individuals and groups.

In one famous early study in 1968, Seligman and colleagues conducted a study using dogs.[7] Under experimental conditions, the dogs became helpless and passive. With retraining, however, the dogs learned to become proactive and put in effort to overcome challenges in which they had previously been passive. The study gave rise to the expression *learned helplessness*, which led to the phrase *learned optimism*. In his popular 1991 book of the same name, Seligman outlined his thinking on the importance of optimism and discusses how explanatory style can affect pessimism and optimism in the face of different events.[8]

Optimism helps resilience

In 1990, Seligman applied his theory in a competitive swimming environment. He wanted to know how swimmers would deal with a challenging event that he created in collaboration with coaches at the University of California at Berkeley. In one part of the study, 33 high-performance athletes including national and world record holders were asked by their coach to do a time trial for their best event.[9]

The coaches were instructed to provide false (slow) times to the swimmers after their effort, with the intention of producing disappointment. The coaches then gave the swimmers 30 minutes' rest before repeating their effort. Seligman found that, in general, athletes with an optimistic explanatory style did at least as well in their repeat effort. The performances of swimmers identified as having a pessimistic style after simulated defeat, however, deteriorated. Swimmers with a pessimistic explanatory style were also more likely to go on to perform below expectations during the season.

Seligman concluded that 'explanatory style predicted swimming performance. Optimists performed better than expected and pessimists worse than expected, particularly after defeat.' It was also suggested that 'explanatory style predicted swimming performance beyond talent'.

This study has a range of implications for coaching athletes on mindset skills, including coaching positivity and optimism. It's particularly relevant for dealing with defeat, disappointments or perceived setbacks. How an athlete explains the event to themselves affects their resilience. The optimistic swimmers who went faster may have thought: 'it's a one-off', 'the time may be wrong', 'I need to lengthen my stroke' or 'I'm better than that — I'll go faster next time'. The pessimistic swimmers may have thought: 'it's not my day — I'm tired', 'I struggle under time-trial conditions' or 'it's not fair to get only 30 minutes' recovery'.

Fast forward to 2002, when a paper by sport psychologists Robert Schinke and Wendy Jerome provided an overview of three general optimism skills that can be taught as part of a broader, comprehensive resilience program.[10] They recognised that with specific mindset training, performance can be improved in challenging settings through targeted cognitive or thinking skills. They discussed 'evaluating personal assumptions' (along the lines of explanatory style), 'disputing negative thoughts' and 'de-catastrophising' as three key skills to be taught to enhance resilience in athletes. They noted that the interventions are also appropriate for staff, including coaches and administrators, particularly given that athletes' resilience becomes more robust when they are placed in 'resilience-producing environments'.

These studies emphasise the importance of how events are interpreted. Indeed, in a number of the sports I have been engaged with I have given groups the opportunity to choose a range of topics under a 'performance mindset' banner to reflect on and build skill in, and optimism has been a frequently chosen topic. How events are debriefed, interpreted and explained is part of the education process. At times I also co-present with athletes from the group to share how they remain resilient, positive and optimistic. Their stories become powerful not only for increasing connection and cohesion within the group, but also as a natural and specific learning experience. Importantly, when discussing resilience in these circumstances, specific examples that relate to the athlete and sport are of most benefit. I'm not referring to deeper personal factors here. Shared sporting experiences normalise challenges, provide specific strategies and increase potential avenues of support within the group.

Reflecting, reviewing, debriefing and feedback

Managing self-talk and deciding who to listen to and who to ignore are also relevant strategies when looking to build resilience. With the emergence in social media of public commentary on athletic performances, this inescapable external noise can be a real challenge for most athletes. So a key skill for athletes is to take control, managing their own thoughts and filtering out irrelevant external information, to deal more effectively with situations and remain resilient.

Perspective needs to be layered into reviews and evaluations. As noted, very few athletes win consistently. Athletes not at the top of the mountain in their sport, including those regularly on the fringe of selection, or on the fringe of qualifying for a national competition or event, make up the bulk of aspiring and performing sportspeople.

Debriefing and reviewing at an appropriate time after an event is underrated as a strategy for learning and building resilience. Many athletes appreciate an effective review. Reflecting on an event enables them to process their thoughts and emotions. Debriefing need not be reserved for major events. Ideally it is incorporated into regular practice. Viewing the situation from a rational rather than emotional mindset helps. Understanding *why* something happened can help. These strategies assist athletes let go and move forward. Reviewing and debriefing can embrace emotions as well as facts. These processes can keep an event in context or perspective. Athletes are vulnerable to holding on to a negative interpretation of an event for too long. Having said this, at times simply moving on from a performance is necessary. Over-reviewing can be draining. This reflects the art of coaching and performing.

Working with individual athletes or squads, I often ask them to review and reflect on events and experiences. Building these processes into post-training and performance routines, as well as into annual or other cycles, should become habit. There are many ways to do this. One exercise I use is to ask athletes for their reflections under three categories: *self, others* and *environment or circumstances*.

Some people tend to overly attribute poor or disappointing performances to themselves. It is good to take responsibility for poor performances, but not when the performance is not necessarily very bad or can be attributed to other factors. Broadening the review under these three banners allows a more accurate picture of a performance to be drawn. Resilient athletes do not evaluate themselves purely and simply on winning or losing. They do not judge or explain their performances as simply good or bad — or, more extremely, as 'great' or 'terrible'. Appreciating that performances can fall short at times shifts how a review is conducted, and a plan to re-energise can then be developed. Avoiding extreme, emotive terms in reviews nurtures consistency and can sustain both physical and mental energy. There is a lot of space between great and terrible. Remember the adage, 'You're rarely going as well or as badly as you think you are.'

Some athletes may at times struggle to accept responsibility for their performance or situation. They blame others or circumstances — the weather, a coach, an opponent or anything to avoid taking personal responsibility. This self-protection mechanism can hamper progress. Honesty can be difficult, because if the athlete made a big effort but their performance was poor, it can be confronting to consider what this says about their capacity. Taking responsibility is the beginning of a learning process. Being honest, and knowing when to take and accept responsibility, leads to growth, and this requires resilience. Athletes have to be comfortable with putting their hand up and saying 'my bad', 'my mistake', 'my responsibility'. Understanding when and when not to do this is part of a performance mindset.

I often encourage athletes to conduct their own review of their performance, preferably before their coach's. This strengthens responsibility, enables them to be more open to feedback and facilitates more meaningful conversations with the coach. Reviewing helps them confront small or large challenges as well as small success within a win or loss and stimulates growth. This doesn't mean the reviewing style should be confronting. The style can be supportive which, can help confront the performance. A simple strategy to manage this is to review *what has been done well* and *what has been learned*. It should also identify *what is required to move forward physically, mentally, technically or tactically*. For many athletes I work with, I often mandate reviewing what has been done well and what has been learned, regardless of outcome.

Recording these thoughts facilitates the debrief strategy. Reflecting on the information collected provides another learning opportunity. Patterns in performance are more easily detected in a structured review. This exercise, as noted, remains constant for wins or losses. As well as reviewing specific events, reviews of blocks of training and performances in the lead-up to major competitions, events or finals series can narrow the focus and enhance motivation. Such reviews can be summarised as 'major learning', 'what I'm proud of' or 'why I can do well'. In effect, the purpose of these reviews is to emphasise key actions to move forward.

To summarise, the following are questions I have used at different times in athlete debriefs and reviews to facilitate learning and resilience:

- What are the details including score, conditions, opponents?
- What happened overall?
- What did you do well?
- What did you learn?
- Did you execute your plan, or how did your plan go?

- How was your mindset?
- What are you proud of?
- How have you/we grown?
- Based on this experience, what do you need to do, or what action needs to be taken at training, as well as in your next performance?

Of course, I'm not suggesting all of the above are necessary in a review. They are simply examples to reflect on. I recall asking athletes to identify what they could have done better and what they have learned from strong winning performances, not just losses. When wrapped in a package that embraces growth, accepting and confronting performances and emotions becomes easier. High-performing athletes don't want their reviews sugar coated. But they are less likely to become deflated or despondent after honest evaluations based on facts and embracing lessons to move forward. This can be empowering and foster resilience.

Team resilience

Team resilience is important. How well equipped individuals are to handle adversity, and how well the group is educated to support one another, impacts team resilience. This can be taught as a specific concept and incorporated into team performance planning and reviews, so team members are aware of their impact on the resilience of other individuals and of the collective.

Research insights

'Team resilience was defined as a dynamic psychosocial process which protects a group of individuals from the potential negative effect of stressors they collectively encounter,' a 2013 study outlined. 'It comprises of processes whereby team members use their individual and combined resources to positively adapt when experiencing adversity.'[11]

These researchers identified four main resilience characteristics of elite sport teams: *group structure, mastery approaches, social capital* and *collective efficacy.*

- *Group structure* includes topics such as group values and norms, shared leadership roles, communication channels and group accountability.

- *Mastery approaches* involve learning processes and effective behavioural responses, such as not dwelling too much on setbacks and managing change.

- *Social capital* is about group identity, perceived social support and prosocial interactions, such as a no-blame culture and frequent positive interactions.

- *Collective efficacy* includes drawing on past mastery experiences, group cohesion including qualities such as fighting spirit and commitment, and social persuasion that relates to feedback.

All four areas are important for team resilience. A no-blame attitude and shared responsibility can lead to more efficient and effective problem solving and growth.

There are many challenges to team resilience, including external influences such as pressure from media, administrators and supporters. A demand for immediate results increases pressure in sporting environments. In these instances, team resilience and unity is vital. When unmanaged, pressure can lead people to become protective of their own turf and can fracture teams and negatively impact performance. Pressure is a time to increase resilience and unity.

At these times, communication becomes an important component of helping resilience. If athletes know and understand what is happening, they feel empowered. When there is a lack of information or communication, people can feel vulnerable.

Increasing communication within a group can help resilience, in and out of competition. If one person is struggling with performance, other team members can support them through instruction or encouragement, enabling them to hold their ground and helping the team to remain strong.

Navigating transition and other vulnerable times

As noted in the introduction, transition is a particularly vulnerable time for many athletes. It often brings new or unexpected challenges. Advancing from junior to open categories, returning from injury, a change in coach, changes of technique and physical changes are all times of transition. Moving to a new city or country, changes in relationships and changes in personal life circumstances can all impact coping.

How transition is navigated becomes important. Patience and an eye on the bigger picture also helps, as does staying positive. All contribute to a resilient mindset. When 16-year-old Storm Sanders moved from Perth to Melbourne, she didn't have as easy a path as she might have wished. However, she embraced these strategies to work through a challenging phase.

After the move, she quickly got down to work. Being at the National Tennis Centre and home of the Australian Open was inspiring, but it wasn't a fairytale transition. 'I had challenge after challenge,' she remembers. 'It was not an easy road. I had injuries, setbacks and poor performances. From 19 to 23 I didn't get a full season on tour and felt like I was starting over multiple times. In 2018 I got a shoulder injury that wasn't able to be diagnosed for about four months. I couldn't lift my arm above my shoulder and didn't hit a ball for seven months. For a while there was no timeline and no certainty of recovery. I thought about giving up being a player and taking up coaching. But I decided to look for a positive. Resilience is finding a positive, even in adversity.

'I wanted to find a way to get better at *something*, even if it wasn't tennis. I studied for a Bachelor of Science in Psychology. I also started doing match analyses of players on tour. It enabled me to see the game from a different perspective. I began to thrive in that tough and challenging situation. It also affirmed what I wanted to do — to get back to playing tennis. It definitely helped me when I started playing again.'

Unable to train, or restricted to minimal training, Storm was determined to stay positive. She used the experience to sustain her motivation going forward. Without knowing it at the time, she was also able to use the experience to her advantage in competition down the track. The more challenges she navigated successfully, the more resilient she became.

Adaptive perfectionism and flexibility

Striving for constant perfection can lead to burnout, dissatisfaction and misinterpretation of challenges. This may sound counter-intuitive, given that the highest-performing athletes must be relentless in their efforts to achieve the greatest success. But research with elite athletes has identified *adaptive perfectionism* as an important quality common to those who succeed at the highest level. That doesn't mean taking it easy. It does mean some flexibility to help resilience. I often use the analogy that if a rigid piece of wood is bent it snaps. Bend a piece of wood with some flex, however, and it will return to its original shape after being tested. Make no mistake, resilience is about flexibility and adaptability. This takes people beyond black and white, good or bad thinking.

In 2002, Daniel Gould and colleagues undertook a very interesting study with a group of athletes that provided revealing insights into performance.[12] The study involved in-depth interviews with 10 Olympic champions from both Winter and Summer Olympics between 1976 and 1998, who between them had won a total of 32 Olympic medals including 28 gold. They were, in other words, the best of the best. The paper identified 10 common psychological characteristics within the group. (This is discussed further in step 7 on performance.) One of the 10 characteristics was adaptive perfectionism.

The authors found that adaptive perfectionism was positively associated with achievement. Furthermore, the athletes in the sample were moderately high or high on personal standards and being organised but, interestingly, low on concern for mistakes. This indicates not that they weren't concerned with errors and challenges, but that they could contextualise them.

The athletes also reported that adversity, such as losing or frustration at training, was interpreted as teaching skills and attitudes important to psychological development. The authors noted that adversity contributed to teaching 'how to lose with grace, mental strength, [and] determination as well as understanding that frustration comes with success'. Adaptive perfectionism helped resilience.

In 2018, a review of perfectionistic studies in sport was conducted by Hill, Mallinson-Howard and Jowett.[13] In their paper they distinguished between 'perfectionistic striving' and 'perfectionistic concerns':

- *Perfectionistic striving* had a positive impact on performance, motivation and wellbeing.
- *Perfectionistic concerns* was related to maladaptive motivation and wellbeing, rather than to enhancing performance.

These findings reinforce the importance to 'strive high', without becoming overly self-critical. When these two factors sit in balance, resilience can be maintained more effectively. Irrational self-criticism along the lines of perfectionistic concerns makes resilience difficult to maintain.

Some athletes believe being perfectionistic helps them because it leads to obsessiveness and improvement. The studies mentioned, however, suggest that, taken too far, it can be counterproductive. Being too rigid and unforgiving of oneself can limit resilience. Resilience is not just about dealing with challenges and pushing on. It is also about knowing when to be flexible and forgiving. This approach helps athletes confront their fears and new uncharted territory that is a constant in their journey. Resilience is about finding a balance between when to push and strive and when to slow down, reflect and adjust. It helps to aim and push higher.

Summary

Resilience is about dealing with challenges, bouncing back and keeping going. It encompasses how a person thinks and what they do. It is a skill that can be developed through experience but also through specific strategies.

All athletes experience ups and downs and challenges, big or small, in sporting events or in life. Appreciating that many challenges including injuries, disappointments and setbacks are a part of sport is helpful and necessary. Athletes who see themselves as adventurers, always looking to scale new heights and embrace challenges, are often more resilient.

Focusing on learning, using supports, and remembering motives and goals can help build and sustain resilience. Debriefing — reviewing performances and events — can influence resilience. Learning how to manage explanatory style, being optimistic and balancing perfectionistic tendencies can help athletes remain resilient.

BUILD YOUR RESILIENCE

- Look to build resilience proactively into goal setting.
- Break challenges down into manageable parts to help address them.
- Consider resilience in different scenarios, such as in the moment, as a performer overall, in sporting life and in life outside sport.
- Consider adapting a learning approach to your journey.
- Consider supports available and take a big-picture view whenever possible or relevant.
- Be prepared for injuries, setbacks and disappointments, appreciating that they too are part of the journey.
- Respect the fine line between winning and losing, and learn how to lose.
- Manage explanatory style.
- Stay optimistic.
- Debrief, reflect and review in the right way at the right time.
- Maintain a flexible mindset, applying adaptive perfectionism.
- Reflect on how well you have managed challenging events historically. Record one to three occasions when you have been resilient, and consider why and how you were resilient as well as how it helped.
- Reflect on your plan in the short, medium and long term, and consider whether you need to adjust the plan as a result of an event. How can you maximise the change in timeline?
- Create a filter. When considering a wide range of opinions related to feedback from an event, choose the ones you believe are relevant, prioritising the views of people you trust.
- Reflect on resilient stories from others you can relate to in order to sustain your own resilience.
- Create opportunities for success to build resilience.
- Reflect on the strategies presented in step 6 on wellbeing.

STEP 3

SHARPEN YOUR FOCUS

Have you ever tried just standing still in one spot for even two, five or 10 minutes, let alone a full hour? In May 2002, in New York's Bryant Park, David Blaine was lifted by a crane onto a platform only 55 cm wide and about 30 metres above the ground. He had no harness, no safety net, no food. The platform had two handles to hold onto for stability in wind gusts. He wore a catheter so he could urinate. David stood there for 35 hours. It wasn't a magic trick but an endurance challenge that required, among other demands, that he block out all distractions. Standing still was a test of focus. The crane lifted him onto the platform about midday and he stood there until about 11 pm the next day. Fatigue, the height and changing weather conditions across the day and night were some of the potential distractions. But perhaps the hardest to conquer would have been his own internal thoughts.

David's training for this very specific task began at least 18 months earlier, standing on objects such as an upside-down pot at ground level, gradually progressing to standing on different surfaces at increased heights. Other mental challenges he had trained for before this one likely helped him to develop focus techniques.

The challenge David set himself was clearly a physical as well as a mental one, but his training centred on building concentration. It illustrates powerfully how focus is something you can train and develop over time, like muscle. The more you train, the sharper your focus will become and the longer it will last. The less you train it, the more vulnerable you will be to distractions and fatigue. Lapses in concentration can be costly.

Another lesson we can take from David's remarkable feat is that concentration can be developed with a quiet and calm mind, regardless of what is happening around us. Being able to concentrate in the face of noise and fatigue requires a still, quiet and calm mind. It is not dissimilar to staying on task when studying at the kitchen table while dinner is being prepared or working in a busy open-plan office.

To emphasise the importance of focus to active athletes, I have occasionally introduced standing still as a basic activity. Some find standing still for five or 10 minutes challenging as their attention drifts. Part of the purpose of the activity is to coach them to redirect their attention and to stay on task, as well as appreciate focus. Another activity to develop powers of concentration is to study an inanimate object for several minutes, noticing as much as possible about it. Skill in such tasks improves with practice. Both activities centre on keeping attention in the present and can also be regarded as an exercise in *mindfulness*, which is discussed further in step 6 on wellbeing.

Experienced athletes and their coaches know this script too well: at times the mind is willing but the body is not; at other times the body is able but the mind is not. Focus or mentally staying on task is a key skill that needs to be learned and maximised for performance. Typically, this skill is developed inadvertently during training, and during competition itself, but it can be learned purposefully through a wide variety of methods depending on the sport, the athlete, and the coach and performance psychologist who are part of the team.

Self-talk: you are what you think

Self-talk, which includes the use of cue or trigger words, is one of the most common and effective methods of building and managing concentration. Its benefits include portability and accessibility: you can use it anywhere, any time.

On August 18, 2015, Australia was playing New Zealand in an Oceania Olympic basketball qualifying game. A win against the Tall Blacks would secure an Olympic berth for the Australian Boomers in 2016 and an assault on an elusive Olympic medal. The Australians started well, but with the support of a parochial crowd on home soil in Wellington, New Zealand clawed back to within five points late in the fourth quarter. It was to no avail, however, and Australia held on to win 89–79. Matthew Dellavedova top scored with 14 points, with Dave Andersen contributing 11 and Andrew Bogut sinking 10. The 2016 Olympics beckoned.

Dave had been instrumental in game one only three days earlier in Melbourne, equal top scoring with Patty Mills on 17 points. Dave's outwardly relaxed demeanour masked an inner determination. 'I was in a leadership role in that series,' he reflected. 'I had a mindset to be *aggressive* and it kept ringing in my ears. *Influence* and *impact* were two other words I used. I missed some shots early and remember getting a serve from the coach at half-time. I could have gone into my shell but in the second half I was aware of how important my self-talk and catchphrases were. I stayed aggressive and helped the team win a high-stakes game.' Australia won the series and qualified for the Rio Olympics.

'Over my career self-talk was really important. It gave me a better mindset when playing at the highest level. The competition is always tough, so you need inner-talk and catchphrases and to keep adjusting them. You need to keep phrases that are relevant. Mine changed over the years — I used things like "sharp", "aggressive", "smart", "work rate" and "leadership". They helped me get into the right frame of mind for games and to deal with the big picture. I used self-talk in the gym or late at night if I was doubting myself. One of the main reasons I used it so much is because I wanted to stay on the front foot and not just be reacting, especially as my career progressed.'

Dave's story suggests that self-talk is relevant at any level, to help performance as well as away from the performance environment — he used self-talk on court, at the gym and at night.

Whether you realise it or not, a constant dialogue swirls around in your mind. Athletes like Dave know too well that this dialogue needs to be managed. Extensive research has also indicated that in sport self-talk is an essential skill.

Although self-talk is not easy to assess and measure, most people understand it as how a person speaks or thinks to themselves – either in a reflective, general or directive manner. Self-talk has been described as an articulation of an internal position, so that it is recognised in consciousness.[1] This description is built on earlier work that suggested self-talk is reflected by verbalisations or statements addressed to oneself.[2]

In essence, self-talk comprises of thoughts or conversations, either brief or long that occur in your own mind. Along similar lines, trigger or cue words are single words or short phrases that people can think or say to themselves. These can be planned or spontaneous. Their intent is to manage and direct thoughts, emotions and behaviour.

Research insights

A 2014 study of 41 young Greek swimmers found that performance improved in a group that was coached in self-talk over 10 weeks between two competitions, compared with a control group that had no self-talk coaching.

The athletes were coached in motivational and instructional self-talk, and to use specific cue or trigger words, before and during training sessions. Motivational cues included 'let's go' and 'strong', while the instructional or technical cues were based on different swimming strokes, such as 'deep'. All cues were developed in collaboration with the coach and tailored to individual swimmers.

A sheet with the self-talk cues was placed at each swimmer's lane during training. The results found the group coached in self-talk outperformed the control group at the second competition.[3]

'The little voice'

I have referred to Herb Elliott's *Winning Attitudes*, which was used to support athletes in their preparation for the Sydney 2000 Olympic Games.[4] The book collected comments on a range of psychology topics from Australian Olympic and high-performing sports champions. It observed that some athletes call self-talk 'the little voice'.

For example, Debbie Flintoff-King, gold medallist in the 400 metre hurdles at the 1988 Seoul Olympic Games, explained that 'the little voice is the one that tells you you can't do it, and the one that tells you you can. I had both. I always had this little thing in my head feeding me negative ideas. I had to keep clearing my head saying "rubbish, I don't want to listen to that". I used to work a lot on affirmations, talking to myself. The little voice can either make you or destroy you.'

In 2014, after his Wimbledon victory over Roger Federer, Novak Djokovic spoke about reassuring himself in the epic five-set battle against his rival. He reflected that when he lost five games in a row to lose the fourth set and missed two match points he knew he needed to reset. 'I had a chat to myself,' he said. 'I was loud to myself, saying "believe, believe in yourself" ... It's not a cliché. It really works even if you don't feel like it at times to say positive things to yourself ... that's exactly when you should do it.'[5]

In 2021, after defeating his other great rival Rafael Nadal in the French Open semifinal, he went on to defeat Stefanos Tsitsipas in the final after being down two sets to love. After the final, Djokovic said in his press conference, 'There's always two voices inside. There's one telling you that you can't do it … That voice was pretty strong after the second set … I told myself I can do it. I encouraged myself.'[6]

These reflections indicate that destructive negative self-talk needs to be tamed or it can spiral out of control. It also shows how powerful self-talk can be to keep a person level, steady and on task, or direct them back to task.

Technical, tactical and emotional self-talk

In my work with athletes, coaching self-talk is discussed often. Depending on the situation, I describe it as *technical*, *tactical* or *emotional/motivational*. Self-talk can use one or any combination of these categories to help an athlete obtain an optimal emotional state or performance. Following is a brief description of each of these areas:

- *Technical self-talk* might be 'forward', 'early', 'footwork' or 'over' for a tennis shot, or 'smooth' or 'rhythm' when running. The choice of words is as broad as the different technical aspects of any sport. Over time, the behaviour is associated with the word and becomes instinctive, reducing the need to use it regularly. However, the word can always be reused when the athlete is struggling with, refining or mastering a particular technique.

- *Tactical self-talk* often relates to a race or event plan and may be built around strengths or a strategy that maximises performance. For example, in a 10 kilometre run the plan may be to go out 'steady' to set up a desired pace, then to 'settle', before 'working' to get home over the last

2 kilometres. I have provided a more detailed example on tactical self-talk in the chunking and race plan section that follows. It could also relate to a team strategy being employed for a specific game. It may be used by a cricket batter or bowler at a particular stage in a match. Clearly there are many examples of tactical self-talk, depending on the sport and situation.

- *Emotional or motivational self-talk* relates to the self-encouragement needed to sustain composure or focus. Basic examples include 'breathe', 'relax', 'now', 'switch on' and 'you've trained for this' or 'make it happen'. Tennis player Lleyton Hewitt's and high jumper Nicola McDermott's famous 'come-on!' is another. Emotional and motivational self-talk can be spontaneous in the heat of battle but is often pre-planned and rehearsed.

Dylan Alcott is one athlete who has described the benefits of positive emotional self-talk. In his empowering book *Able: gold medals, grand slams and smashing glass ceilings,* he described his rise to world number one wheelchair tennis player and his mindset in his first Australian Open final in 2015. He was leading 4–1 in the second set and was two games away from winning when rain interrupted play. 'Suddenly I was thinking too much, and the weight of the occasion began to get the better of me. After the rain delay, I lost the next two games. Now I was leading by just one game. At that moment, self-talk came to the fore with phrases such as "don't let this moment slip. You can do this!" The positive self-talk worked and, in the end, I proved too strong'.[7]

The simple nature of some triggers is highlighted in a case study of champion Welsh Rugby Union player Neil Jenkins, the first player to score 1000 points in international matches.[8] Researchers found that Jenkins used several strategies in the competitive environment to help cope with distractions. For example, he coped with negative self-talk by swearing at it or imagining putting it behind him in a black box. 'I don't always do it because if things are going well, I just feel confident and then I've just got to keep going.' In his kicking routine he used 'rhythm' as a key trigger. As he had used this trigger at training, in matches he imagined that he was on his own, kicking at training.

Positive, negative or neutral and curious self-talk

Other than fitting a specific category such as technical, tactical or motivational, I often discuss that self-talk or trigger words can be *positive, negative or neutral*. If the self-talk that scrolls through your mind is negative or destructive, this has to be identified and challenged. It's a confrontationist approach. Many psychologists coach their clients to use self-talk strategies to counter negative thoughts and replace them with more useful and rational ones that will help them to maintain focus, confidence and a sense of control and calm.

Other than reacting to and dealing with negatives, self-talk can also be proactive. Proactive self-talk is usually positive and revolves around statements such as 'I will', 'keep going', 'I can' or 'it's okay'. It aims to ensure that your thinking through the day and during performances moves in the direction you want it to. It's about self-encouragement. While positive self-talk can be very powerful, there is another important type of self-talk that can be beneficial—neutral self-talk.

Neutral self-talk is, at times, a much easier space to come to terms with than positive self-talk. Many athletes prefer not to be too positive, especially if they feel it may not be warranted, and this can be healthy. It can be difficult and feel false to tell yourself that you will win when the competition is very strong. To be realistic can be peaceful. 'Let's see', 'I'm not sure how I'll go, but I will have a go', 'I can focus only on what is in my control', 'I might be OK' or 'I will focus on my own performance' are all examples of neutral self-talk.

Scott Draper used this as one strategy in his rapid rise from a tennis ranking of basically zero to top 100 in less than a year. A turning point was in 1994 when Scott lost in the qualifiers of low-rated satellite circuit events in NSW for three weeks in a row. Not long after, he flicked a switch and won 42 consecutive matches that took him to the final eight players at the Japan Open in Tokyo in 1995, facing off against Andre Agassi. 'I was the same person, with the same physique, skills and equipment,' he told me. 'I worked with my sport psychologist, Michael Fox, and decided to get serious. I agreed to show no negative emotion. No headshake. No negative language. Show nothing and focus on playing. If I messed up, I would say, "Isn't that interesting". It helped me not to punish myself. It stopped me from getting caught worrying about my own demons.'

After his tennis career, Scott turned his hand to golf and secured his professional card using the mindset skills he had refined in tennis. He earned his Australasian golf tour card in 2004, but it wasn't easy. 'The top 30 players got their card,' he reflected. 'The top five also got additional benefits, so after I was in the top 10 on the last day of playing for my card, I started thinking about the top 5. As soon as that happened my game started to struggle, and I learned that golf is a sport that can get ugly very quickly. I rapidly went from three under to three over with three holes to play and suddenly I was thinking I'm not going to make the top 30 after almost being in the top 5. I got to the 16th hole and my tee shot went into the bunker. From the tee to green I was in constant self-talk mode. I told myself to "stop the bullshit and get back to process". I reinforced my routine with self-talk. In my practice swings I focused on feeling the shot and trusting. I told myself: "Pick your spot. Pull your head in. Commit to the shot." Incredibly I holed the bunker and birdied the 16th. It released the shackles for the last two holes, and I finished 12th to get my card.' Scott's stories in tennis and golf are classic examples of using self-talk and routines to stay process-oriented and focus a performance.

Along the lines of neutral self-talk, I also encourage athletes to embrace curiosity about a performance. It can open up a calming space and minimise distractions. I often ask athletes, *Can you be curious about the situation you're in or about an upcoming competition?* One possible question to ask to get into a curious and neutral space is *I wonder how I will go? Let's see how my training translates to competition* is another interesting way of looking at an event to help reduce tension. This approach can elicit a calming effect and problem-solving strategy and, as many athletes will attest, problem solving and executing are constant mindsets that help performance.

Mantras

Self-talk that revolves around a common phrase can take the form of a mantra. Mantras have been described as a word or group of words intended to create a certain state or lead to a desired action.

Ideally, mantras and trigger words become so ingrained as to trigger the behaviour almost instinctively. They become more than words, helping to bridge the gap between mind and body.

I've worked with many athletes who have created a mantra to assist their focus, composure, performance and wellbeing. They include a race car driver with a mantra of 'smooth, clean, consistent' and a swimmer who incorporates 'my lane, my plan, my race' into their pre-race routine.

In an interview immediately after her 1500 metres semifinal run at the Tokyo 2021 Olympics, Linden Hall shared her mantra for the Games: 'top five, stay alive'.[9] It referred to her focus on finishing in the top five to qualify for the final. This was on the back of not qualifying in her semifinal at the Rio Olympics five years earlier. The goal drove her and the mantra focused her. In an article for *Australian Runner* magazine, Debbie Flintoff-King said she received this mantra-like message from a friend the day before her final in 1988 in Seoul: 'be as tall as a mountain and flow like a river'.[10]

Mantras like these, as well as cue or trigger words, can be practised away from the event so they become associated with emotions that can be reignited. At times, athletes will write them on a sheet of paper to read before or during competition (where possible) or on their wrist or even equipment (where possible) to reinforce their plan and maintain their focus.

Internal or external focus

One way to consider concentration is to view it as either internal or external. This relates to where attention is directed. For example, an athlete with an external focus diverts attention away from how they feel physically towards something external, such as the next tree when running a road race, an opponent behind or ahead, a distance marker or the finish line. This is probably one reason why some people speed up for the last part of a fun run — because they can sense or even see the finish!

Internal focus can include attending to breathing, efficiency of technique, pace, levels of comfort or discomfort, execution of a plan, and trying to be physically and mentally calm and relaxed. Internal focus methods have been defined as monitoring sensory input. They are termed associative, whereas external focus methods are termed dissociative.

In some sports a combination of internal and external methods helps to maximise focus. In golf, for example, being aware of grip, relaxed shoulders and swing are internal factors, while being clear about the trajectory of the ball and where it is going to land are external. In football, the feel of the ball and the momentum in a run-up are internal, while choosing a target for the ball is external.

Following the running boom and the upsurge in interest in fun runs and marathons in the seventies, eighties and nineties, internal and external focus methods came to be used to help runners at all levels maximise their performance. Kevin Masters and Ben Ogles undertook a review of studies in this space and reported that associative or internal focus was the preferred method of elite runners.[11] These runners used more sensory information–related cues, which helped them adjust their pace and race in events from 400 metres to marathon distances. Less experienced runners used dissociative or external focus methods to direct attention away from their bodies, and potential pain. It may be argued that novice athletes don't have the experience or skill to understand and interpret physiological sensations and manage their performance accordingly.

I have found it takes experience to know how to both interpret and manage physical discomfort. Worrying about exhaustion levels, high heart rates, dizziness and muscle soreness to the point of getting the shakes are easy to misinterpret.

It is unlikely that there is one clear-cut internal or external concentration method that can be applied in all situations. The event itself, its duration and the athlete's level are factors that influence which focus method may best maximise performance. In light of this, I suggest it is useful to be able to use different internal and external methods at different times. In my experience, high-level performers become skilled at switching between different types of focus, depending on what is required at the time. An example might be switching between a focus on your own performance and on that of an opponent.

Narrow or broad: switching focus

The concept of broad or narrow focus is part of a model Robert Nideffer championed in 1976 in *The Inner Athlete: mind plus muscle for winning.*[12] Nideffer considered that in different sports and at different times in a sport, athletes are required to shift focus, depending on shifting demands.

Broad focus refers to assessing information, and narrow relates to being on task. Racing-car drivers on a qualifying lap without traffic predominantly stay narrow, but if they are making a passing move in a race, they have to assess what is happening with other drivers, which requires broad focus. In a practice session, the focus is broad as they assess their car's performance in order to provide feedback to their race engineer. A narrow mindset is required as the driver focuses on a rock or section of track they use as a braking marker.

There are many other examples in different sports where athletes switch between broad and narrow focus. Sports that pause or have breaks provide ideal opportunities for shifting between broad and narrow focus. Even in continuous events such as swimming there is opportunity to be narrow and focus on oneself or broad and briefly assess where an opponent is, such as on a turn. Knowing what type of attention to use and when to switch can significantly aid performance.

In field sports, the ball being at the other end of the ground may create an opportunity for a player to go into broad mode as they assess what will be required of them when the ball is back in their area, at which time they will switch to an appropriately narrow focus. In cricket there are many opportunities to switch between narrow and broad focus. The key skill is to know when to switch and to effectively apply the appropriate mode.

Getting in the zone or flow

Many people speak about getting in the zone or flow when mind and body are linked in an optimal state for performance. A flow state is one where everything seems to slow down and the performance effectively feels easier. Many athletes report that this experience is rare, however.

When I asked Nicole Pratt about flow, she said, 'I can count on one hand how many times I got into the zone in almost 20 years of my tennis career. When it does happen it's special. Most performances in my career were about working to stay switched on. But the few times I felt flow it was from a combination of being highly emotionally charged and added meaning. The match that comes to mind is my first round at the 2000 Olympics in Sydney. I always wanted to be a tennis player, but the pinnacle of my goals was to get to the Olympics. It was the Mecca. I wasn't expected to win as I was ranked about 50 or 60 and my opponent was ranked about 14 or 15 in the world.

'As I was walking onto the court for the coin toss the whole crowd stood up and started singing "Waltzing Matilda". I was so overcome with emotion I started crying. I remember thinking, Nicole you need to pull yourself together — this is not the state you need to be in to try to win this match. Because I actively said that, it transported me into another state. Then, halfway through the match, I realised, hey I could win this, so it was the same thing. I had to say, pull yourself back together again.' Nicole won the match, which ended up extending her career, because it automatically made the next Olympics in Athens a big-picture goal.

Psychologist Mihaly Csikszentmihalyi began his studies in this space as far back as the seventies and his book *Flow: the psychology of happiness*, published in 1992, is a classic in the field. He studied people in various fields including chess players, performing artists, musicians, athletes and surgeons. He conceptualised flow as 'the state in which people are so involved in the activity that nothing else seems to matter; the experience itself is so enjoyable that people will do it even at great cost, for the sheer sake of doing it'.[13]

In 2017, researcher Christian Swann described flow as a highly desirable state due to its contribution to peak performance, as well as enhanced wellbeing and self-concept, but one that remains elusive. Based on the studies he reviewed, skills to assist flow revolved around 'thorough preparation, task-focus, coping strategies, goal-setting, motivational exercises, confidence building and arousal manipulation'.[14]

Research from 2014 involving 17 elite Australian athletes who had competed at world championships or Olympic games in rowing, swimming or diving investigated the optimal psychological state for peak performance.[15] Interviews suggested peak performance is characterised by the automatic execution of performance. It was determined that the idea of an 'optimal state for peak performance does not depend on achieving a specific psychological state for all athletes but requires a highly developed ability to identify and then self-regulate a range of cognitive, emotional and behavioural factors relevant to the individual athlete and the requirements of the specific competition environment.'

Self-regulation, taking control and trust in ability helped athletes act on psychological experiences to transition to the automatic state for peak performance. Psychological experiences included the presence of nerves, a focus on execution and having a clear mind.

As already alluded to, the game, race or competition scenario itself can contribute to flow states. One way I perceive flow is that a person is so absorbed in what they are doing, they become disconnected from the outcome. It follows that a flow state can help performance but a situation can also help contribute to reaching that state. In one of the Hawthorn AFL Grand Final victories, I overheard a player say after the game that they were able to relax and enjoy the moment *with about five minutes to go*. At that stage, the team's lead was over 50 points. An observer thought the game was over by quarter time. It is interesting to note that it doesn't feel like that for athletes when they are absorbed in the contest.

Self-regulation

When distracted, one aim is to redirect attention back to what's important. Self-talk is just one of a range of strategies athletes use to achieve this. Self-regulation is the overall capacity to manage and adjust emotion and focus to a desired space. As a skill it should be prioritised. The first part of the skill of self-regulation is recognising the physical or mental state you are in and whether it is desirable for performing or not. You may be too comfortable or relaxed when the situation demands more focus and energy, or conversely, you are too pumped and physically tight when the situation requires composure. The second aspect of the skill is making the necessary adjustment to fit the circumstances. The best athletes do both well.

I have worked with many athletes who have started poorly and had to adjust their mindset to enhance their performance. Alternatively, some athletes start well before their performance level drops, necessitating an adjustment. Self-regulating back to a desired state or level of performance is easier to achieve when following a predetermined plan. It helps composure and provides clarity.

Being calm assists many athletes to focus on maintaining and directing or re-directing energy. There are many techniques to assist both mental and physical relaxation.

Referring to a relaxation strategy he developed, Dylan Alcott reflects on the lead-up to the 2016 Rio Paralympics.[16] He was ranked number one in the world in his sport. It was a hard-earned and well-deserved ranking. But, he writes, 'As every top athlete knows, rankings mean very little once you're out there. It all depends on what happens on the day. At that level, anyone can beat anyone. That's why you get upsets, when newcomers and long-shot players turn into giant killers. So, I wanted to leave no stone unturned in order to be ready. I talked to my sport psychologist to develop some skills to ensure I didn't freeze on court. I wanted to be able to perform at my best, no matter what might happen. We determined to think of something that had no negative connotations at all.' It turned out that the answer was Dylan's cat, Chad. 'No matter what was going on, thinking about Chadymoongies would always put me in a good mood', so he thought of Chad 'as a tool to clear my head, to relax and to smile. It was a tool that would come in handy in a couple of weeks' time'. This strategy worked to assist Dylan to direct and re-direct his attention and emotions as needed and he went on to win his first Paralympic gold medal.

DISTRACTIONS

Distractions may be external, such as competitors, position, scoreboard or weather including wind or heat. And distractions may be internal, such as worry, fatigue, not letting go of an error or uncertainty where to direct attention. Physical discomfort is another internal distraction that many athletes contend with, particularly when striving for optimal performance. Mental strategies can be deployed to manage both kinds of distractions.

Physical strategies, too, such as diaphragmatic breathing or focusing on one muscle group, have been found to be beneficial in minimising distractions. Relaxing face muscles or shoulders can help delay fatigue before it sets in, as well as manage it when it arrives. Embracing discomfort is a strategy to employ in this situation to stay on task. Rather than viewing discomfort as a negative, identifying it as the space where maximal work rate is occurring can help limit the discomfort. In essence, the attitude towards discomfort either exaggerates or diminishes it. Of course, this relates to discomfort from exertion and not an injury, where athletes need to listen to their body.

I have been at competitions where athletes have expressed concern about cramping. Once all medical factors have been ruled out, at times I have responded with 'good, you know you're working'. From there the discussion has even led to encouraging the athlete to 'try to cramp. If you do and can't run any more, that's the time to deal with it'. Part of the conversation is based around cramping being feedback that the athlete has given everything. This includes recognising that the physical sensation and discomfort is temporary. It's about embracing and not fearing the physical discomfort and minimising the distraction.

Worrying about a performance and getting caught in an evaluative mindset, such as overly assessing how things are going, is another common distraction. Being worried about feedback or commentary post performance from coaches, social media, journalists or even fans can dissipate attention. It correlates with focus being off task and too broad.

Being distracted is a totally normal human behaviour. Focus fluctuates, fades, drops. The challenge is to recognise when this may happen or has happened and get back on task quickly. Recognising potential distractions in advance is a simple and clever way to help maintain focus. Forewarned is forearmed. Is it fatigue? Is it the opponent? Is it the weather? Is it an error? Is it the crowd or lack of crowd or the event itself — is it, for example, a final or the first round? Is it the stage in the match — for example, the beginning, middle or end? As I have discussed with many athletes, because distractions can be difficult to address on the spot, it's important to acknowledge in advance that they will occur, and to rehearse strategies at training for overcoming them.

Secondary errors

One of the most significant distractions for an athlete can be an error. Whether or not it's obvious to others, athletes may be conscious something is not working. If errors dominate thinking and take over, they can diminish focus and performance. Not surprisingly, missing a game, set or match point in tennis, missing a kick or goal in football or bowling a poor over during a cricket match can be situations that athletes do not let go of and negatively impact immediate future performance. Managed effectively, experiences like these can also assist future performance.

I call the thinking from an initial error that leads to another a secondary error. The secondary error occurs because the first one created a distraction. I have said to many athletes, accept and learn from the first error and adjust to prevent a second.

This is a strategy Garth Tander mastered to assist his consistency and performance. 'I developed a review process during races that really helped me improve my focus,' he said. 'Early in my career frustration took over after mistakes, and that contributed to another mistake. What I learned to do was if I did something

88

in the car that was even the slightest bit off, I would aim to learn from it, which helped me stay calmer and reduced any other mistakes. I had triggers to keep my performance at a high level and prevent mistakes as well. I used to race and not think much or enough. When I started using that strategy it turned my career around.

'I developed the skill to the level where even the slightest error would be something to learn from and adjust. This evolved to the point that when speaking to the engineer and looking at data after the race, I would refer to a time in the race when I recognised something was amiss, and it wasn't even showing on the data. Eventually, I would be aware if I might be vulnerable for a mistake to occur and at that moment made sure I adjusted to avoid it altogether.' Keep in mind that in Garth's sport this skill is being executed at high speeds, so 'the margin for error is very small'. Mastering this skill elevated Garth from being one of the many who are very good to one of the elite in his sport. 'It was a step that I felt separated my performance from others.'

The skill was needed and used in Garth's 2011 Bathurst Enduro win. It is a challenging 1000 kilometre event over 161 laps held at Australia's most famous racetrack. Garth was teamed up with Bathurst rookie Nick Percat. 'We had a fast car for the whole race that was capable of winning. But in the last 30 laps the conditions had changed and our car performance deteriorated. Craig Lowndes was catching me and I knew it would be a challenge to hang on. With about eight to ten laps to go, I tried to counterpunch by pushing too hard and made a small mistake. It was after the chase, which is the fastest part of the track at about 300 km/h and I braked a fraction too late and went slightly off the track. It ended up slowing me down, rather than speeding me up. It cost about one second, which was significant.

'I instantly switched back on by telling myself, "No more errors and no more counter-punching!" I had to get back to focusing on the detail of my own performance and not get caught up on

Lowndes. He got to my rear bumper with three laps to go and I managed to hold him off. It came down to a mental strategy and mental strength.' The winning margin was a mere 0.29 seconds after almost six hours and 27 minutes of racing. Garth's story illustrates how important it is in the heat of battle to have a pre-planned focus strategy to maintain performance.

Being in the present

Focusing on being in the present and staying in the moment is another method of remaining relaxed, minimising distractions and maximising attention. Being in the present is a mindfulness technique that is also used for building and maintaining wellbeing. (Mindfulness is discussed in more detail in step 6 on wellbeing.) The best strategies for staying in the present depend on the sport and the individual. For runners, strategies may involve attending to rhythm and breathing; for swimmers it may be feeling the water; for team sports it may be communicating with teammates.

In cycling, focusing on smooth power on the pedal may be the strategy, whereas in some ball sports it may be watching the ball early, while in motorsports it may be constantly looking ahead for good lines to stay in the present. Thinking of the next contest, the next corner or the next point is also a strategy to direct or redirect attention to the here and now. There are many options, but an effort to stay in the present will assist focus.

Attention to detail

Paying attention to detail, ascribing importance to the smallest task, can help focus. The slightest lack of care or attention to detail can reduce focus and performance. It can happen to the greatest athletes. Cricketer Donald Bradman discussed how a small lack of care cost him in his final match and left him with a career batting average of 99.94, just below 100.[17]

The fifth cricket test of the 1948 Ashes series between Australia and England was the last match of his stunning career. Bradman remains an outlier in the history of the sport. His 99.94 average is so far ahead of the second-best average in the history of the game, that it has been suggested his is the single best sporting career of any sportsperson in the history of *all* sport. In his last innings he needed to score only four runs to achieve an average of 100 over his career. As he walked out to bat, the England team gathered around the pitch to welcome him to the crease, and the English captain, Norman Yardley, led three loud and resounding cheers. Bradman was then bowled for a duck after edging the ball onto his stumps.

Bradman later reflected, 'I was not aware that it was going to be my last innings. Neither was I aware at that stage that I only wanted four runs to have a test match average of a hundred ... if I had taken a bit more care, I would have got away with it.' The story shows that even one of the greatest can have lapses in care or attention that result in errors. It has also been suggested the opposition team pitch applause was a contributing distraction. I wonder what would have happened if Bradman had realised he only needed four runs to better his average. Would he have taken more care and his focus been more finely tuned?

Focus on what you can control

All athletes and coaches discuss the importance of focusing on what they can control rather than what they cannot control. It is a waste of energy to focus attention on the temperature, the draw or competition schedule, referee calls, the crowd or, at times, an opponent's behaviour.

A strategy to think about what you can control is to focus on two specific elements: effort and execution of a skill or plan. I have worked with many athletes to direct their energy into these two areas. When this is done, after the event it is possible to evaluate effort and execution as well as the outcome. Given that these two areas are within a person's control when those specific areas have been the focus, the likelihood of a positive performance is higher.

Visual and physical cues

A visual cue can serve as a trigger to sustain or refocus an athlete. The cue may be a sign, the scoreboard or someone in the crowd. Such an external stimulus can be used to sharpen or refocus attention. It can also help to relax and ease tension. I have encouraged some athletes to use a particular letter on a sign, or a word on a sign to remind them of a cue word. Looking at a support team or teammates can also act as positive visual cues.

Using physical triggers such as touching a foot on a line, tapping hands on thighs, clapping, or bouncing on the spot are other strategies used to maintain or switch focus. All these physical movements can send a message or cue saying, 'switch on', 'this one' or 'now'.

Shaking and loosening muscles is another physical strategy to trigger a sharper focus or to help be relaxed and ready. Swinging arms, tuck-jumping or fast running on the spot are also strategies employed. These strategies may be built into routines that are used regularly before an event, used during an event to aid the execution of a skill or used intermittently to redirect attention and energy.

Body language

Being conscious of body language is another strategy used to maintain focus. Historically, body language has been presumed to reflect thought and emotions. Rightly or wrongly, a person walking slowly, eyes downcast, is likely to be interpreted as feeling flat.

Someone whose face looks tense as they smash their equipment would be interpreted as angry! Recent thinking recognises a two-way, interactive relationship between body and mind. How a person is thinking or feeling can be reflected in their body language, but how they hold themselves physically can impact how they think and feel.

Observers constantly assess athletes based on their body language. Athletes are coached to focus on specific types of body language, like standing tall, being loose in the shoulders and face, projecting an image that is relaxed and composed or switched on and ready. This is less about the way the athlete is perceived and more about helping them to be alert and ready.

A comprehensive review of body language in sport in 2019 found that body language does play an important role in sports, 'both as a predictor of behaviour and, maybe most importantly, as a factor influencing the formation of impressions and expectancies, which in turn may impact performance'.[18] In other words, body language not only serves to influence a person's own mindset but can impact how an opponent behaves. Athletes inevitably monitor the fatigue and emotions in their opponent's body language, which can either spur them on or discourage them; impressions and expectations conveyed through body language can influence the player and their opposition. To stay switched on mentally, it's important to be switched on physically.

Use of time

Many sports are not continuous. They are stop-start, for varying lengths of time. Netball, basketball, soccer, football codes and many team sports are broken into halves or quarters. Cricket stops and starts between each delivery, while tennis has a break between each point and game. In a team game, even when a player remains on the field, they may have less intense intervals when the play is not near them. Events such as high jump, archery, surfing, BMX and pole-vault are only some further examples of stop-start sports.

In many continuous sports, there is also time between heats and finals. In some events, there may be hours or days between events. How this time is managed becomes an important feature of performance.

While it's clear that the time when an athlete is performing is the most important, the importance of down time is underrated. In a competition, down time is an ideal opportunity to refresh focus. Mini-reviews and refocusing can make all the difference in how a performance unfolds. It is a significant skill to manage this time effectively. Coaches often have input but are not always able to.

Thinking of time as a vital ingredient to managing focus has taught me that 30 seconds is a *long* time in sport. Even how five seconds of 'down' time is used can have a positive or negative impact. A review of the Australian Tennis Open in 2021 determined that for all the men's singles matches the average game time was about two and a half hours, with the ball in motion for only 36 per cent of the total match time. The remaining 64 per cent fell between points, games and sets with the game stopped. This equates to 96 minutes of no physical demand or non-playing time and 54 minutes of physical demand.

The average length of the women's singles matches in 2021 was just over one and a half hours. The average time the ball was in motion in those matches was 39 per cent, while the play was stopped for 61 per cent of time. This correlates to about 55 minutes of down time and 35 minutes of action. The 96 and 55 minutes is an intriguing and important part of the match that when used well can have a significant influence on the remaining time and outcome.

Down time can be used in many ways to assist performance: reflecting, learning, letting go, relaxing, composing, planning, organising or energising—however it is used, it is a clear opportunity to maximise when the game is not in motion.

In the AFL Grand Final of 2021 between the Melbourne FC and the Western Bulldogs FC, I calculated the time the game was in motion and when it was stopped in the course of the pivotal third quarter. Even when the game clock stopped only briefly, I included those moments for accuracy. The most down time occurs between goals and at boundary throw-ins. For that third quarter, from the first bounce to the siren, the game was in motion about 60 per cent of the time and was stopped for about 40 per cent.

With about nine minutes left in the quarter, the Bulldogs had a 19-point lead. After Melbourne kicked their first goal of the quarter to reduce the margin, the clock stopped, showing eight minutes and 42 seconds. From that point on to the end of the quarter the game was in motion for only about 50 per cent of the time, and Melbourne kicked a further six goals. There is no knowing whether, if the Bulldogs had more effectively managed the approximate eight minutes of down-time when the game was stopped, they might have been able to arrest Melbourne's momentum.

Chunking and race plans

A plan can help to direct attention. It doesn't have to be complex. At times, the simpler the better. The plan could emphasise what a person wants to do, how they want to go about it, or both. The 'what' may involve technical or tactical elements.

A basic plan may be the ball coming out of the sweet spot of the racquet in tennis or the middle of the bat in cricket. For a bowler it may be hitting the mark on the pitch for the specific delivery they want. The plan may also involve a strategy, such as bowling three specific deliveries, with a target delivery on the fourth ball. For a swimmer it may be holding a streamline position and keeping the stroke rate up. For a golfer it may be achieving the flight they want in the air or having the ball land where they want it to. The options are endless depending on the sport and athlete.

In many continuous events, having a race plan is a common focus method athletes use. Basically, this involves breaking an event down into smaller chunks that can be more easily envisaged and managed. Imagining the whole event can be overwhelming. For example, it can be easier to attack a 42 kilometre marathon as three 10 kilometre blocks, two 5 kilometre blocks and a 2 kilometre burst or hang on to the finish. Sometimes the distance or terrain of a course or event can dictate chunking. Many athletes assess and plan a course, whether it's a running, cycling or triathlon event. It is a common method for swimmers, too, although the course is constant — always a flat 25 or 50 metres of water. In some sports it may be a focus on each quarter or half or smaller blocks of time.

THE TAN

A classic example of chunking a course I've run many times myself is Melbourne's famous 'Tan'. It is a 3.827 kilometre undulating gravel and bitumen track around the outside of the Botanical Gardens near the city centre. Such is the prestige of the Tan that the Council has built a clock at a start-finish point so runners can monitor their times. There is also an honour board recognising the fastest laps. The board reads like an Olympic middle-distance final, with Australian runner Craig Mottram at the top of the list. His time of 10 minutes and 8 seconds in 2006 is in my opinion Olympic medal level. Interestingly his time was run when he was training with an AFL team, not from an official race or time-trial with runners of his calibre. Included in the top ten are Olympians such as 1500 metre Olympic gold medallist from Sydney 2000, Noah Ngeny, who ran 10.22 in 1999 and Australian 2021 Olympic 1500 metre runner Stewart McSweyn who ran 10.09 in 2021.

The reason I know the Tan so well is because of a squad I coached and ran with, The Nail. So many sessions were pounded over the pavement there that long-term friendships endure to this day. On a day I hadn't planned to run, I managed to post a time of 11.30. I got talked into it by AFL umpire boss, Jeff Gieschen, to 'pace the umpires' for a time-trial, when I was working with them as high-performance manager.

The standout runner in The Nail was David Ruschena, who ran an 11.00 and went on to run for Australia. Dave was a mentally strong athlete who regularly worked on his mindset. He managed to run a personal best 5000 metres track time of 13.37, pushing on after having a sore foot at the 3 kilometre mark that turned out to be a broken bone. To help Dave on the day of his 11.00, we placed Nail members strategically around the Tan to pace him. It gave him something to look towards and a runner to work off.

Here's one way to attack the Tan. Keep in mind it's only one approach, but it's an example of developing a race plan or chunking an event.

First section, from the start to the first corner — a gentle uphill about 800 metres

Go faster than you think you can. Very uncomfortable to be in that mindset, so encourage and reassure yourself to keep the pace high. Establish good breathing. Resist the urge to slow down and be comfortable. There's a fine line, though, between running fast and running too fast!

The hill

Steady but not too fast. Shorten stride to keep a lid on the pace after the first fast section.

It is only a small part of the total distance so don't get sucked into going too fast and building too much lactate and fatigue. Lean forward, use your arms, keep good technique and don't fight it.

Off the top of the hill — easing gradient, flat then some down

Maintain power and work hard off the top of the hill. Turn right and lengthen stride to use the down gradient to maximise speed on the downhill section.

Slight down, then flat around the back

Focus on rhythm. Not quite halfway yet, so fast but as relaxed as possible. Get breathing right. Focus on technique. Smooth. Rhythm. Relax shoulders. Look forward. Beware of gravel track and loss of traction and slipperiness.

Observatory to Government House Drive — slight downhill

Force the pace — focus on short-term goal of Government House Drive, because after that it feels like you're in the home straight. Danger to slow down here and pay attention to potential discomfort and fatigue.

Government House Drive to driveway of Sidney Myer Music Bowl

Focus on breathing and maintain pace. Keep balance on downhill section — good technique. Stay composed and encourage yourself.

Sidney Myer Music Bowl to finish

Kick and hold on. Crack the whip on yourself. Look forward and look for (through) the line. Think 'all the way'. Encourage yourself ... no outs. Good to collapse after the line — it means you gave everything.

ADOPTING AND ADAPTING A PLAN

Over time, the plan may be reduced to a single word for each section and minimal conscious thought will be needed. As the process becomes intuitive, energy can be focused on remaining composed and just pushing the pace with only a few triggers needed to activate the full plan.

Other environments will of course require different methods for breaking down the event, such as quarter by quarter or half by half, as mentioned, but the idea remains the same: to think only about the short block rather than the whole event. Corner by corner or lap by lap for a racing car driver. Jump by jump or throw by throw for a field athlete. Minute by minute or contest by contest are strategies used to keep athletes and teams switched on to the present. Chunking information or reducing a whole into smaller blocks is a strategy used by many people, not only athletes, to enhance focus and enable performance. Consider a working day or an impending deadline. The best time to take a break or what should be achieved by a certain time are just two factors for chunking. Using information from the last block to help the next can also be important.

It can take courage to stick with a race or game plan. If your plan is to conserve energy early and kick finish, doubt can creep in if you're behind. It can distract from the focus on the plan or how well it is executed. To counter this, plans and sections of plans can be rehearsed in training, such as surging under fatigue at the end of a repetition. Practising being in front or behind is another. Not only is the physical application and demand being rehearsed but so too is focus. The challenge with committing to plans is to realise when to adapt them. This is when switching from a narrow focus of executing the plan to a broad focus to determine if a switch is necessary becomes relevant. It can also be a trap to be too rigid and not adapt quickly enough to the situation at hand.

Routines and clarity

Managing routines in the lead-up to, immediately before or during competitions is another way to help manage emotions, focus and performance.

Often, the lead-up, whether the week, night or just before a competition, can be a challenging aspect of performance, while the actual event itself can be the easy part. To assist athletes develop routines, I have often used the term 'big' and 'little' routine to drive conversations about preparing for and managing a performance. Big routines relate to the week, day and night before a competition. Balancing rest, training, finalising mental plans, eating well, and relaxing physically and mentally are all components, as are unrelated tasks such as organising tickets for family and friends. Watching movies, playing video games, listening to music and trying not to over-think are relevant in this space. Effectively using music to relax or for a performance is a common practice, particularly considering the portability and accessibility of music. Choosing and using the right music at the right time using a playlist is something that many athletes are skilled at. It can help to influence mood, relax, calm or energise.

Little routines relate to times an athlete has more control over and include the one to five minutes or short time before the start of a competition. Little routines can also relate to times during an event. Little routines are about narrowing attention and directing energy to what is important. It is about simplifying everything. At these times the performance should be viewed as being as simple as possible. The work has been done.

Storm Sanders had a rapid rise after a year away from sport due to injury in 2018. In 2021, she was in a doubles semifinal at Wimbledon and she reached the quarterfinals of the doubles at Flushing Meadows. 'To stay focused I use routines,' she reported. 'My routine includes breathing, looking at my strings and certain thought processes to review and plan, which help me to stay switched on. I aim to use the time I can control to reset. It's hard to practise these things, so I try to dedicate time in training to being aware of that level of focus. Sometimes in training you go through the motions, but there are times when I try to make training harder than matches. Then, in front of a crowd, no matter what the scoreline, I can draw on that. It's all part of being aware that there are so many variables, and you have to focus on what is in your control. My routines, including the small ones, help me feel in control which helps me feel clear and comfortable.'

When Geoff Lipshut put a 10-year plan to Jacqui Cooper, they recorded it on a piece of paper. 'He told me to read it every day. If you are driving somewhere in a car, you look at a map to see where you're going. For me it was the same in sport. Reading the plan helped me manage any negatives and taught my inexperienced self to believe in the journey. I read it 10 times a day, every day for 10 years until I got to world number one. That was one of my routines.

'Immediately pre-event, my routine involved not getting in my own way. At the top of a ski run, the only person who can unravel or mess it up is yourself. A lot of people let themselves down through self-sabotage. They get in their own way. I made sure I got rid of any negatives. I worked on having a clear mind and very few processes — keep it clean and simple immediately pre-event was a mantra,' Jacqui explained.

The concept of a routine, either pre-event or during the event and before executing a skill, is that it maximises the likelihood of achieving a desired level of performance. A routine can focus attention on what is important and block out distractions, but because it is a repeated and predictable pattern of behaviour, it can also allow a person to feel comfortable in different situations. And like self-talk, a routine is portable.

Pre-competition or in-competition routines are very powerful. Routines can incorporate physical and mental strategies. Shaking and loosening muscles, physically practising a movement, or bouncing on the spot work together with self-talk, mantras, visual cues, deep breathing, or rehearsing a race plan to bring a routine together.

Research insights

Pre-performance routines involve an intricate combination of cognitive strategies coupled with behavioural responses that prepare for the execution of self-paced motor skills. A routine can help set up an activity to be more automatic.

Three considerations in building routines are the nature of the task, the skill level of the performer and the performer's own preferences.[19]

Nicole Pratt, Storm's coach, used a different type of routine to help her on the professional tennis tour. 'I was religious with routines. I would wake up and do something physical every day. A positive start to the day gave me confidence. It created a consistency that enabled me to be ready for the day and maximise it. The second part of my routine was to ask myself every night whether I had maximised the day. I found an accumulation of "Yes, I did all I could do" helped me sustain a long career.'

It is evident from these stories and strategies that although the specifics can be quite varied and individual, routines are an effective and often essential means of sustaining motivation, focusing attention and assisting performance.

Summary

The capacity to concentrate in the face of multiple external and internal distractions is a learned skill. While athletes have used numerous strategies over many years to sustain concentration, this chapter has outlined some methods that can help sharpen focus. A key strategy is to develop a range of self-talk techniques. Switching between a narrow and a broad focus can also help. Another strategy is to strive for a flow state and self-regulate emotions during an event. Positive body language, the effective use of time and building race plans and routines all help to maintain concentration to assist performance.

BUILD YOUR FOCUS

- Consider technical, tactical, motivational or emotional self-talk, as well as trigger words. Mantras and mottos are another form of self-talk used by athletes that can be built into thinking.

- When necessary, aim for a neutral mindset, using curiosity where appropriate, to remain open-minded and focused.

- Consider broad and narrow focus, when to use each, and when and how to switch effectively between them, depending on your sport or event.

- Consider using objects and strategies such as a towel, drinks or music to help relax and/or direct and redirect attention.

- Develop some visual and physical triggers, such as tapping your leg or bouncing on the spot, to energise or signal something.

- Consider and rehearse positive body language.

- Consider how to maximise down time, breaks and time between efforts during competition.

- Have a race plan, and where appropriate use chunks or blocks to break focus into sections. These may be based on natural factors, or any chosen blocks based on strengths or the event and competition.

- Identify what a flow or optimal state is for you and develop strategies to move towards this space.

- Recognise what is in your control and what is not to assist directing energy into what is.

- Build general, big and little routines for pre-competition or within competition, and rehearse them at training.

- Consider daily routines that help provide structure and an overall positive mindset.

- Recognise concentration as a learned skill to build over time.

STEP 4

CHAMPION YOUR LEADERSHIP

Leadership in sport is often underrated. Many athletes are placed in roles of captains, vice-captains or leadership groups without satisfactory support or leadership development. Leadership is far more than captaincy. The impact of effective athlete leadership is significant in many ways including assisting athletes to navigate their own path, as well as impacting other athletes and people around them in both personal and performance spheres.

Diamonds: leadership by example

Liz Watson was appointed captain of the Australian Diamonds netball team in September 2021 at the age of 27. It was an honour that came with responsibility that she embraced. 'The appointment came from both the coaches and the squad,' she explained when I interviewed her shortly after she took on the role. 'I take confidence from that. It drives me to want to lead well for them.'

Having been in netball development and leadership roles before, Liz sees her leadership as having grown across her journey as an athlete. 'My leadership has definitely advanced as my game has and as I have physically developed from gym work. The more you work on your leadership each year, the better you get at it,' she said. 'A blessing for me was the early years with the Vixens. Even when not a leader I still had different roles and responsibilities, and that helped me become a leader. You don't even know it's happening. Simple things, like taking the warm-up of a training session. When you first do that it's nerve-racking with the older players, but the more you do it the more natural and comfortable you feel.'

In 2014 she was still a young player in her debut year with the Melbourne Vixens, 'I had great role models in Bianca Chatfield as the captain as well as other senior players. Bianca really involved all the younger players in leadership chats and planning and gave us different roles. I learned that in netball, with only 10 players, you have to share the load. When I first started it was never the youngest or newest in the team doing jobs no one else wanted to do. We shared it all and rotated jobs around. I asked questions all the time and another senior player Catherine Cox told me to keep doing that.

'Now as an older player I keep saying to younger players there are no silly questions when trying to learn. Even speaking in reviews after games. Catherine said to me, "I love that you're speaking up as an inexperienced player". She appreciated that I was really invested in what I was doing. I was probably annoying but I was trying to find out as much as I could.' As it turned out, in 2014 the Vixens won the championship, but it would be another six years before they lifted the silverware again. By then, Liz was in the role of captain.

Of their 2020 championship win, Liz said, 'Kate Moloney and I were co-captains and what we learned was that we needed everyone to help. The whole squad needed to buy in, and everyone in the team had to feel like a leader. We also wanted them to be themselves and be part of the team, because that's when people perform at their best.

er this.

'In everything I've done as a leader, as captain, vice-captain or in a leadership group, I have always tried to lead by example — and I still try to hold on to that. I couldn't respect a leader who told me to do things they didn't try to do themselves. You don't have to be the best player, but you do have to show you are trying to live the values and culture and that's what is important. I'm most comfortable leading on the court in a game. That's when I'm most calm and controlled. Off-court leadership that involves things like selection and dealing with people's emotions and the highs and lows — that's something I'll keep learning about and growing my leadership in.

'I think the most important quality to have as a leader is to be worthy of trust. It's about the relationships you can build because as a leader you have players who come to you whether they're struggling or going well. They need to know they can build a relationship on and off the court and trust you with whatever they're saying. If you have the team members' trust, then you can build a relationship on- and off-court and everything else flows from that. Trust is the basis of a club and its culture. It's the trust that I'm doing the work and anything I say to people they'll take it for what it is, and the relationship will get stronger and then we can have a conversation about whatever we need to deal with. That's why I took confidence from being appointed the captain of the Diamonds. It reflected the players' trust in me.'

Although Liz describes her most comfortable leadership space as on the court, during her 2021 season with the Vixens in the Super Netball League, Liz faced a different off-court leadership demand. In April, shortly before the start of the season, Liz had a foot injury that required surgery. 'I missed the whole season. It was different and a struggle at first. Training alone, away from the group, didn't make it easy. I created some structure on what to do. The coach asked me to be on the bench for games so I sat courtside to assist and provide feedback to players. It enabled me to be a supportive voice. What I learned the most was that you can get a feel for how the group is going. I focused on helping any way I could. I also learned that you could get a different feel for the group by watching training rather than being part of it. You can see who is more or less engaged, who is flying and who is struggling. You don't notice as much when you're out on court because you're so focused on the drill. That was great, as I could give feedback to Kate and other players.'

Liz's story reinforces the importance of positive role models and of being given responsibility to assist leadership growth and development. It also illustrates the importance of leading in a variety of circumstances — at training, in games and away from the game — and of leading by example on and off the court, regardless of performance.

Influence

I see leadership as principally about influence, and that influence can be positive or negative, often without the leader being aware of it. This influence may be from the position of a formal leadership role or from someone not in a formal role. It can also be passive or active. For example, an athlete who sets a benchmark for professionalism and training standards models high performance simply by example, while an athlete who calls individual squad members to check on their welfare or calls a meeting within a squad to discuss goals and performance is clearly active.

Great leadership is also *proactive*. The influence is deliberate and involves conscious energy in a planned direction to individuals, groups and the environment. I see leadership as a dynamic, action-oriented interaction between an individual and their surroundings.

How influence is exerted varies. Some leaders are more extroverted than others. Some are more directive; others more introverted and some lead by example. Good leaders use a range of different styles depending on the situation. Variation in styles means leaders can connect and interact with different stakeholders. This is one benefit of having leadership groups. Varying styles can encourage discussion and reflection within the group, which in turn helps effective decision making and leadership growth. A leadership group also provides important support to those in a captain's role.

Leadership styles may lean towards being task-oriented or people-oriented. Historically in sport, leadership has gravitated to overtly focus on results and outcomes, sometimes at the expense of the individual, but this is no longer acceptable practice. Results and outcomes will always be relevant, however, the best leaders focus not only on performance but on relationships as well as individual and group wellbeing. I see effective leaders as influencing thinking, feeling and behaviour, as well as processes.

In sporting environments, many of the concepts discussed by athlete leaders take place in collaboration with coaches. A coach may, in essence, lead a sporting team, but there are many layers of leadership. Even coaches report to boards and managers. For coaches and athletes in leadership roles, the balance is important. It is a shared mission, particularly because athletes still have to focus on performing. For athlete leaders the balance is about maximising people as well as their own and others performance.

Research insights

A 2019 study found that leadership in sport is effective when 'a leader succeeds in creating a good team atmosphere, strengthening the team's cohesion and communication, and establishing a strong work ethic. This effective leadership is, in turn, an important driver of the team's functioning and effectiveness; that is the team's ability to develop adequate cognitive, motivational, affective and coordinative processes'.

The study reflects and affirms the broad nature of leadership, which extends well beyond direct performance factors.[1]

The *what* and the *how* of leadership

It can help a leader to have a guide to the many demands and challenges along the way. I try to provide a roadmap for the leaders I work with to help them navigate the expected and unexpected scenarios they will encounter. As a starting point, I recommend simplifying leadership to the *what* and the *how*. Exactly *what* are you leading? What are you aiming to influence? And *how* are you going about it? Being clear on both aspects can help guide leadership decisions, energy and action (see figure 4.1).

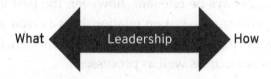

What ← Leadership → How

Figure 4.1: understand your what and how

Over the years in the course of my own leadership roles, work and study I have developed the Self-Culture-Others-Situations (SCOS) leadership model in the form of a pyramid (see figure 4.2).

Foremost and at the base is leadership of self; second is leadership of culture, then leadership of others and finally leadership of situations. I advocate working from the base up, although each layer is as important as all the others. For example, when leading situations, how a crisis is dealt with can have a lasting impact on the way the leader is viewed by those around them. However, too often leaders are reactive rather than proactive, so their time is spent dealing with situations that have already developed. It's like firefighting. Certainly, effective leaders manage situations that arise well, but putting energy into the other layers of leadership, starting with self, is likely to prevent or reduce the number of challenging situations that need to be managed.

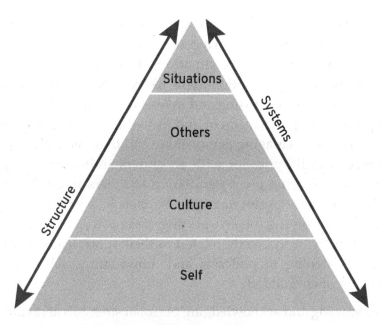

Figure 4.2: the SCOS leadership pyramid

Leading self

The model locates 'leading self' at the base of the pyramid. It's an imperative for all athletes, whether or not they are in a leadership role, because every athlete is ultimately responsible for how they train and perform. But leaders, in particular, need to look after themselves before they can lead others effectively. (Think of an airline's emergency instructions to put on your own oxygen mask before helping others.) Those in formal leadership roles are likely to be more heavily scrutinised than the rest of the team. They shoulder the main responsibility for a wide range of factors including performance and culture. Leaders are also accountable for each of the other stages in the model: culture, others and situations. So it begins with the individual. Leading self is the foundation and includes taking responsibility for every other layer in the pyramid.

Leaders are role models, so if a leader's own house is in order they can more effectively drive and contribute to culture, help others flourish and manage situations. If leaders are struggling, culture, others and situations will likely struggle too. Leading self, then, means prioritising and investing in one's own personal and professional management and growth, including wellbeing. This extends to managing personal life and time, as well as health and rest. A healthy leader with an understanding of managing their own wellbeing gives permission to others to do the same. Investing in self-development can happen in a variety of ways including observing other sporting codes, watching material either directly or indirectly related to their sport, using mentors, reading, listening to podcasts and, importantly, self-reflection and being open-minded.

Recognising and acknowledging personal strengths and vulnerabilities can help lead self. This facilitates accepting vulnerabilities and being comfortable with help-seeking and utilising support staff, colleagues and teammates. Strong, effective leaders recognise they cannot do everything. They empower others and share responsibility and credit. Leadership teams and groups support this process. Being comfortable with your own style helps you to be authentic. It is too hard to try to be something you're not or something others want you to be.

Leading self contributes to taking responsibility and being accountable for your own behaviour. In sport leadership this may be (a) during performance, (b) away from performance and (c) away from the sport. I refer to leading self away from the sport as *leading when no one is watching* — for example, decisions being made when you're socialising, either with peers or away from the group or when alone. Standing firm on personal and organisational values that guide and direct decisions and behaviours is important. Leadership is a full-time responsibility, not a part-time role. This is because, as already noted, leader behaviours and actions have a ripple effect on others both in the sporting and personal landscape.

Most importantly, leading self means being accountable for your own performance. Leadership doesn't mean always being perfect. It doesn't mean always being the best performer. A trap a team can fall into is to nominate as captain their best performer rather than the person best able to guide and support culture, others and situations as they arise.

Liz Watson reminded us that leadership begins with self when she said, 'I couldn't respect a leader who told me to do things they didn't try to do themselves'.

Thoughts on leading self

- Invest in your own personal and performance development.
- Prioritise your own wellbeing.
- Role-model standards.
- Take responsibility for your actions.
- Acknowledge your strengths and vulnerabilities.
- Share and allocate responsibilities.
- Continue to seek and use supports.
- Reflect on your leadership and growth in this space.
- Lead in competition and away from competition.

Leading culture

Good leaders recognise the importance of culture and their influence on it. All athletes in a squad or team influence the culture they are a part of. Being aligned with a positive culture contributes to enhanced performance. Regardless of how a culture has evolved, athletes in a sporting environment are the custodians of that culture as they both represent and influence it. A poster on a wall with the word 'respect' is useless if coaches, athletes and staff do not model respectful behaviour.

Leading culture means upholding a group's values and behaving accordingly. Over time, in a positive environment, personal and sporting values are and should be more aligned. This facilitates comfort and I see this alignment as a performance enabler. Team leadership is difficult if personal values conflict with those of the club or team. I often ask athletes and coaches how personally aligned they are with the values of the organisation they are in, since lack of congruency creates stress and becomes unhealthy for both the individual and the sport. Conversely, when personal and sporting values are aligned, the environment is positive and people thrive. Athletes who drive culture have a contagious impact on their squad or group on both a personal and a performance level. Culture is sometimes defined as the minimum standards a leader accepts. These standards may be related to values and behaviours set, communication and language used or other standards strived for by individuals or a team.

Culture relates to behaviours. Leaders live the values that guide all athletes and staff. Leaders facilitate conversations with individuals within existing cultural parameters. For example, if respect is a value within a culture, when an individual behaves in a respectful manner, it can be acknowledged and rewarded. If, on the other hand, an individual exhibits a lack of respect, the culture's values can be a starting point for a discussion. Step 5 discusses culture in more detail.

Dave Andersen told me, 'I've always been a quiet leader. My focus was inside the locker room. Checking on the culture was a big part of my leadership. I saw myself as a person in the team who would try to reinforce the culture and help others, whether I was the leader or not.'

Thoughts on leading culture

- Live and role-model identified values and behaviours within and beyond the competition arena.
- Educate and support others to do the same.
- Hold others accountable to the culture, and celebrate people living culture.
- Use values and behaviours from culture to drive conversations.
- Contribute to reviewing the culture to ensure that it is relevant and healthy.

Leading others

Positively influencing, supporting and facilitating others' growth, personally and professionally, is important for each member of an organisation, as well as for the organisation as a whole. Leading others involves recognising that all athletes in a squad or team have the capacity to influence each other, directly or indirectly. The impact of mentoring and supporting others can be profound. The traffic is not all one way. Senior, more experienced athletes draw energy from the enthusiasm of those who are younger; younger athletes thrive on the generous guidance of more experienced athletes. Many leaders have reported to me how much they learn when they teach and how they grow when they help.

At times leading others may involve investing considerable work and time. On other occasions, it involves no more than checking in and acknowledgement. Many times athletes have told me their stress increases when athletes or coaches in leadership roles haven't spoken to them for a while, even though they train together every day. A check-in and a short talk can go a long way. Leading others also involves asking questions and active listening.

Good leaders respect individual differences and strengths within a squad or group. Some athletes may have higher game IQ, some have better fitness and physical management experience or better personal skills. Leading others enables athletes to develop each other more rapidly and respects individual differences.

When leading others, I consider personal and performance relationships. Building personal relationships contributes to maximising performance relationships. Of course, there will be different levels of personal relationships within any group based on a range of factors. Age, common interests, circumstances and personality influence this. Showing an interest in others outside of sport contributes to wellbeing and likely performance. Some athletes are more private and have tighter personal boundaries than others. But that doesn't mean a leader shouldn't show interest or care for them as individuals.

Leading others shouldn't depend on how an individual performs. I have worked with many leaders who are reluctant to speak up or follow up personal or performance conversations with others if they feel they themselves are not performing particularly well. Leadership demands conversations are initiated anyway. That's another reason why leading self should be prioritised. Leading others is about being invested in others and building unconditional relationships. That's not always easy. Highly effective leaders don't have relationships that are conditional on whether everything is going okay for them or others.

Effective leading requires an appreciation for the power of language and words. Long after contracts have expired, words and conversations are recalled. When from a leadership role, these have additional punch. Effective use of language includes managing tone, volume and timing and being aware of the influence of these variables, as well as the content. Who is present when conversations are held is something else good leaders consider.

Leading others also assists others to grow. It rewards and recognises small, not only big efforts and achievements, provides others with opportunities to lead, invites others to speak openly, as per the trust that Liz Watson spoke of.

Jacqui Cooper described her return from injury after 2002 as 'my second career'. Over the time she was injured, she gained a renewed perspective of herself and her sport. 'I reinvented myself. One thing I did was to become more involved with the team. I would room with junior athletes to help them. It ended up giving me more energy, because we all supported each other and none of us ever felt on our own. From the shift in culture, aerial skiing emerged as a powerhouse. Our culture became one in which experiences were shared, success was shared, and respect was shared. When you've got that and you turn up, you can turn it on. In that environment it's easy to be happy when you don't win but your teammates do.'

Thoughts on leading others

- Listen actively. Sometimes not much needs to be said.
- Show interest in others and be empathic. Appreciating different character styles and individual challenges in a sport environment is not always easy, but feeling understood can assist others personally and performance-wise.
- Check in on how others are going personally. Give or recommend support when needed, at and away from competition.
- Check in on how others are coping with performance. Give or direct to support when needed.
- Provide opportunities for others to grow and recognise when to share responsibility and credit.
- Check in on how others are going with culture (including their values and behaviours).

(continued)

- Appreciate and monitor the power of language—choose your words carefully.

- Be prepared to challenge in the right way. This may take the form of encouragement, or directly discussing a concern. Good leadership of others ensures that what needs to be said is said.

Leading situations

Leading situations is a necessary aspect of leadership, because even when the other tiers are going well, it may be required to manage a wide range of scenarios. These could include a demoralising defeat to poor behaviour. Some situations are draining and distracting and can undermine performance. This brings us back to the analogy of preventing wildfires by investing in culture and others rather than having to spend time constantly putting out spot fires.

But no matter how strong the group or culture, incidents will happen. Athletes are for the most part young people learning about life as well as sport. Sport, particularly at the highest level, can be very challenging and can bring out both the best and the worst in people, especially when emotions are heightened. A lot depends on, for example, how extreme pre-event anxiety or bitter disappointment after a loss are managed. How victories are celebrated is also of relevance. For some athletes, high performance and attention can lead to an inflated sense of self and lack of respect that in turn leads to challenging situations. Hence, leadership during highs and lows is equally relevant.

Many sporting groups spend extraordinary amounts of time together, often while travelling or while experiencing deep fatigue or performance pressure. In these circumstances, input from more experienced leaders can help. Sometimes allowing time before dealing with an incident can help. I recollect a phone call at about

6 pm about an athlete who was in trouble. The coach felt the incident should be dealt with there and then, but after we'd discussed it we agreed to deal with it in the morning. The next day after a pre-briefing with the coach, he expressed gratitude for sleeping on it. On another occasion, though, I called a meeting at 11 pm. Key leaders were all on deck to deal with a situation that couldn't wait.

It's important to identify what procedures and protocols exist for managing incidents. If there are no guidelines, an effective leader will ensure critical incident management plans and connections with professionals are put in place before they are needed. Leaders are often judged on how they handle an emergency; it's a moment when their leadership is under the microscope.

A situation might arise when a team or squad are entering a hostile opposition environment, or before the final game after an extended time on the road, or in the lead-up to the final game of a season, which must be won to make the finals. It may be an in-game situation relating to momentum, a referee or an opponent. These, too, are situations in which leadership is important and on which a leader will be judged. These are experiences and situations that good leaders are prepared for and embrace.

At times, leaders also need to know when to relax and when to ease tension. Flexibility based on a situation is important. Leadership is not always about being serious. Having fun is essential, and knowing when to be serious and when to kick back and have a laugh is an important skill. Adapting your leadership style in different situations, as mentioned earlier, is a skill.

Brigitte Muir knows 'summit fever' can grab you when you get close to your goal. 'But it can't get in the way of making the right decision. You must be flexible enough that you can change a plan, even if you have told people the plan. If you wake up in the morning and it's obvious that the plan is no longer the right one, you change it. I've found that if you explain the reasoning, people will accept it. You need to listen to people and take advice, but the leader still has to take responsibility and make a decision.'

That many situations are often utterly unpredictable is one of the appealing and intriguing aspects of sports and leadership of different situations in sport.

Thoughts on leading situations

- Consider a range of scenarios beforehand to assist preparation for and management of different situations – both within and beyond the competition environment.

- Direct, guide and support other athletes and stakeholders in different situations.

- Sense and manage momentum in competition, taking control and adjusting accordingly.

- Deal with performance challenges the opposition may strive to create, such as intimidation.

- Deal with personal challenges of team members as they arise and utilise supports and appropriate resources as necessary.

- Be flexible based on circumstances – 'read the room'.

- Take responsibility for decisions in different situations.

Leading structure and systems

Structure and systems impact how leading self, culture, others and situations evolve.

Structure and systems relate to processes as well as who is in what position. This could include any role that is created within a team, as well as reporting lines and responsibilities. Is there a leadership facilitator in the structure and who is it? In sport leadership, if there is a leadership group, who is part of it? One captain and two vice-captains or vice-versa? Is there an emerging or developing group of younger or newer leaders, or is every athlete or player involved in the squad or team involved in leadership education? Perhaps there are no leadership groups. How often do leaders meet? Establishing effective leadership structures depends on group maturity and specific factors within a sport. Getting the structure right can have an impact on leadership opportunity and capacity.

Systems can either enable or limit leadership opportunities. I often advocate creating opportunities that encourage leadership capability to grow. Athletes are not necessarily natural leaders. They are typically selected on performance, not only leadership qualities, which means that establishing systems to facilitate growth not only makes sense but is essential.

Leadership growth

Many athletes are young. In junior sports, captains and leaders are teenagers. Even in open sports athletes can be placed in leadership roles in their early or mid twenties. Clearly leadership is more difficult for those with limited life and sport experience, which means it must be prioritised and taught.

One benefit of sport is that it encourages leadership simply through participation. It begins with tasks as simple as packing the right equipment for training or for the game, and includes the more complex tasks of preparation and organisation. Hence leadership development is to a degree inherent in sport participation.

I have watched athletes in leadership roles grow with education and experience. All the athletes I interviewed for this book reinforce this. It is the same for coaches. In the AFL, player leadership groups typically meet weekly pre-season and in-season. Taking account of annual leave and other strategically planned breaks, this can amount to 40 leadership-facilitated sessions each year. These meetings do not include the leadership opportunities that occur naturally in a sporting environment or are manufactured to enhance growth. Growth becomes inevitable.

Again, Brigitte Muir's experience is salutary. 'Leadership is so important because a team is only as strong as its weakest link.

Leaders need not worry what others will think if they choose the right thing to do. My leadership style has changed over the years. It used to be partly ruled by ego. As a leader you have to assess many factors and the biggest obstacle to objective assessment is ego. As I became more experienced, I became more caring. I saw more of people's fears, loves and everything about them. I became a better leader.'

Sam Mitchell, too, sees leadership as an evolving skill. 'The natural component may be as low as 10 per cent. Ten years of focus, work and discipline on improving gets you a very long way. My natural style of leadership was around discipline and driving a high standard, but I lacked empathy. I didn't understand different backgrounds, personality traits and motivation. When I became team captain at 25, my life experience was quite narrow, but my expectations were high. I tried to be more rounded. By the end of my career, I still had a natural hard edge, but after 15 years of education and learning around relationships, my empathy and efforts to understand people individually became more of a strength.

'I understood I wasn't a perfect leader and took on feedback. Feedback is the lifeblood of any high performer, so I looked at what I needed to do to improve. I got people around me I trusted to analyse me, to make me more aware so I could grow in the direction of my focus. I tried to improve as quickly as possible. When Hodgey (Luke Hodge) became captain at Hawthorn, I stood right back. I wanted him to do a better job than I had. While I was out of the leadership group for two years I shifted my focus to leading in a one-on-one model, rather than in group sessions. I put my energy into assisting players one-on-one by sitting with them and watching and learning from game vision together or working with others on goal-kicking in training sessions. I think that helped them and helped me with my leadership.

'One of the key qualities for leadership is emotional intelligence. For me it was about having the ability to recognise how others feel and controlling your emotions and behaviour to get the best out of each person. That's often quite subtle. Before the game I used to think of it as temperature control. Sometimes the temperature in the room before the game was too high or too low. I would read my own gauge and the gauges of others, and if necessary I would try to adjust the temperature. Knowing how to get the best out of others at key moments was crucial. I'd talk to some players about their opponents. If I saw someone was uptight, I deliberately joked with them to get them out of their own head. Sometimes it also helped calm me down if I was too intense. As a leader, you need the emotional intelligence to read your own temperature but also that of the group.

'There's a fine line in leadership between driving expectation and supporting people. Getting the balance right is important. I'm better at it now, but the learning is ongoing.'

These stories reflect the need to keep learning. The best leaders I have worked with are always looking for opportunities, formal or informal, to learn and grow. Having a mentor or leadership facilitator can help — someone to bounce ideas off — but reading, formal assessments, doing workshops and courses, and listening to and observing others are all growth opportunities. I have facilitated leadership groups and conducted assessments with many leaders in both the sporting and corporate worlds. There are many leadership assessment tools to choose from. Some focus on skills and competencies, for example, while others focus on style. And leadership groups can informally provide feedback to each other to stimulate growth.

I often ask leaders to rate themselves on the specific leadership behaviours they are striving to attain and then get other leaders or teammates to rate them. It is a basic form of 360-degree evaluation. Strong leaders are comfortable with feedback and use it to reflect on their leadership. In this realm it is important to keep in mind that providing and receiving feedback effectively are stand-alone skills. Leaders and groups should be provided with education in this space to maximise the opportunity and experience of giving and receiving feedback. Too often feedback is not managed as well as it could or should be and becomes counter-productive.

In my leadership work in sport, a common ingredient I have identified is an appetite for improvement. Good coaches and athletes in leadership roles don't take their leadership for granted. As part of their pattern of growth, as alluded to, I encourage them to set specific leadership goals and then ask for feedback from colleagues in order to monitor their progress. It's a simple but effective measure. Again, the key is to embrace learning opportunities and remain open to continuous growth. Strong leaders recognise how important this is.

Formal and informal leadership

Dave Andersen held both formal and informal leadership roles during his career. 'Leadership grew on me as I got older. I also tried to be a mentor as my career went on. My leadership role changed. As captain I was like a coach liaison as well as a player leader. As a general leader, whether or not I was captain, if people were not playing well, I would try to cheer them up. I tried to maintain harmony in the squad, and a lot of that work is done behind the scenes.'

Mat Hayman talks about the challenge of formal leadership. 'I had been a domestique my whole career, and I learned that there's a big difference between a domestique and a leader. I was comfortable being someone who works for the benefit of the whole team. When I was made the team leader, it was very hard to switch to having others work for you. It was a different mindset and I struggled with it. When I won the Paris–Roubaix, I wasn't in that role. I wasn't trying to be someone else; I was totally free in that race in 2016. A true leader has the best interests of the team and organisation and that thought sits above them.' Mat was highly effective as a leader in an informal role, but balancing performance and formal leadership was a challenge. When he came back from injury in 2016 he wasn't in a formal leadership role, and that contributed to his outstanding performance at the Paris–Roubaix.

For both coaches and athletes, ensuring that people in formal leadership roles are comfortable and willing to grow is relevant. I often ask leaders whether a formal leadership role will help or hinder their performance. Even great athlete leaders' contracts are not renewed when their performance drops below a certain level for some time. For other athletes, being in a formal leadership role can fast-track and enhance their performance. They thrive. It is the responsibility of both coach and athlete, as well as leadership facilitators, to work out how best to manage this process. This is totally different from other environments where the role is purely to lead — that *is* the performance. For example, a school principal doesn't teach classes, but leads the staff and school. While they don't have to be the best athlete, an athlete in a leadership role has to perform and lead.

I sometimes refer to athletes in informal leadership roles as *silent leaders*. Silent athlete leadership recognises that not all athletes will want to be in formal leadership roles. Some, however, have extensive experience or demonstrate strong leadership qualities. Silent leaders do not necessarily proactively influence individuals and groups. Their influence is subtle, even inadvertent. They may be the person the captain turns to for advice.

Research insights

A 2006 study into the nature of athlete leadership was conducted with 258 varsity athletes from 13 teams. The researchers suggested that 'athlete leadership may be viewed as an athlete occupying a formal or informal role within a team who influences a group of team members (minimum of two) to achieve a common goal'.

(continued)

Three types of leaders investigated in the study were *task, social* and *external* leaders.

- *Task leaders* help the team focus on goals and clarify responsibilities.

- *Social leaders* contribute to team harmony and ensure teammates are involved in different events.

- *External leaders* promote the team in the community and represent it in meetings with coaches or other officials.

Most task, social and external leaders held formal leadership roles and were predominantly starters, or players who featured regularly in the starting line-up. It may not be crucial for 'social leaders' to be starters.

The study concluded that there are different types of leaders in both formal and informal roles.[2]

Research insights

A 2013 study investigated the benefits of having formal and informal leaders on a team. The participants were 104 varsity athletes from basketball, hockey and volleyball. Athletes felt leadership should be spread among teammates. Specifically, they thought that approximately 85 per cent of a team could hold some form of leadership role. Specifically, they felt that 19 percent could hold formal leadership roles, while almost 66 per cent could occupy an informal leadership role.

'Athlete leaders on a team influenced a variety of group dynamic constructs, including team member attributes (increased resources), team structure (enhanced role clarity), cohesion, team processes (better communication), individual outcomes (more satisfied), team outcomes (performance enhanced) and leadership behaviour (both transactional and transformational behaviours exhibited).'

The study found that athletes felt it was beneficial for a large number of participants to be involved in either formal or informal leadership, and that athlete leaders can have multiple benefits to a sport.[3]

Harnessing the energy of these people in a squad or team environment is relevant because they impact a group in a range of ways. Whether because of their humour or knowledge, or experience and respect they command, others listen when they speak. Silent leaders who are aware of their impact can assist formal leaders and coaches as well as other athletes.

I have regularly developed leadership programs for all athletes, not just for those in formal leadership roles, and my experience has been that it enables a variety of leadership groups and growth to emerge from the specific education created.

Leadership density

A model I have regularly applied to teams and squads is what I call *leadership density*. It involves maximising leadership in all athletes, whether in a formal role or not, and encompasses maximising *leading self* in the SCOS pyramid as well as the additional leadership layers. This is in addition to a senior leadership group, and often means a new and specific leadership program must be tailored and built.

Such a program enables formal leaders from a senior leadership group to be involved with or rotate through other leadership meetings with athletes. In the process, they experience new leadership opportunities and build leadership capacity. It also creates relationship-building opportunities that are important both personally and for performance.

In the leadership density model, I have allocated assistant coaches to facilitate small groups, providing them with additional opportunity to build personal and performance relationships with athletes outside the typical training environment. The number of groups will vary depending on the nuances of the sport, the athletes, resources and other circumstances. At times I have mixed groups of inexperienced and highly experienced athletes together. On other occasions I have grouped athletes based on more experienced, mid-tier and younger. Leadership density can also incorporate the whole squad as a group, depending on circumstances.

Topics discussed in leadership density meetings can vary widely, and may include:

- leadership assessments and feedback to help players understand themselves both as people and as athletes
- 360-degree feedback sessions
- silent leadership education
- mentoring education
- fun and social activities to build relationships
- education on personal management, including topics related to being away from sport such as finances or balance
- public speaking or general communication and relationship education
- specific education on what leadership is and on different types of leadership
- scenario and contingency management.

While formal senior groups meet regularly, leadership density groups I have developed typically meet less frequently — perhaps monthly or quarterly. Being creative and flexible in developing such a program ensures it is enjoyable and beneficial. The ultimate purpose is to enhance personal and performance growth, and its success depends on a performance psychologist or other dedicated staff member coordinating and managing the program. Keep in mind that no athlete wants yet another meeting, so the correlation to performance and personal benefits has to be clear. Keep sessions brief and be sure to get the support of senior coaches and other leaders to maximise the benefit of such a program.

Liz Watson was describing a leadership density model when she discussed her experience with the Diamonds. 'At the Diamonds, we speak about a squad mentality for leadership. The whole squad is part of the leadership journey. It's not just the captain and vice-captain. We need leadership across the whole court. It's really important when you are planning games and reviewing and in chats between quarters and time-outs. Once in the game you can get tunnel vision, so input from other players is important. We bring other players into meetings and give them responsibilities to lead and help them feel like they want to lead. It's important because at the Diamonds' level everyone has to be a leader and show that, with or without an official title. In the Diamonds group many of the players have leadership roles in other environments, so they are comfortable and understand leadership and that helps,'

Leadership groups

Leadership groups are beneficial in a number of ways, including in:

- developing future leaders
- supporting senior leaders, such as captains and coaches
- sharing responsibilities that accompany leadership.

As with any group of people, a variety of styles will be represented in an athlete leadership group. This is beneficial not only because it encourages strong debate but because different leadership styles are modelled. Some lead by example; some are introverted, others extroverted; some have a higher sport IQ, others have great people skills.

Who facilitates athlete leader group meetings is important. The head coach typically plays an important role here but to ensure athletes are exposed to a range of voices and perspectives,

I also recommend having a specific facilitator to encourage leadership growth.

In addition to senior leadership groups, 'emerging' or 'developing' groups can be created to support identified future leaders. Another way to develop leadership beyond a formal senior leadership group is to rotate emerging leaders through senior leadership programs.

Of course, it is up to senior staff, coaches and senior athlete leaders to determine whether a leadership density model, leadership group model or hybrid is the best fit for their sport. I'm advocating a range of options for sports to consider, not suggesting all of the above need to be implemented.

Captain class

Lists of leadership qualities abound in many fields. Studies of education and corporate environments identify skills, competencies and a range of other qualities. These lists vary widely; there's no single definitive list of leadership qualities in any field.

In *The Captain Class: the hidden force that creates the world's greatest teams*, Sam Walker reviews a large number of sport teams from around the world, including the English Premier League, Olympic sports and the AFL.[4] He then determined what he considered to be the 16 most successful performing teams in sport history. These included The New York Yankees in the Major Baseball League from 1949 to 1953, the Boston Celtics in the NBA from 1956 to 1969, the Soviet Union Men's Ice-Hockey Team from 1980 to 1984 and the New Zealand All Blacks rugby union team from 2011 to 2015. Two teams from Australia were on his list: The Australian Women's Hockey Team from 1993 to 2000 and the Collingwood Magpies AFL team from 1927 to 1930. When discussing his selection criteria, he identified leadership as one crucial element.

Walker emphasised that in sport the captain isn't necessarily the primary leader. It may be the coach or even someone at a level above the coach. This is one reason why there are different theories and models around leadership in sporting groups and teams. He did, however, advocate on the importance and impact of the leadership of a captain.

From his research Walker listed seven traits of elite team captains. These were:

- extreme doggedness and focus in competition
- aggressive play that tests the limits of the rules
- a willingness to do thankless jobs in the shadows
- a low-key practical and democratic communication style
- motivation of others with passionate nonverbal displays
- strong conviction and the courage to stand apart
- ironclad emotional control.

Walker describes each trait in detail. Whether or not you agree with his list, it is thought-provoking on what specific qualities may best apply in any particular environment. Some sports and teams could identify their own list and work towards growing in those areas. This is work I have done on several occasions.

Leadership qualities

In developing my own leadership assessment tool to drive discussion and coaching on this topic, I created the following generic list of eight qualities. As mentioned, there is no definitive list, but having a structure and a goal to strive for provides a useful starting point. You might try to evaluate your own experience against each of these qualities. Otherwise, create your own list and include associated behaviours so you and others can review leadership more clearly. Leadership qualities are different from styles, which may be autocratic, democratic, transformational, more casual or a coaching style, to name a few. Effective leaders adapt their style according to their situation to maximise their leadership qualities.

Your list may be quite short, limited to qualities that are specifically relevant to you and your environment. They may be leadership goals or a leadership brand you are striving for. They may be three from the following list or include any number of other qualities you consider most relevant.

CONTRIBUTOR

Being in a formal sport leadership role includes being proactive and action-oriented. This involves a willingness to take on extra responsibility, work with coaches, promote the sport and work with external stakeholders. It also includes role modelling suitable on- and off-field behaviour, setting high standards and assisting future leadership growth. There are many different ways a person can contribute, but you cannot have leadership without an overall contribution to the team and sport organisation.

SPORT INTEGRITY

This involves representing the sport well, taking responsibility for actions, and speaking with the team or other athletes about concerns or issues. It involves using your leadership position for the benefit of the team and sport rather than your own benefit. Integrity also includes being prepared to hold others to account.

TEAM AND OTHERS FOCUS

Team focus emphasises the welfare of the collective and being prepared to sacrifice individual goals for team goals. It means nurturing, monitoring and contributing to the health of the team or squad. Empathy is a big part of a team or squad focus. It is vital that team members know leaders understand them and their situation. Proactively organising team activities, monitoring the vibe of the group and being aware of the wellbeing of its members is incorporated into team focus. It also means contributing to others' performance through encouragement, coaching or inspiration. Team focus encompasses a willingness to live and promote the culture of the team as well as building personal and performance relationships with stakeholders, particularly teammates and coaches.

COMMUNICATION

Leaders' communication skills will vary, but with time leaders should be comfortable speaking one-to-one with teammates and coaches, to the whole group and even in public forums. Note I emphasise comfort rather than polish. Inviting, listening to and appreciating others' opinions and asking questions are important receptive skills. Leaders must develop the skill of communicating with a variety of stakeholders, from corporate sponsors and administrators to new and young teammates, and they must be savvy when it comes to managing media and social media. Communicating with clarity, decisiveness and brevity is particularly relevant in competition. Managing how points are expressed, as well as what is expressed can be impactful, as often people will not take in all the words but will lean on the emotion. The words leaders use are powerful and often underrated, as discussed earlier. Good leaders manage and monitor their language.

DETERMINATION

Good leaders perform their role well but are also determined to lead well. They are competitive and drive the group to perform, not just win; and they are task-focused. They have a strong work ethic, resilience and the determination to make a positive impact.

COMPOSURE

Leaders have added layers of responsibility and embrace this. Good leaders lead themselves well, as discussed in the SCOS Leadership model. They learn to maintain composure in a range of circumstances, whether in or out of competition. Sometimes it will be tempting to give way to negative emotion and feel overwhelmed, but effective leaders will remain calm, being aware that their composure and demeanour will influence others. This assists leaders to be aware of momentum while in the heat of battle, and helps with effective decision making and directing others.

POSITIVE PERFORMER

As we've discussed, in sport, leaders do not need to be the best performers, but they do need to be involved and interested in performance. They need to be reliable contributors to performance and they need to be courageous. They have insight into the team's momentum and the capacity to manage it. Their body language remains consistent and they remain optimistic. Sport leaders inspire through their actions, whether steady or in one-off acts that impact others. They are positive performers both at training and in competition. Positive leaders strive to put their best foot forward.

SELF-BELIEF

Leaders recognise their capacity to lead and influence. They trust and back their own judgement and believe they have something to offer others. Their self-confidence enables honesty and open-mindedness, which means they can continue to take advice and develop. Leaders are confident enough to show vulnerability without fear of being seen as weak. Self-belief means being comfortable in your own skin and authentic. Leaders don't try to be someone else. Most importantly, leaders are comfortable to make and back a decision. They are comfortable to acknowledge their strengths and what they are good at, yet they remain humble. This confidence provides comfort to others to follow.

You'll notice I haven't included 'inspiration' as a category. This is because when a leader practises good leadership behaviour, they are authentically inspirational. *Trying* to be inspirational for the sake of it is likely to be counterproductive.

Summary

Athlete leadership is highly relevant in both individual and team sports today. I have seen young athletes develop to become highly capable leaders. This can enhance their own performance, the performance of others as well as benefit the environments they occupy. These leaders have exhibited an appetite for learning and growing, and are comfortable asking for help and sharing responsibility and recognition. I've also seen such leadership extend beyond a sporting career.

Strong leaders are proactive in managing themselves, driving standards and supporting others. They bring emotional intelligence to balance their drive for high standards. Leadership takes many forms, whether formal and informal. Regardless of official roles, all athletes should be aware of their capacity to influence others.

There are many different pathways to building leadership in sporting environments that ultimately reward both individuals and their sporting organisations. They will not always lead to runs on the board, but they will provide people with opportunities to perform at their best. There are many leadership qualities. Consider what qualities you are striving for in any specific environment to maximise leadership growth and to positively impact those around you.

BUILD YOUR LEADERSHIP

- Appreciate the proactive nature of leadership and the potential influence of one leader on individuals and a group.

- Consider *what* you are leading and *how* you are going about it.

- Consider the SCOS leadership model and leadership of self as a priority.

- Recognise leading culture, others and situations as additional important aspects of leadership.

- Invest in growing leadership across a sport program.

- Recognise the power of informal or silent leaders.

- Consider integrating leadership density and group programs into a program and training schedule.

- Be clear on what a leadership group is leading, and consider obtaining feedback from a squad or team about what they want from formal leaders.

- Consider the style and qualities that are most relevant to you as a leader in your role. Think about behavioural definitions of these qualities, and monitor your progress through reflection and feedback.

- Consider having a specific leader, mentor or facilitator to support and assist growth in the role.

STEP 5

FOSTER YOUR CULTURE

Australia's swimming team made history at the 2021 Tokyo Olympics when it won more gold medals than any previous Australian Olympic swimming team. The Dolphins won 21 medals in Tokyo (including open water), nine of them gold. This was a far cry from the 2012 London Olympics where Australia had its worst swimming team performance, with 10 medals overall and only the women's 4x100 relay team winning gold. The performance raises curiosity about the team's rise at Tokyo.

Culture in practice

When Rohan Taylor was appointed as head coach, replacing Jacco Verhaeren, his clear focus was to continue an overt and very deliberate culture build. Rohan had discussed this with Jacco in the transition to his 2020 appointment, in the midst of the COVID pandemic and only 12 months before Tokyo was scheduled to take place. 'From my experience in a previous role as head coach at Nunawading Swimming Club in Melbourne, I knew the importance of culture,' he told me when I interviewed him after Tokyo. 'I took lessons I learned from there to the Dolphins.

'To begin with I looked back to London, when the team's culture had been labelled poor. So I asked myself, what is culture? I see it as a living environment. What people see, feel and hear. It's the collective behaviours of people. I realised that historically there had been a focus on values, but not on behaviour. In London there were also a lot of silos due to an overemphasis on independence.'

Rohan emphasised three factors for the Dolphins in the lead-up to London. 'Early into the role I worked with the athlete-and-coach leadership group and we discussed which practical examples of athlete behaviours we wanted to foster.' The discussion was based on a premise of three areas he had determined to emphasise in the culture build: (1) Recognise the core reason we are here — to perform; (2) Understand that each person's behaviour influences the rest of the team; (3) Central to this change was athletes' buying into the culture and wanting to do things for the team rather than doing things because they had no choice.'

Trust and relationships were a priority. 'I felt that, historically, people only understood the first of the three principles. The personal relationships hadn't been there when they needed to. I emphasised that supporting each other mattered most. This level of investment is necessary should pressure start to derail performance.

'I didn't want to throw out or change the values that were in place. I aimed to align existing values (courage, excellence and unity) with the three principles I was introducing. Courage related to influencing others and respecting their individuality. Excellence related to preparing to the best of your ability. Unity was about recognising others, regardless of their performance. Unity was the fabric.'

When he took on the role as head coach, one thing that Rohan also wanted to create was a 'legacy statement'. He reflected on a time when he had done some swimming coaching for the Hawthorn

AFL team between 2005 and 2009. A quote he saw in the elevator at the club made a lasting impression on him. It read: 'If you embrace Hawthorn, Hawthorn will embrace you.' Drawing from that experience, in a coach-and-athlete leadership meeting in his new role he raised the idea of a legacy statement and relayed the story of the impact the Hawthorn declaration had made on him. After some discussion, the group came up with their own statement: 'We make each other better.'

'I wanted people to have something they could readily check their behaviour against.' The statement was on all the slides used in team meetings and referred to regularly.

A key aspect of the culture build was acknowledging positive behaviours that aligned with the three principles. Highlighting what was working, what was good and fun was important. 'I didn't want to wait until people stuffed up to highlight what we were striving for,' Rohan said.

Following the explicit work on culture, examples of positive behaviours arose almost immediately. Squad members at a training camp who had finished a session jumped into another lane to help other swimmers finish their session. At the games, after a medal swim, Kaylee McKeown didn't have her team runners with her. A message went up to the stands from pool deck asking anyone wearing a size nine shoe to get down ASAP. 'About five people jumped up to help,' Rohan recalled proudly.

This is a summary of the steps Rohan described that he took as part of the culture build:

- He sorted out small things quickly, before they morphed into big things.
- He conducted fortnightly leadership meetings with athletes and coaches from early in the year.
- He considered the coach team for Tokyo carefully. 'They had to have at least one athlete on the team, and they had

to be experienced. This helped the relationship piece.' He recognised the risk of younger, less-experienced coaches focusing on their own athlete's needs at the expense of the whole team.

- He appointed an experienced senior assistant coach to help him.
- On arrival at Tokyo, he inducted the whole group into the venues, facilities and support structures.
- On their first visit to the pool, he arranged for the team to perform a chant on pool deck as a sign of unity in front of others.
- He designed the team's area to feel like a home away from home.
- At the pre-departure camp at Tokyo, he reinforced positive behaviours and reflected on why the team were well prepared.
- In Tokyo he conducted routine check-ins every morning with athletes and coaches. This typically took 30 minutes, but 'if needed I was prepared to give more time to stay and have a conversation. It wasn't token'.
- He proactively sought out individuals identified as possibly being vulnerable.

The proactive emphasis continued to be practised after the Games in the form of a specific debriefing. This debrief format started after the 2018 Commonwealth Games. That competition, the Pan Pacific Games and the world championships were all debriefed with an emphasis on opportunities for future action noted. That information was used to assist the build-up to Tokyo. The specific debrief from Tokyo included two opportunities: to 'protect what we know works' and to 'apply our learning and experience to Paris in 2024'.

There was one major point regarding culture that Rohan was determined to highlight. 'We wanted people to feel they were part of a great experience, regardless of performance. We didn't want people looking back at events like the Olympic Games and not have great memories as their dominant reflection.' Simply by using the word 'we' rather than 'I', Rohan showed he was living the values and behaviours he encouraged.

Evidence of the successful culture build was reflected in performance. 'The historical data leads us to anticipate that medallists are most likely to come from the top five ranked swimmers going into the meet,' Rohan explained. 'At London and Rio we had a conversion rate of top five ranked swimmers to medals of about 30 per cent. At Tokyo, we were able to shift that conversion to about 68 per cent. I attribute that to a wide range of factors predominantly based on the culture shift.'

So when watching the Australian Swimming Team or many other teams and athletes on screens, look beyond the performance to what lies behind it. Culture work is reflected in how coaches and athletes interact with each other and external stakeholders. It is reflected in how they hold themselves in times of inevitable challenges and losses, as well as positive performances.

Rohan's story reminds us that performance does not exist in a vacuum. It is founded on a wide range of influences that make up a team's environment and culture. Some of those influences are self-evident but those that aren't are no less vital. Culture is an important cog in the performance mindset.

Thinking, decisions and behaviour

I like to view culture informally as the 'personality' or vibe of an organisation, be it sporting, corporate, educational, not-for-profit or governmental. It can also reflect what an organisation stands for, what matters most. Culture is often viewed as a shared pattern of behaviours, beliefs and values understood by organisation members. They impact a wide range of factors such as creativity, learning, thinking and decision making. As I discuss with groups when working in this space, effective culture should guide *thinking, decisions* and *behaviour*.

More formally, culture has been defined as 'the social and psychological environment that maximises individual and team ability to achieve success'[1] and as 'a shared pattern of assumptions that guide standards and expectations in performance and behaviour'.[2]

Viewed from a structural perspective, culture can include a vision, a mission statement, values, purpose, priorities and behaviours. The range of terminology used when discussing or building a culture can be confusing, but the important thing to remember is that organisations are clear on what they are building and the language or narrative around it. Good cultures are sustained on processes being integrated into structures, communication channels and operations. It also involves all stakeholders being clear on the terminology and how it applies to the organisation and to them.

In sport, one interesting nuance related to culture is creating a single representative team out of individuals who may typically live in different cities and compete against each other. Track and field and swimming teams are two examples. Individuals from national soccer, netball, hockey and basketball teams, too, may compete against one another from week to week and unite only briefly before competing as a single team against other states or countries. Establishing a lasting culture in these circumstances can be challenging. This is in contrast to teams and squads that train and compete together on a weekly basis and compete seasonally.

Regardless of how a team is established, a strong and supportive culture is a competitive advantage, so I recommend that its development be by design rather than by default.

Looking back on his Paris–Roubaix victory, Mat Hayman reflected, 'Special things happen to special teams. Knowing how supportive everyone was as a group was special. It was a great team for two years leading into that race. We were underdogs but a very close-knit unit, and that helped me and was the special part.'

Sam Mitchell also believes that culture is vital to team success. 'Most people are a reflection of their environment and perform at a level that parallels that environment.'

There is little doubt that individuals in teams and organisations feed off the culture of which they are a part. Yes, individuals contribute to culture, but the impact of culture on people cannot be overestimated.

High-performance environments

Culture is one component of an environment. One model identifies four components essential to a high-performance environment.[3] These are:

1. leadership (vision, support, challenge)
2. performance enablers (information, instruments, incentives)
3. people (attitudes, behaviours, capacity)
4. culture (achievement, wellbeing, innovation and internal processes).

The authors recommended that practitioners working in the high-performance and culture space take a holistic view and consider coaching leaders, facilitating performance enablers, engaging people and shaping cultural change in order to impact the whole environment. Their findings supported the contention that 'a performance environment that is created in elite sports teams is equally as important as the people performing within it'.

I have always advocated for organisational structure as a source of competitive advantage in a sporting environment. What positions exist within such a structure, and who holds them? For example, is there a person responsible for culture development and management, or does that role fall to the coach? Is it a dual-management role? Is there a leadership group of athletes who actively support the culture? Is data related to culture collected? What funds are directed towards staff capable of establishing a high-performance culture? If a person is identified as highly capable, is a position created for them within the structure? These questions remind us that many factors need to be considered if structure is to provide a competitive advantage.

Nicole Pratt reflected that, 'Environment is incredibly important. It breeds positive culture. I craved to be in a world-class environment. I went from being a country kid to the Australian Institute of Sport, and that was really stimulating. Later I moved to the USA, to Harvard, and that environment was incredibly positive. There was recognition that all the athletes were doing something amazing. At times, in Australia I felt that being ranked 30 in the world was not recognised, but in the US at the time everyone thought it was amazing. That gave me breathing room, because what I was doing was celebrated and I took joy in what I was doing there. I had a real sense of belonging in that environment. After being a top-ranked junior, my senior ranking was 340. After two years in the Harvard environment, I got to 140. Then I moved to Orlando, another great environment, and I progressed to 35. Both US environments had a culture of excellence, positives and a process focus that enabled everyone to achieve what they were capable of. It helped my career progression.'

These positive environments were one reason Nicole loved playing for her country. It was a different experience from that of being an individual on the grinding tennis tour. 'Playing Fed Cup and at the Olympics was always a priority because I wanted to strive to be a national representative. I played my best tennis in those environments. I was highly charged and emotionally invested. When we played Colombia in Wollongong, we were down 1–2 and I hadn't played a match yet. Fifteen minutes before the last singles,

Evonne Goolagong Cawley told me I was playing. It meant so much to me that even with limited preparation I went out there and won. Australia went on to win the doubles and the tie. It was an amazing experience, similar to the Olympics.'

Nicole's story is one of many that support the view that a healthy environment and culture can be a uniting and driving force that contributes to motivation, performance, engagement, positive experiences and personal growth.

Individual athlete and coach influence on culture

During his basketball career, Dave Andersen was part of no fewer than 22 national championship–winning teams in a list of countries that included Italy, Russia, Spain, France and Australia. With only five players on court at a time and squads of about 12 in a season, one person's impact on a team's culture can be significant. 'I had a goal in every team I played for to be the "glue-guy",' Dave recalls. 'My mother was from England and my father was Danish, and I was born and raised in Australia, so it was bred into me to be culturally open-minded. So when there were people from several nationalities in one team, I always deliberately tried to get them working together so we were all on the same page and it definitely helped.'

This may be one of the reasons why NBL team Melbourne United called Dave and re-rostered him as a backup player just before the final series during a COVID-impacted 2021 season. As it turned out, he didn't get court time in that final series, but he was at every training session and on the bench for every game, educating and supporting. So his 22nd and final championship was won without any court time. Such was the value of the glue-guy.

In a 2010 study, researcher Peter Schroeder investigated how much team improvement was related to (a) a change in team culture and (b) the leadership behaviours inculcated by coaches in this process.[4] He interviewed 10 NCAA Division One head coaches who had guided previously unsuccessful teams to championship level within five years. He found that 'coaches started the cultural change process by creating core sets of values specific to their teams. To ingrain these values, coaches taught them with several tactics, recruited athletes who would embrace team values, and "punished" and rewarded consistent with the values'.

Cultural change was achieved reasonably quickly, in most cases by the third year. This fits with my own experience. Intent to build a culture is essential, along with investment in resources. Certainly, I have seen culture change quite rapidly when leaders have positive intent, have skills and resources and are united in their efforts. In my experience, positive culture change can occur as rapidly as across one or two seasons. Rohan at Swimming Australia is testament to this.

This study also identified two environmental effects on team cultural change. Some environments created an 'aura' that heightened the importance of team culture, which meant coaches did not have to spend as much time helping athletes understand and adhere to core values; hence the environment contributed to rewarding the values. But in environments that didn't have the resources to foster team culture, coaches had to spend much more time defining and teaching core values. These environments didn't reinforce core values, and in some instances even diminished their importance.

This study reflected the importance of valuing culture across an organisation. When all parties, from the boardroom to the last selected athlete to support staff, understand their influence on culture, everyone benefits and performance improves.

As athletes become more mature, appreciating and understanding their influence and impact on the environment and culture is of relevance. Engaging with their environment in a positive way to maximise the resources available to them can assist progress. Creating their own small positive sub-cultures with supports, family and friends within the larger environment they are part of can also be of benefit. It is part of recognising reciprocal influence, a concept modelled by esteemed psychologist, Albert Bandura and his work on reciprocal determinism. The model outlines that psychological functioning involves continuous reciprocal interaction between behavioural, cognitive and environmental influences.[5] Reciprocal influence acknowledges that people both influence and are impacted by the environment and culture they are in.

Cultural consistency

The study mentioned earlier confirms the importance of resources and broader buy-in to building and sustaining culture. I have observed sports in which administrative staff force particular organisational values onto coaches and players. This approach is fraught with danger, since the values developed by organisational staff may have minimal application for competitive athletes. In addition, values must have 'behavioural definitions' associated with them that can be attached to on- and off-field performance.

In my experience, values must be shared across an organisation in a way that allows specific behaviours to be adapted to suit different areas, including the athletes and coaches. This means the entire organisation will operate according to consistent cultural values. Each part of an organisation, including coaches and athletes, not only is accountable to the whole but grows in response to shared values with specific and differing codes of behaviour to them. This facilitates alignment, with people across an organisation being on the same page and directing their energy towards a common goal. Of course, this may not always be an option, but it's a model worth considering.

Research insights

Six university team-sport coaches in Canada who between them had won more than 30 national titles were interviewed about their strategies.

The researchers identified behaviours that created a culture of on-going success. These included:

- hard work and disciplined daily attention to detail

- effective emotional management of themselves and their athletes that included implementing team activities to promote relaxation and managing coach and athlete emotions before and during competition

- continuous self-assessment and self-education, including self-reflection. Coaches 'believed that engaging in self-reflection on past experiences at national championship tournaments, reading books, attending conferences and interacting with other coaches, as well as having a more experienced mentor, were all sources that helped them modify their coaching skills and enrich their knowledge'.[6]

The finding from this study on effective emotional management supports a broader concept embraced by some sport teams and adapted from corporate environments: *psychological safety*.

Psychological safety

In 1999, when Amy Edmondson, Professor of Leadership and Management at Harvard Business School, published a paper titled 'Psychological safety and learning behaviour in work teams', it is unlikely she would have known the ripple effect her study would have.[7] She defined psychological safety as 'a shared belief held by members of a team that the team is safe for interpersonal risk taking'. Her research was based on an investigation of 51 small teams within a large manufacturer of office furniture that, at the time, had about 5000 employees. Her findings led her to conclude that a combination of structural and interpersonal characteristics influenced learning and performance in teams.

Structural features consisted of 'a clear and compelling goal, an enabling team design (including context support such as adequate resources, information and rewards), along with team leader behaviour such as coaching and direction setting'. Learning involved seeking feedback, discussing errors and using this information to improve. Interestingly, and overlapping with sport, Edmondson noted the need for learning in teams as increasingly critical due to the growing complexity in fast-paced environments that requires learning behaviour to make sense of what is happening and to take action.

Edmondson also noted that team psychological safety is distinct from individual psychological safety. Team psychological safety alleviates concern about the reactions of others and promotes a team's willingness to point out and learn from errors. Team members are willing to speak-up about errors if they feel they will not be rejected by the team and that the team is capable of using the new information to improve.

About a dozen years after the publication of Edmondson's work, Google embarked on a similar assignment: to identify what made their best internal teams effective. 'Project Aristotle' reflected Aristotle's aphorism that *the whole is greater than the sum of its parts*. Over three years researchers analysed 180 teams from engineering and sales. Their findings concluded that the most important ingredient of success was how teams worked together and that psychological safety was paramount. Other important factors were dependability, structure and clarity, meaning and impact.

Edmondson's and Google's work highlighted the importance of psychological safety to culture. Since then, emotional intelligence has also been highlighted as assisting the promotion of psychological safety.

Learn and grow

Athletes spend countless hours training physically. Therefore, it is inevitable that, barring injury, they'll develop and improve in that way. The challenge is the rate of improvement. The goal is to steepen the development curve over time. Yes, training harder, better resources and a range of other conditions contribute, but an often-overlooked ingredient to shift the rate of improvement is the capacity to grow and learn faster. It is less about the shiny new facilities and more about coaching competence and a culture that contributes to growth. Another important element is engagement. And positive culture enhances engagement, which in turn enhances learning. Work plus engagement results in higher and faster development. In essence good cultures embrace and create a learning environment. The learning applies to all members of an organisation.

To assist fast-track growth, at times I have conducted assessments on athletes and coaches to identify preferred learning styles. This information can help coaches to coach better and help athletes to contribute to and engage in their learning. Some people learn better by reading, others by watching and some by doing. Taking such considerations into account only enhances the growth and experience of athletes and coaches. New Zealand educator Neil Fleming has researched how kinaesthetic, visual, aural and read/write are learning styles that can be adapted to maximise the benefits of coaching and, in turn, athletes.[8]

Effective cultures and learning environments balance individual and collective needs well, including catering for a wide variety of approaches to learning.

In 2008, Amy Edmondson expanded her work on psychological safety by presenting a model that incorporated a 'learning zone'.[9] She discusses this further in her book, *The Fearless Organization*.[10] Within her model, the learning zone occurs when high psychological safety and high standards combine. In contrast, an anxiety zone evolves from the interaction between high standards with low psychological safety (see figure 5.1).

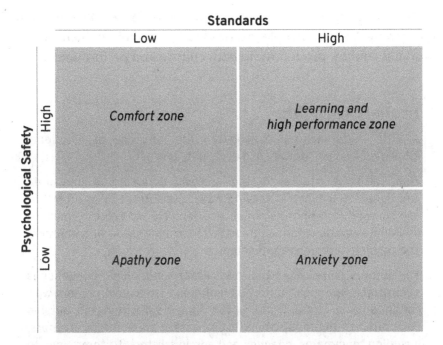

Figure 5.1: psychological safety and performance standards

Source: Amy Edmondson, *The Fearless Organization* (Hoboken, New Jersey, John Wiley & Sons, 2018)

Edmondson also differentiates between execution as efficiency and execution as learning.

- *Efficiency* includes leaders providing answers, feedback being one way, and staff asking questions when unsure, with problem solving rare.

- *Learning* involves leaders setting direction and articulating the mission, feedback being two way, and problem solving being constant on the basis of information provided.

It becomes apparent that creating a learning environment is important for success over the long haul. This aligns well with learning in sport, considering the length of time it takes to be able to perform consistently at a high level. It also highlights the importance of a learning environment to be ingrained in the culture of sport. Too often the time pressure for results creates an environment where people are predominantly told, which in turn becomes counter-productive to both culture and performance.

Research insights

A 2018 meta-analysis investigated the influence of emotional intelligence on performance in competitive sports.

While different studies in the analysis defined and measured emotional intelligence in varying ways, the authors drew on Mayer and Salovey's definition: 'the ability to perceive and express emotion, assimilate emotion in thought, understand and reason with emotion, and regulate emotion in self and others'.

The authors emphasised that one reason emotional intelligence is important in sport is that it's an emotionally laden environment with continual stressors and challenges from both within and outside competition. Athletes also have to be aware of the emotions of others, including teammates, coaches and administrators, to communicate and work with others to get the best out of themselves. This review found a small but significant relationship between emotional intelligence and sport performance.[11]

Emotional intelligence

In sporting environments, psychological safety can be thought of as a cultural variable and emotional intelligence as a quality that contributes to it. In many environments I have worked in, both coaches and athletes have had emotional intelligence assessments and education, either in groups or one-to-one. Emotional intelligence helps groups and teams who have to work together in often unusual and unpredictable circumstances. Teams also usually contain a wide variety of personalities, and emotional intelligence encourages empathy, understanding and respect of others, which contributes to a positive culture.

As a concept, emotional intelligence was popularised by Daniel Goleman, who has written extensively on the topic. His early work in this space began with his book *Emotional Intelligence: why it can matter more than IQ*, which was published in 1996.[12] I have often used emotional intelligence as a topic to assist the personal development of both athletes and coaches in sport, as well as in corporate environments. Emotional intelligence can be coached and developed in athletes either directly or indirectly and benefits both personal interaction as well as culture and performance.

> For some insights into emotional intelligence, I recommend an early article by Goleman titled 'What makes a leader?', which is the first chapter in the *Harvard Business Review's* 2011 book titled *On Leadership*.[13]

In my experience, psychological safety and emotional intelligence are both vital to culture. Emotional intelligence skills, such as effective communication, empathy, stress management and being open minded also contribute to psychological safety.

Research insights

In an investigation into the potential benefits of psychological safety in sport, 289 handball players were recruited from national and regional level competitions in Belgium and Holland.

It was found that coaches, formal leaders and informal leaders who contributed to creating a strong team identity fostered a psychologically safe environment that paved the way for optimal team effectiveness and contributed to wellbeing.

From a practical perspective the authors suggested that their findings highlighted 'the importance of fostering an environment that encourages athletes to voice their opinions, engage in decision-making, ask others for help, seek feedback following mistakes and take risks'.[14]

Research insights

British athletes from a wide variety of sports, including hockey, rugby union, soccer, basketball and cricket, were recruited for this study.

Researchers found that athletes felt valued, connected, confident and comfortable because of a positive relationship with the coach and feelings of psychological safety. Such an environment contributed to athletes' feeling that they could flourish and thrive both in sport and in life.[15]

Relationships and communication

Effective communication and relationships are a cornerstone of a positive culture. They bring to life and sustain any values and behaviours as well as enable conversations and interaction to thrive. I often consider relationships in sporting environments as being either personal or performance based, as mentioned earlier. The stronger personal relationships are, the more thorough performance conversations can be. In turn, relationships, are built on a foundation of effective communication and positive experiences built over time. With strong personal relationships, however, one has to be sure not to be a 'yes' person and fail to provide honest feedback when necessary. There are many examples of successful sportspeople being surrounded by 'yes' people who want to be associated with them and avoid being honest for fear of the consequences. Strong cultures enable honest and direct communication without fear of repercussion.

Considering the variation of personalities, life experiences, ages and interpersonal skills people have, communication cannot be taken for granted. Good cultures are sensitive to these variations and establish processes to facilitate effective and appropriate communication education and channels. From a practical perspective, nurturing communication and relationships within squads and teams, as well as between athletes and coaches, can be done through designated activities and high-level coaching practices. Such activities may be social and as simple as sharing meals or investing in a variety of tasks, including playing non-specific games, having mentor and buddy systems, using small groups for different activities or allowing time for individuals to get to know each other better. Bringing emotional intelligence and social sensitivity to tasks can also help. As discussed in step 4 on leadership, it is not just *what* is done but *how* it is done that matters.

Additionally, specific education on communication and relationships can benefit individuals in squads and teams. There are a wide variety of avenues to enable this, depending on a range of factors including age, level or time together as a group. In sporting environments, understanding how to give and receive direct feedback is of utmost importance as the next challenge is always just around the corner. One aspect of this education should encompass providing feedback on behaviour, as distinct from on the person. Timing is another relevant aspect of providing feedback. Whether feedback should be in a group or individual environment also has to be considered. Tone, volume and language used are typical ingredients of communication education. Another consideration: is it assertive, aggressive or passive? Is it clear? Is there follow-up?

Good communication and strong relationships enable athletes to be comfortable with acknowledging vulnerabilities and admitting errors that are a natural part of any sporting performance. Being able to put your hand up and accept responsibility for errors without feeling judged either by yourself or by others is powerful. Emotional intelligence and psychological safety encourage this openness, which is why they are important elements in effective cultures of all kinds and in sport specifically. It doesn't mean that all team members become best friends, but it does confirm the benefits of knowing the person as well as the performer.

As Garth Tander developed his driving skills, he also developed his leadership and understanding of the importance of culture. It is likely his appreciation of culture is another factor that enhanced his performance. 'Team culture is so important because the individuals that make up the team are so varied. As I developed, I realised the need to respect and appreciate differences in people and other people's roles. I went from being young and brash and not appreciating others who helped me to being someone who did. As my career progressed, I learned to build personal relationships across the team with different staff. I asked them about personal interests to develop a deeper and more genuine connection. I realised it's really important to show appreciation for the people you go into battle with. Once a good culture is embedded and lived there is more harmony and efficiency. There are also fewer internal challenges and distractions. It also helps communication and avoids wasting time on things that don't help winning.

'When I was doing high-level physical training, if I'd had to do it on my own, I wouldn't have worked as hard as I needed to, but when I was training with others in a small-group environment it was both more enjoyable and a better quality. It was a healthy competitive environment that helped me learn to push myself way harder. And it gave me a goal and enjoyment beyond racing.'

Individuals coming together in squads or team sports are there because they can perform, but Garth reminds us people can learn to appreciate others and that everyone contributes to a culture. A group performs better if there is a culture in which appreciation and gratitude are articulated and not taken for granted. Coaches and facilitators play an important role here to initiate conversations and foster relationships, particularly with junior athletes, which also contributes to the team's wellbeing.

In my own practice, I invite people to consider how they come across to others, as well as what formal and informal opportunities there are for communication and relationships to develop. At times I also conduct brief communication surveys that encourage reflection on the impact of different communication styles, such as predominantly assertive, positive, fun and jokey, or more serious. The key is to be aware of different communication styles and how one person's communication style impacts relationships and the culture.

Mastery climate

The concept of a mastery climate has its origins in the achievement goal theory that differentiates between an athlete's task and ego focus, which is discussed in step 1 on motivation. A mastery climate is characterised by learning and mastering skills and emphasises maximising effort or trying to do one's best. It goes without saying that sports environments are highly focused on outcome — athletes exist to win. However, an overemphasis on performance outcome to the detriment of mastery can have negative consequences.

The notion that a perceived mastery climate increases enjoyment and a belief that effort leads to achievement was identified in an early study from the 1990s with 105 basketball players from 9 varsity teams.[16] This was further supported in a study with a small number of elite winter Olympic athletes. These athletes were high in task focus and moderate-to-high on ego, but felt the climate should have an emphasis on mastery and be accepting and caring to enable them to maximise success. The athletes also emphasised the importance of the coach as the creator of the climate.[17]

Emphasising mastery does not mean outcomes and results are set aside. Athletes and coaches know too well performance demands, and at times outcomes will be front-of-mind. Outcome goals and focus are often strong motivators. A mastery climate is about the day-to-day *atmosphere* around these outcomes. It embraces all that is needed to achieve a goal without unduly emphasising the outcome. It encourages reflecting on how to learn and improve as fast as possible in order to reach the highest possible standard.

It emphasises self-referencing when striving to develop and goals including mastering a craft. A skill of coaching and support teams is to know when to emphasise outcome within a mastery environment to maintain maximum motivation, effort and wellbeing.

Research insights

Research on mastery and motivational climates in sport has included investigating the impact of these environments in youth sport. One study investigated the relationships between a coach-created motivational climate and athlete engagement in 260 adolescent soccer players in England. The authors found that 'engagement was predicted by a mastery climate and that a mastery climate offers a means of promoting higher levels of overall engagement'. They also noted that athlete engagement is 'an enduring and relatively stable experiential state, which refers to generalised positive cognitions and affect about one's sport'. The study also emphasised the link between engagement and culture.[18]

Mastery's significance to wellbeing and performance of individuals and groups is often underrated. It is a key element of culture. Winning and losing can too easily detract from maintaining a mastery climate. Outcome cultures also have a use-by date. Mastery climates emphasise sustainable targets that stand the test of time and stay relevant beyond winning and losing.

The New Zealand All Blacks

The culture of the New Zealand All Blacks rugby union team has been discussed a great deal. It is explored in detail in James Kerr's 2013 Legacy.[19] A year later the University of Otago's Ken Hodge collaborated with former All Blacks Head Coach Graham Henry and Assistant Coach Wayne Smith on a journal article for The Sport Psychologist that gives an excellent overview of the development of the All Blacks culture from 2004 to 2011, culminating in a World Cup victory over France in 2011.[20] The victory was on the back of

New Zealand's worst ever World Cup performance in the previous tournament held in France in 2007, when for the first time they didn't reach the final four teams. The result created uproar in their rugby-loving home country and was likely a contributor to an even greater emphasis on a team mindset and culture build that contributed to New Zealand securing back-to-back Rugby World Cups and lofting the trophy at the next opportunity in 2015.

In relation to motivational climate, Hodge, Henry and Smith signposted eight themes: (i) a critical turning point, (ii) flexible and evolving, (iii) dual management model, (iv) 'Better people make better All Blacks', (v) responsibility, (vi) leadership, (vii) expectation of excellence and (viii) team cohesion. They summarised their practical suggestions for coaches: 'involve athletes in meaningful leadership roles via a version of the dual-management model, adopt a mindset for transformational leadership via focus on individual consideration, inspirational motivation, intellectual stimulation, fostering acceptance of group goals, high performance expectations and appropriate role-modelling, learn how to be an emotionally intelligent coach by developing interpersonal and intrapersonal competencies of perceiving emotions in self and other and implement autonomy-supportive coaching strategies'. The paper quotes Wayne Smith: 'we worked on their strengths, rather than just their weaknesses. We wanted them to understand that they were there because of what they were good at.'

In the documentary *Chasing Great*, the then captain, Richie McCaw, explained that the team thought 2007 would be their moment, but they ignored the lessons from 2003.[21] Richie, who went on to have one of the most decorated careers in rugby union history, said of the 2007 quarter-final loss, 'It didn't come down to talent. It came down to when the heat was on we weren't able to find a way to win. Training harder or being fitter wouldn't have helped. We had to admit we didn't have the tools in the box that we needed. We needed to not just pay lip service to the mental side. We addressed the elephant in the room and went to find the people and put time into the mental stuff.'

Of the 2011 World Cup victory, Richie said, 'Instead of being scared I was embracing it, thinking bring it on.' There's little doubt that the All Blacks had built an effective learning environment. 'A key to whatever you do in life is to have a challenge and learn. If you stop learning, you can get sick of what you're doing. If you can get better, that's why you keep turning up.' That mindset carried over to the 2015 World Cup, about which Richie said, 'You want to be in that situation to test yourself. This is the 50-foot wave I've been wanting.'

Building culture

There are many factors to consider when building a culture. It's one thing to hang a poster on a wall with some values printed on it, but to live a culture is altogether different. There are many ways organisations and people can do this. Here are a few thoughts from my experiences working with a wide variety of sports, schools and corporates on creating a culture.

TERMINOLOGY AND ENGAGEMENT

Commit to building a values-driven culture. Engage and involve all stakeholders across the organisation in the importance of culture, and encourage them to contribute to culture build and reviews. Be clear on how you want to frame the culture: Is it more fun? More serious? More outcome or more process?

Start with the end in mind. Will it be framed in terms of mission, values and behaviours? Variations include: Purpose–Vision–Values–Behaviours and Purpose–Values–Behaviours. I've seen some organisations come up with phrases like 'why we exist' or 'our manifesto' or 'our DNA' to define or reflect a focus or an enduring component of their culture.

Once a structure is determined and the components propagated, be clear on how culture will be integrated and reviewed. Engage a range of stakeholders in order to maximise buy-in, and emphasise culture at recruitment and in the course of induction. I recommend specific staff or consultants, such as performance psychologists, be nominated to facilitate this process.

I have asked sporting squads and groups engaged in a culture build questions like: 'How is the group currently perceived?', 'How do we perceive competitors?', 'How would we like to be perceived?', 'What do we stand for?', 'How can we live the culture?', 'What behaviours are required?', 'What examples of positive behaviour do we have?', 'What are the benefits of working on culture?' and 'What gets in the way of our living culture?'

CLEAR VALUES AND BEHAVIOURS DESCRIBED

Many people are annoyed by vague values and behaviours that are difficult to relate to, too abstract, not relevant or not lived. Ensure that the culture includes clearly comprehensible terminology and values and behavioural definitions. The culture should stand the test of time and be relevant beyond one season. Specific team goals, such as a certain number of wins in a season, a ranking or a position, are goals that a culture may help the team achieve, but they are *not* a part of the culture. Goals are a part of a broader strategic plan that also includes culture.

SUPPORT PEOPLE AND PERFORMANCE

Support of both people and performance is essential in sport. Processes that enable athletes to maximise their capacity to perform, including access to resources, training and competition opportunities, should be available. Healthy cultures foster and compliment athlete determination and help them achieve their goals as well as be comfortable and grow as people. More on the people aspect in step 6 on wellbeing.

LEADERS LIVE, MODEL AND DRIVE CULTURE

While each person in an organisation influences its culture, and ultimately everyone is responsible for culture, its leaders have the greatest influence on how it is presented, lived and prioritised. Critical components are how much culture is valued and how it is built into processes. Coaches and leaders in particular can determine whether the culture shines and thrives or becomes murky and fades into the background.

COACHING, CELEBRATING AND ACCOUNTABILITY

Develop individual, small-team and larger-group education related to culture. Integrate reflection on culture into formal performance reviews as well as more informal conversations. Ideally, culture should be integrated into the organisation's narrative, its stories. Create opportunities to celebrate people and processes that exemplify and strengthen culture.

Culture can help ease the tensions experienced around performance conversations. Use culture to discuss behaviours that do or no not align with what is desired. Pointing out that a behaviour is not aligned with the culture doesn't reduce individual responsibility, but emphasises behaviour that is not aligned to culture.

DISPLAY AND SHARE

Ensure culture is reinforced internally and, when appropriate, externally. Determine as an organisation what is to be displayed, how and where. What exemplary stories will be shared? Will culture be reinforced on letterhead, in presentations, email signatures and websites? External stakeholders are far more interested in culture now than ever—they want to know what a sport stands for to ensure they are comfortable being aligned with it.

INTEGRATE INTO PROCESSES

At interviews, explain culture and assess cultural fit. Selected meetings can reflect on culture. Seasonal reviews and exit interviews are an opportunity to obtain feedback. At times a culture coordinator may facilitate cultural conversations. Careful consideration should be given to who will be formally charged with integrating and maintaining culture.

MONITORING AND EVOLVING CULTURE WITH DATA AND MEASUREMENT

Culture can be assessed quantitatively either by directly rating specific elements of the culture or by indirectly assessing related aspects like wellbeing, engagement, social-emotional constructs and performance outcomes. There are many benefits to this kind of analysis, including recognising strengths and development areas, maintaining accountability, and balancing qualitative reflection or impressions about culture with real data. The data can be collected simply by creating a survey for people to rate and comment on, for example, how well they think values and behaviours are being upheld. In collecting data on culture, I have often used independent surveys that reflect culture, including engagement, as well as the specific rating of self and groups on the values and behaviours a sport adopts.

VALUES CONGRUENCY

As mentioned in step 4 on leadership, people whose values align with those of the organisation are often better able to contribute. They are usually more comfortable in the organisation. I often illustrate this with the example of the stress that would be experienced by a health advocate working for a tobacco company. Culture and individuals thrive when the values of team members, including staff and athletes, are congruent with the values of the organisation.

DIVERSITY

Hiring based on culture and values congruency doesn't mean everyone in the organisation should be the same. Effective cultures thrive on diversity, whether in gender, race, age, experience or thinking.

Challenges to culture

There are many challenges to building and living a culture. Here are a few elements that I consider when investigating the maximum impact a culture can have.

PHYSICAL ENVIRONMENT, GEOGRAPHY OR SIZE

Leading and building culture can be simpler if everyone is in one place, just as a staff of 500 poses difficulties that a staff of 50 may not. And, as we've discussed, ensuring that values are relevant to athletes, as well as to coaches, support and administrative staff, can be a challenge.

Overestimating the impact of the physical environment, with its multiple meeting rooms, top-shelf whiteboards and shiny signs, can cause us to forget for a moment that culture is created and reinforced by people and their behaviour. Mindset towards culture is the most important aspect. Physical structures reinforce culture but they do not create it. On the other hand, people do need a physical environment in which they are comfortable if they are to work productively and interact effectively.

CHANGE

Without ongoing commitment and maintenance, disruptions such as changes in leadership, organisation direction and staff can all dilute culture. New leaders often want to create their own mark on a team or organisation, including shifting culture. The foundation of a culture should remain reasonably constant, with recognition that at times some shift may need to occur for it to remain progressive and relevant.

At times, a lack of change can be as counterproductive as too much change. Effective organisations strive to retain competent staff who live the culture, and to part ways with staff who sabotage it deliberately or inadvertently. Many teams experience renewed energy when establishing a culture but find it difficult to sustain the commitment that keeps it alive, particularly considering the constant changes that often occur in sporting environments.

COMPETITIVE—COLLABORATIVE BALANCE

A genuine balance between competitiveness and collaboration is a key ingredient to sustaining a solid culture. As many high-performance oriented individuals know, a healthy internal competitive environment can help drive high standards. Competition for selection or simply competitiveness at training can be extremely helpful and healthy. However, this becomes counterproductive when competitiveness overrides collaboration. Competition may be between athletes, coaches, support staff or administrators. The competition may be over results, a contract, for selection, attention or credit. Unhealthy competitiveness can drain people and culture and erode performance. Collaboration can keep competitiveness healthy.

INTENSITY—ENJOYMENT BALANCE

Something to keep in mind when building a sporting culture is that if it's too businesslike and formal it can stifle individuality and suffocate performance. The intensity involved in sport needs to be balanced with fun and enjoyment for culture to be sustained. Everyone needs a laugh at times. Sometimes fun happens inadvertently; at other times it's planned. A sporting culture is not based simply on a code of behaviour characterised by rules and curfews. Behaviour management is at times a relevant aspect of culture, but it's not the culture. Understanding how to balance intensity and enjoyment is a relevant aspect of culture in sport.

Building a good culture is hard; keeping a good culture is harder

Thinking about how difficult it is to build and sustain culture in sporting environments, Dave Andersen had some interesting observations on the NBA. 'In my experience only about five teams in the NBA have an effective team culture. We place a much bigger emphasise on culture in sport in Australia than do other places I've played, including Europe and the USA,' Dave told me. This may be one reason why the Australian men's basketball team were looked upon so fondly at the Tokyo Olympics. Like the swimming team, they exemplified a deliberate culture build that had started years before.

The men's basketball team achieved their best-ever result with an inaugural Olympic bronze medal in a highly competitive environment. Patty Mills, who was team captain along with coach Brian Goorjian, placed great emphasis on culture. Immediately after the bronze medal victory, Mills spoke emotionally to Channel 7: '… it's our culture … Australian culture, our Aussie spirit … we have been able to build our Boomers culture by understanding the lay of the land that goes far beyond basketball … always giving back … understanding where we come from … living in the present, and who we represent.' Mills' speech was applauded globally and reflected just how much a positive culture adds to a team.

The culture was built on the foundation of a heartbreaking loss by just one point to Spain at the 2016 Rio Olympics. In Rio, the Boomers were leading by one point with under 10 seconds remaining, only to lose by one point. It was their fourth fourth place at an Olympic Games, which added to the meaning and importance of culture at Tokyo. Mills, who had played in that game in Rio, had additional fire. Dave Andersen, who played in 2016, was one of several Australian players not at Tokyo, which meant they ended their careers without an Olympic medal.

Of the Boomers' culture, Dave Andersen said, 'Definitely the culture footprint was planted as far back as 2008 at the Beijing Olympics, with Brett Brown coaching. Patty Mills was only 20 years old and playing his first Olympics. We had a goal to try to keep the nucleus of the team together and to carry it forward from then. We wanted to make and keep Australia competitive on the world stage.

That created a camaraderie that was off the chain, and it was fun as well. So, the success in Tokyo started back then.'

Summary

Time, energy and resources are needed to build and sustain a positive, effective culture. Performance doesn't happen or exist in a vacuum. It is part of a dynamic psycho-social system that affects people, how they operate, learn and maximise what they have trained. Its impact on people personally and on their performance cannot be overestimated. There are many ways to build and sustain effective environments and cultures, depending on the sport, the size of the group and how often they come together.

A key priority is to ensure leaders drive culture. Psychological safety and emotional intelligence in relationships and communication are vital ingredients. An emphasis on learning and mastery, as well as being aware of what helps build or challenge effective culture, are other ingredients that contribute to maximising culture.

In strong positive cultures everyone is on the same page and everyone is growing. That enables opportunity for people and performance to thrive.

BUILD YOUR CULTURE

- Commit to building and working on a culture that supports people and performance.

- Strive to building and sustaining a values-driven environment and culture.

- Emphasise both values and behaviours within a culture.

- Allocate staff to facilitate and proactively manage culture.

- Consider the importance of psychological safety and emotional intelligence on culture.

- Embrace a learning environment as part of your culture.

- Ensure relationships and communication are prioritised as skills that contribute to a positive culture.

- Emphasise a mastery climate.

- Be aware of factors that may assist or challenge culture.

- Use data and metrics to monitor culture.

- In the building and maintenance of culture, reaffirm that every person contributes to and feeds off culture.

STEP 6

PROTECT YOUR WELLBEING

Tayla Harris is one of the most recognisable players in the Australian Football Women's League (AFLW). She was an inaugural player with the Brisbane Lions when the competition started in 2017 and an all-Australian representative in 2017 and 2018. After she transferred to Carlton in 2018, she became the leading goal-kicker that year and the next and in 2021 she continued her career at Melbourne in the AFLW. She has also been a high-performance boxer, having had eight professional bouts at the time of writing.

One of Tayla's strengths is her kicking. In a match against the Western Bulldogs in 2019, she powered into a trademark kick that was captured by photographer Michael Wilson. Tayla was in full flight, propelled off the ground by her strong action. When the photo went viral, Tayla became a target of online trolls and harassment that is hard to fathom. 'It was totally unexpected,' she said when I asked her about the incident. 'I couldn't have imagined anyone would think anything other than "there's an athlete playing their sport". I tried to understand it but couldn't. I found it very frustrating.

'I decided that because it was totally unacceptable I had to respond. [Tayla retweeted the photograph with the comment, 'Here's a pic of me at work … think about this before your derogatory comments, animals']. I also did it because my biggest fear was that young girls seeing the negative comments would avoid or stop playing sport. I was okay with responding because the public support was amazing and powerful.

'I have a very close circle of supporters. As soon as it happened, they did whatever it took to help me. I'm not afraid to ask for advice or suggestions. That meant as well as my closest supports I got some great advice from other people I respected. Because of that support from everyone, the situation became more uncomfortable than bad.'

Tayla's story offers lessons on many levels. The importance of established supports to nurture athletes' wellbeing is paramount. The importance of seeking help is another. Her capacity to reframe the situation from bad to uncomfortable on the back of support also reflects how she managed her narrative through that time. The community support led to the creation of a statue of Tayla in mid kick that symbolised, among other things, the importance of respect — for women in general and for athletes simply plying their trade. It also symbolised the importance of respect on social media. Inappropriate, even toxic commentary on social media has become an additional layer of stress for many people, including athletes, as this medium has gained momentum over the past decade. 'It doesn't matter if you're a man or a woman, young or old — everyone has a right to do what they love,' Tayla said at the unveiling of the statue.

I have worked with athletes who have been abused on social media for their performances. Some comments have been crudely disrespectful, as in Tayla's case. Some threatening messages are from frustrated and angry gamblers who have lost money wagering on an event. Some supporters who are frustrated with an athlete's performance feel they have the right to abuse and threaten them. Such behaviour is totally unacceptable and should not be tolerated.

It adds another stress that athletes have to deal with — another challenge to their wellbeing.

Tayla should be applauded for how she handled the situation, as well as how she managed her own wellbeing. But it never should have come to that. Sporting teams and bodies have started to do more to support people in this situation. In my opinion, this work has to continue and increase. The subject of athletes' wellbeing has gained increased attention in recent times and should continue to be a priority.

No one is immune

The reality is that no one is immune to emotional, mental health or wellbeing challenges, certainly not high-profile elite athletes or any person involved in sport. Proactively looking after their wellbeing and mental health should be an ongoing priority.

The positive human spirit can find strength even in seemingly dire circumstances. Challenges that feel insurmountable can be overcome. Having worked with many athletes through extremely difficult emotional situations, I have the utmost respect for their effort and capacity to deal with adversity and recover and return to strength. I know that many people draw inspiration from their stories.

Wellbeing enables exceptional positive personal and professional experiences. Nothing is as important as you — not a job, an exam mark or a relationship, not winning, not even sport itself. Drawing on positive spirit, as well as using supports and a range of other strategies, can help sustain wellbeing. From there, performance in any field is easier to maintain.

Performance does not grant immunity. Winning doesn't protect against wellbeing challenges either. Winning can actually add layers of stress, with increased external attention and scrutiny compounding the personal pressure athletes put on themselves to perform. 'As an athlete I always felt like I wasn't good enough,' Nicole Pratt admitted. 'I didn't recognise the importance of celebrating. I was caught up in pushing on. For example, when I won my one and only WTA career title in India: it was a solid draw and a hard-fought tournament win, but there was no one there to celebrate with. It should have been a great moment, but I felt horrible without anyone there to share it with. It was a bit hollow. That night after the win I spent in my room crying. From that experience I realised that sharing is more important than winning.'

Nicole's story speaks to the emotional toll that elite sport can take. Many athletes are relentless in their pursuit to perform, often at the cost of their own wellbeing. Wellbeing has to be prioritised above performance by all. Recognising that no one is immune to wellbeing challenges, managing them must be a daily task. Sometimes this is intuitive; at other times it has to be deliberately managed. Wellbeing cannot be taken for granted. It's a skill that should be prioritised. This chapter discusses some of the factors surrounding wellbeing and strategies to maintain it.

Find the positive

Sport creates many exciting and interesting opportunities for athletes and other people involved. It can foster and build wellbeing by creating lasting positive relationships and experiences that can be reflected on for years to come. Training with teammates or squad members, learning new skills or simply doing something they love to do are some elements that can make a sport enjoyable, even away from competition. A healthy sporting environment can also be a place to develop life skills and personal growth. This may be one reason why it has been suggested that athletes make great employees.

On managing wellbeing, finding positives in what you are doing is a good place to start. A positive doesn't have to be a huge achievement. It can be a small task. This is why I ask athletes to identify and record *daily positives*, as discussed in earlier steps. It's incredible how difficult this is for some people. But once they are able to recognise daily positives, they become more attuned to noticing small things they enjoy. They notice positives in others as well. This is different from gratitude, which we'll discuss later in the chapter. Examples of daily positives can include:

- did something well or enjoyed at training
- had a good chat with someone
- made a nice dinner
- complimented a teammate
- started a conversation with an athlete or coach I don't often speak with.

Keeping such a record doesn't need to be ongoing. It can be used intermittently to develop the habit of noticing positives and thinking positively. Noticing positives also contributes to building *wellbeing hygiene*. I see wellbeing hygiene as a product of developing protective mechanisms that contribute to sustaining wellbeing and enhancing resilience to deal with challenges through thinking positively and putting structures in place that protect wellbeing.

Person first, athlete second

Scott Draper experienced his share of challenges, both personal and sporting, as described in step 2 on resilience. These experiences contributed to his prioritising wellbeing. 'If you have your life in order, it is so much easier to compete,' he told me.

A consideration in sport, as well as other fields, is that wellbeing and mental health don't exist in isolation. It would be convenient to compartmentalise our lives, but the reality is that wellbeing and mental health exist within a larger dynamic system that all of us, including athletes, operate and exist within. Life and sport coexist, and it is difficult to block out one for the sake of the other.

Athletes are people first and are subject to the same wellbeing and mental health concerns as anyone else. Difficult relationships, family worries and other personal issues affect athletes just as they do everyone else, and these issues need to be recognised.

Many sports provide little or no financial return or security for athletes. As a result, many athletes have 'dual careers', studying or working while training and pursuing their sporting ambitions. In these circumstances, a high-performing focus that exists in sport can carry over to other areas of life, which can be good but can also create additional pressure and layers of challenge. I have seen athletes thoroughly enjoy studying or holding down a job to balance their sport, but it can put an unsustainable pressure on them when they feel they have to do as well in that field as in their sport or the workload and demand from each is overwhelming.

A person can only spread themselves so far. In this situation athletes, coaches and supports must recognise that each individual experience should help the other. When it doesn't, changes need to be made. I am typically quite assertive on this. Wellbeing is not a space to be patient in. Training and performance can build slowly. The slightest hint of a wellbeing challenge needs to be treated as urgent. The person is more important than the sport. As I mentioned in step 4 on leadership, there have been times when I have called a crisis meeting late at night. I have learned to drop everything, and have done so many times, to try to prevent a difficult situation from escalating.

At times, sport can be a haven, a space in which to escape life's challenges. It may provide life lessons to foster emotional growth and positive wellbeing. On the other hand, a sporting environment can exaggerate any pre-existing concerns or vulnerabilities and cause frustration and stress.

Recognising different factors that can impact wellbeing is one aspect to help manage this space. Some of these are listed here.

Thoughts on what influences wellbeing

Athletes' wellbeing and mental health are influenced by a wide range of factors. They can include:

- selection or non-selection
- interaction with squad members or teammates
- interaction with coaches and support staff, including coach leadership style and feedback mechanisms
- physical and mental fatigue
- injuries
- the culture that exists in the sport
- financial insecurity or contracts
- demands and stress related to performance (for example, travel, external demands, social or other media)
- personal factors away from sport including living arrangements
- lack of support from a sporting organisation or away from sport
- disappointment with a performance or performances over time
- having to move and live away from loved ones
- personality
- transition after sport.

Athlete-centred environments

An *athlete-centred environment* is one that sees the athlete's wellbeing and personal development as equal to or more important than their performance. It prioritises the person over the sport. Coaching should incorporate working with the whole person, not just the athlete. This approach influences communication, decisions about training and a range of other factors. It guides thinking, behaviour and decisions or operations in a sport.

An athlete-centred environment should be overt and observable, not just a philosophy to be discussed. In this way it can be evaluated and emphasised by all stakeholders in the organisation, including coaches, other staff and administrators, as well as the athletes. It is no different to a people-first culture at a workplace or student-focussed environment that encompasses social-emotional learning at a school.

Research insights

Athlete-centred environments:

- foster holistic development
- create a partnership between athlete and coach as well as the sporting organisation
- contribute to a quality team culture
- emphasise teaching by guiding.[1]

Look beyond the behaviour

When working with athletes on wellbeing and mental health issues, the broader picture needs to be considered. This encompasses reflecting on both the environment *and* the person. What is happening in the sporting environment that may be impacting wellbeing? What systems and processes are impacting wellbeing positively or negatively? What is happening in that person's life? What is impacting their emotions and behaviour? These are necessary questions.

Too often people focus on individuals regarding their wellbeing and mental health without considering the environment. This is unfair. Wellbeing concerns are not simply about the person. For example, if a sport has multiple wellbeing and mental health issues, the environment and system require thorough investigation and likely an overhaul. At times the environment may be fine; it may even support and assist the individual, yet they may still struggle emotionally. Understanding what is affecting their wellbeing, both positively and negatively, gives individuals and the organisation an important insight to assist in navigating people into a better mental space. Don't simply look at the person when considering wellbeing challenges. This insight helps explain why culture is so important, as discussed in step 5 on culture.

Poor behaviour in sportspeople can also reflect stress. 'Look beyond the behaviour' is advice I have long encouraged coaches to consider. Missing sessions, arriving late or underperforming may point to a deterioration in coping. At more severe levels, substance abuse and behavioural issues need to be addressed, but can also be a reflection that something more is going on. In these instances, both the behaviour and the emotional factors contributing to the behaviour must be addressed; otherwise repeat offences will likely occur. This does not excuse poor behaviour that clearly has consequences, more that, when addressing and dealing with poor behaviour, a deeper dive is often necessary.

Wellbeing and mental health

The World Health Organization (WHO) defines mental health as 'a state of wellbeing in which an individual realises his or her own abilities, can cope with the normal stresses of life, can work productively and fruitfully and is able to make a contribution to his or her community'.[2]

This definition has evolved from a positive psychology framework where the capacity to flourish and thrive is assessed. This framework is distinct from historical medical models in which the absence of a mental health issue was itself associated with positive wellbeing. The WHO points out that mental health is more than just the absence of mental disorders.

Sport psychologist Carolina Lundqvist has noted that the construct of wellbeing is both multifaceted and complex and has been poorly understood and defined. She has suggested that 'an increased understanding of wellbeing in athletes is desirable, as this information could potentially address aspects of competitive sports that constitute obstacles and facilitate athletes' ability to flourish and use their full potential as both humans and athletes'.[3]

In a recent overview of mental health in elite sports, Lundqvist noted the 'almost explosive growth in interest in investigation of mental health among athletes'.[4] This has been stimulated in part by a global shift towards greater responsiveness on mental health issues in society overall. Lundqvist also noted that 'wellbeing is increasingly adopted as an indicator of positive mental health'. She noted that single-continuum models have been increasingly described to understand wellbeing and mental health and that in these models individuals typically move along a continuum:

1. normal variations in mood, psychological and social activity

2. normal emotional or behavioural reactions to life-situations, such as being nervous or sad

3. increased levels of psychological harm or injury, such as anxiety, reduced performance, difficulty concentrating and social withdrawal

4. mental illness as a diagnosed clinical condition.

To be clear with regard to wellbeing and mental health, there is a distinct difference between a wellbeing concern and a more serious mental health condition. Often these can be confused. This is when professional advice and support is required. It's worth noting that it's normal to experience a range of emotions, including being sad or disappointed. There is a difference, as the model identified, between normal emotional reactions to poor performances, life events and a clinical mental health condition. Other models, such as the dual-continuum model proposed by Keyes[5], recognise that athletes may be flourishing with complete mental health or still functioning with incomplete mental health or illness. Having a mental health concern does not preclude a person from working or performing. I have worked with many high performers who continue to function in their role while they have mental health challenges.

Destigmatising wellbeing and mental health

In recent times, the greater preparedness of athletes with a global voice to speak publicly about mental health concerns has drawn necessary attention to mental health. It's so important to destigmatise discussion about mental health to encourage people to seek help. We need to get to a stage where athletes are as comfortable saying, 'I'm struggling mentally at the moment', as they are saying, 'I've got a tight hamstring'. These conversations can prevent normal and temporary struggles from becoming more significant.

Athletes with a global profile who have spoken about mental health include tennis player Naomi Osaka, swimmer Michael Phelps and gymnast Simone Biles. This has contributed to creating an increased accountability on sports bodies to manage the overall care of athletes, including their mental health.

Incidence of wellbeing and mental health concerns in sport

Research insights

The Australian Institute of Health and Welfare has identified that in the general community, 16–24 years of age is the demographic with the highest proportion of mental disorders, and 25–34 years of age is the second highest group. In these groups, about 25 per cent or one in four people will experience a mental health disorder at some stage. The rates are even higher for 'distress' in young people.[6]

Adolescence and early adulthood are stages of life that can be immensely enjoyable but can also bring many physical and emotional challenges. These years, of course, correspond almost perfectly with the most active period of an athlete's career.

There is some variation in the research about whether athletes experience a higher or lower incidence of mental health issues than the general population. This is understandable, as it is likely influenced by the sport, the culture and a range of other factors. From my experience, backed by data collected before and after interventions I have conducted or coordinated, I have seen squads and teams improve wellbeing and mental health over time when good wellbeing programs and cultures are in place.

A 2016 study suggested that on the basis of current evidence, elite athletes appeared to experience a broadly comparable risk of mental health concerns, such as depression and anxiety, to the general population.[7] The authors found that greater risk of mental health issues might be experienced by athletes who were injured, were approaching or in retirement, or were experiencing performance difficulty. The study suggested there was a tendency towards greater vulnerability in sports involving a particularly lean body shape and in female athletes. Low social support was identified as a risk factor, highlighting the importance of formal and informal support networks.

Coping, both in and outside of performance, was reported to be important. Managing poor performances, dealing with performance-related anxiety, managing injuries and social media content were some examples noted that impact coping. The authors also argued that assessment and management of mental health and wellbeing needs should be on par with that for physical needs.

Prevention is better than cure

Identifying and acting on a wellbeing concern early can prevent many future concerns. It is important to differentiate between experiencing symptoms associated with stress and a mental health diagnosis. Being aware that people may exhibit different symptoms can assist with early detection and intervention to stop a wellbeing concern becoming a clinical mental health issue. It also helps to differentiate between a more serious mental health concern and an understandable response to a short-term situation.

Behaviours that may be symptoms or signs to look out for may include:

- more isolated or withdrawn than usual (not returning calls or messages)
- less motivated (being late, missing training, diminished performance at training)
- less interested in general or when speaking with others (giving one-word or short answers)
- exhibiting lower self-care (presenting more poorly than usual)
- being angrier or showing less energy than usual and seeming 'flat'.

To assist people to look out for each other, I often consider behavioural, psychological or physical symptoms to be aware of and whether these are persistent, invasive and excessive. Given that athletes and coaches spend a lot of time together, keeping an eye out for these behaviours shouldn't be hard. They won't automatically signal a wellbeing or mental health issue, but a checking-in conversation is always worthwhile.

Whether or not a person is experiencing wellbeing or mental health challenges, good wellbeing hygiene can be developed using some of the following strategies. These are only examples and by no means an exhaustive list.

Self-appreciation, self-permission, self-acceptance and self-compassion

Over a career, feeling that only the highest standards are acceptable every day is emotionally unsustainable. Nobody wins all the time. Even people expected to win might not. That's the nature of competition. Accepting that there are ups and downs both physically and emotionally can be empowering and a relief. It doesn't mean not striving for the best possible performance. It does mean developing self-appreciation, self-permission, self-acceptance and self-compassion.

Athletes are conditioned to strive constantly and absorb challenges, physical and emotional. They are conditioned to set high standards, to push through difficulties and to be hard on themselves. These are generally positive traits for an athlete. But while at times such an approach will serve performance well, emotionally it can create vulnerability, undermining wellbeing and in turn performance. Pushing through mental distress is not the same as pushing through physical discomfort to complete a challenging session, hard training block or tough competition. Because they are accustomed to pushing through discomfort, many athletes I have worked with take the same approach with their wellbeing. This is misguided.

In sport, selection and self-validation can hinge on tiny margins of difference that have significant consequences. That's part of sport. But for an athlete to hitch their sense of wellbeing to such fine margins, although at times inevitable, is unhealthy.

To develop skills in the 'selves', consider appreciating effort, recognising enjoyment, and putting outcome and sport in context. The selves help athletes to be kind to themselves. They're about self-care. They're also about being comfortable with being yourself mentally and physically. Appreciating relationships, opportunities and enriching experiences over and above outcome can help here. Adopting a learning approach can also help embrace the four selves. Striving for high achievement isn't often associated with complimenting oneself. It is typically more related to self-deprecation or put-downs. Self-complimenting is important to sustain energy and is a part of this mindset.

Taking control of your wellbeing means not waiting for others to give you permission to do something that may benefit you. Too often athletes avoid self-care until someone else gives them permission to take a break or do something emotionally nourishing. Certainly, at times this requires negotiation. You can't do anything you want at any time — like just not turning up. But asking for permission to miss a session or giving yourself permission to take a day off and do something that will help your wellbeing is important. It may be as simple as taking a lunch break or going for a walk! Prioritising time in each day for self-care is part of this.

Self-compassion has been a growing area of interest in sport. It is the compassion athletes direct towards themselves when faced with 'painful' or challenging experiences and is linked to adaptive psychological functioning and wellbeing. Negatively comparing themselves with other athletes (I call it the *curse of comparison*) is a common trap for athletes to fall into. These comparisons can relate to body image, development disparity or different opportunities. Its victims often become self-conscious or self-critical to their own detriment. Adopting a mastery or self-referencing approaches and respecting individuality on a performance pathway can help to limit the curse of comparison. It can also foster self-appreciation, self-acceptance and self-compassion, as well as enable self-permission.

Research insights

In a study of swimmers aged between 18 and 25, researchers wanted to determine if self-talk could reduce anxiety and increase self-compassion in athletes.

Athletes who received five coaching sessions on specific motivational self-talk showed incremental changes in the use of self-talk, a reduction in competitive anxiety and an increase in self-compassion levels compared with the control group of athletes who received no training. The researchers found that the benefits of self-talk extend beyond direct performance and include generating desired emotional states in athletes in competitive sports.[8]

Gratitude and kindness

Being grateful is as relevant in the competitive environment of sport as it is in life. There is little doubt that being grateful can help wellbeing. There are numerous ways to show gratitude. There are also a variety of methods of coaching and building it.

Neurologically, expressing gratitude has been shown to contribute to releasing dopamine and serotonin, two important 'feel good' neurotransmitters. Showing gratitude has also been linked to the hypothalamus, which assists with regulating sleep, as well as a range of other functions. Gratitude is more than comparing yourself with people less fortunate. It's about recognising specific elements in your own life or circumstances to be grateful for.

On occasion, I have facilitated specific gratitude education and activity sessions for athletes. These have included identifying who has been helpful on a sporting journey and clearly communicating appreciation to that person. I have also been involved with organising athletes to send Christmas cards to supporters as a form of appreciation. Gratitude journals are a proven strategy for maintaining wellbeing. Keeping a record of what you are grateful for and writing letters of gratitude to bring even small positive experiences to the front of your mind can contribute to your wellbeing. A common activity is to record three things to be grateful for each day. This can be done for a week or a fortnight. It can be a one-off or regularly repeated. The idea is to increase what a person identifies and notices around them.

Even saying 'thank you' as a form of gratitude has been associated with wellbeing benefits. Expressing gratitude can facilitate relationships and input from others. It can help keep perspective by ironing out the highs and lows. It can also contribute to feeling that there is a team involved in the journey.

Similarly, helping others has been shown to be positive for wellbeing, which is why athletes and sporting organisations can benefit from involvement with not-for-profit, community-based activities and charitable organisations. Random acts of kindness, as well as formal pro-social behaviour such as volunteering and supporting charities, have also been shown to benefit wellbeing. A gratitude journal is different from recognising daily positives, although there is clearly some overlap.

Research insights

A meta-analysis in 2020 investigated kindness and wellbeing in almost 200 000 subjects.

The study reported a benefit to wellbeing from pro-social behaviour, which is defined as behaviour that benefits others including helping, cooperating, comforting, sharing, donating and volunteering.

The study found that informally helping others was also linked to wellbeing benefits.[9]

These concepts are about building wellbeing holistically. The focus of such activities, I believe, is on prevention and proactivity in developing wellbeing hygiene through positive emotional mindsets. Such activities, to be clear, are not the primary methodology for treating clinical depression and anxiety.

Journaling

As mentioned in step 2 on resilience, debriefing and reviewing can assist athletes in a number of ways. I have found journals and written records to be powerful tools for many athletes. I once had a follow-up call from an athlete I had worked with some five years earlier. His career had stalled. The enquiry: 'Do you still have the notes we made? I used them for a while but have lost them.' Fortunately, I recalled the conversation and had kept the notes. The athlete agreed that it was time to update the notes based on his current circumstances. It's not too different from Jacqui Cooper looking at her 10-year plan 10 times a day for 10 years. There are many well-regarded athletes who are known for keeping some form of journals for personal or performance purposes.

Many athletes keep a journal for different purposes, such as goal setting, daily positives, gratitude or competition plans and reviews. It may be to record daily training to monitor and feel in control of performance. It may include quotes or mantras. It may be paper and pen or on an electronic device. A journal is a personal diary. It allows an athlete to debrief on their own and organise their thoughts and ideas. It can also help get them out of their head. Journals serve as a powerful reflection tool. Many athletes use and carry journals and diaries with them highlighting exceptional training sessions, work done and a range of other positive and learning features. I myself have kept diaries for many years to monitor my daily training, injuries, goals, events, health and thoughts. While not always for everyone or for every day, it is an underestimated tool on a sporting or any other journey.

Sport relationship and identity

For some athletes, their sport can feel like their whole life, rather than one part of it. This is understandable given that, for many athletes, engagement in their sport takes priority over most other activities. To achieve in most sports requires being fully absorbed. When commitment is high and the activity dominates most days for years on end, it is easy to become institutionalised within the sport. Stepping outside the bubble of their sport can help athletes to broaden their identity and ensure that institutionalisation doesn't occur.

In the worst case, it can feel as though without sport there is nothing. Sometimes this way of thinking requires external validation for recognition that sport is a part of life, rather than all that a person has in their life. This was evident in a Twitter comment posted by American gymnast Simone Biles during the 2021 Tokyo Olympics. During the competition her emotional challenges were laid bare for all to see. She was criticised by some, but she also received what she described as incredible support. She commented that the support she received helped her realise that she was more than her gymnastic achievements.[10]

Her comment provides some insight into why athletes can be vulnerable when things are not working. At times, people who commit so much time, energy and emotional investment in a pursuit can feel that their entire identity hinges on that activity. Clearly, their identity is defined not just by their sport, or by their success in the sport, even if it sometimes feels that way. Sport may be a significant and dominant part of what someone does, but it is about *what they do*, not *who they are*.

For Storm Sanders: 'The biggest thing about wellbeing is to be able to open up to your team and to people you trust. It's so important to check in with yourself and with others. Even when my tennis got better, I always spoke to family back home. Even if you set aside your sport and results for only 10 minutes a day, it helps keep you grounded and that helps your consistency. I try to use down time to do things I enjoy.

'After the semifinal at Wimbledon, after losing four match points and then losing the match, I thought I was still proud to have got those match points. I don't want to forget the journey. I try to recognise what's been good and really appreciate the journey.

'Part of that is to make sure my identity is not just based on wins or losses. I try to make sure I have an identity beyond tennis and results. I have friends and other goals, so if I don't win a match I can keep going. I think if I felt like tennis was my whole and entire life, I would feel a lot more pressure to perform and wouldn't perform as well. It's easy to get stuck thinking you can only do one thing. It's important to dedicate time to yourself regardless of your results.

'When I was injured, I found I could do other things. It helped me to see tennis as one chapter in my life, and not to ignore life after tennis. I realised it would not be my whole life. That probably happened because I had to start from zero again after a year out. I also recognised that you need support after big events, mainly because emotions run so high. It's so important to have the right people and supports around you.'

Storm and Simone, along with many other athletes, have learned how important it is to have an identity beyond sport. It takes pressure off performance and can ultimately help performance, even though that's not the priority.

Taking action

Cate Campbell is a four-time Olympic swimmer with multiple medals to her credit. She is so highly regarded that she was selected as one of the Australian flagbearers (with basketballer Patty Mills) for the opening ceremony at Tokyo in 2021. With rumours swirling about whether the Tokyo 2020 Olympics would proceed in the midst of the COVID-19 pandemic, Cate described the impact the uncertainty had on her in *Vogue* magazine. She received a message in March 2020 while at the supermarket that read 'we're not going to Tokyo'. Cate admitted that 'those words hit me with a physical force ... My life suddenly seems meaningless — what now?'

Forced to stand still for the first time in her life, she decided, 'to do something I have never done: to sit down, to stop moving, striving ... I suddenly had the time and energy to pursue things I'd always wanted to do.'[11] She learned that it's okay to stop and be still; 2020 taught her to swim more for the love of it, rather than out of fear.

Following her performance in Tokyo, Cate courageously and admirably announced that prior to the Games she had consulted her GP and a psychologist and had been prescribed anti-depressant medication. She shared on Instagram her experience, noting that she wished she had got help sooner, and encouraged people to make mental health discussions more common. Her hope was that by sharing her story, it would reduce stigma and help to change people's perception of mental health.[12]

Cate's story reflects that medication is one tool, combined with counselling and other support mechanisms to assist a person to manage their emotions in challenging times. In the past the stigma, and concerns about medications, acted as a deterrent. Over the years medications have advanced incredibly. There are professionals specialising in this space to support and guide people through decisions about the best support path forward. It is much better to be proactive with managing wellbeing and begin intervention early (rather than waiting until a problem is exacerbated). This is reinforced by Cate with her reflection about reaching out for help sooner.

Help-seeking

Help-seeking is acknowledged as an essential component of wellbeing programs that advocate early intervention for athletes. It is a topic that should be incorporated into sporting programs and is a skill for individuals to build. A number of studies have been conducted to identify what assists athletes to seek help for mental health issues.

Research insights

Barriers and facilitators to help-seeking in athletes[13]

Barriers to help-seeking	Facilitators of help-seeking
Mental health stigma	Encouragement from others
Lack of mental health literacy	Previous pleasant interaction with service providers
Negative experiences with help-seeking	Positive attitude of others to help-seeking
	Access to internet and resources

In sporting contexts, one obstacle to seeking help for wellbeing or mental health concerns is the cultural perception that the sporting world is for 'mentally tough' individuals. Athletes are conditioned to 'push through' physical pain barriers and deal with uncomfortable challenges.

In many sports, showing emotional or mental health vulnerabilities is too readily perceived as a sign of weakness. For high-achieving athletes, who typically set high standards for themselves and are often put on a pedestal by the world outside, disappointment about feeling low can exaggerate the issue itself. Acknowledging emotional challenges can feel as though it compromises what an athlete thinks they should stand for. They unfairly judge themselves a failure for not always performing up to high expectations or for feeling anything other than great.

To enable help-seeking to be viewed as part and parcel of high performance, such attitudes need to be recognised and dismissed, both by those around them and by the athlete themselves. Failure has to be redefined.

Mat Hayman began his professional cycling career in Europe when still a teenager. 'I was 19, and it was hard. I was living in Poland and became very lonely and homesick. The only thing that made me happy was training and racing, but you don't train and race all day every day. I was very low mentally. The thing is, when you're down you don't want to do anything. Thankfully my mum and family recognised what was happening and pushed me to do something. I ended up joining a sketching and drawing class. It was totally outside my comfort zone but it helped me change my habits.'

When feeling low, Mat reached out to his family. They identified that he was unusually flat. They encouraged him to be proactive: to begin changing some poor habits that were driving him down. With their support, he said, 'I began to turn things around, but they were scared there for a while.'

Mat makes an important point: reaching out for help is especially hard when a person is feeling low. Their energy level can be at its lowest, and their sense of embarrassment high, which is why many mental health problems such as anxiety and depression too often aren't managed until they are well advanced. It's also why prevention, help-seeking and early intervention are so important. There are many ways to seek help and support such as in person, by phone, through self-education or reaching out to family and friends. Reaching out in the smallest way can be of benefit.

The journey and narrative

Letting go of disappointing performances is a challenge for many high-performing people. With so many variables influencing a performance, disappointments are inevitable. Results can't be changed over time. It's not uncommon for athletes to be unhappy if they come second. Dwelling on what could have been is more common than thinking *I'm lucky I got second*. A body of work in this space, called *counterfactual thinking,* provides some interesting insights. If a past performance is undermining wellbeing and the capacity to perform as a result of overwhelming disappointment, it has to be dealt with, rather than allowed to fester.

Putting a disappointing event, such as an injury or a poor performance, into context is difficult but necessary to help manage an athlete's wellbeing. As discussed in step 2 on resilience, pursuing a sporting career is rarely smooth sailing. There will be varying performances, and many twists and turns. Seeing a sporting experience as a journey can help to compartmentalise these events. A helicopter view helps athletes appreciate positive factors associated with their sport and success and not allow the challenges to dominate the narrative.

I often tell athletes that one single event does not define their journey. They are the authors of the experience, whether it's disappointing or gratifying. Some athletes are able to appreciate disappointments or even a poor performance, knowing they can learn and grow from them and they did all they could. Progress in sport is not linear. It's important to embrace all the experiences that contribute to the journey. The language you use to describe, talk about or remember an experience is a part of the narrative.

Managing a narrative helps you embrace an experience without judging it. An overall narrative is the culmination of a wide range of stories. How you see yourself in those stories and how you tell them can become defining. By effectively managing the narrative, you are the author of your own story. The events are what they are, but you decide how to interpret them. It may be happy or sad, or an incredible adventure with many ups and downs. Although the events cannot always be controlled, you *can* control and own the narrative.

None of this is to say that not winning or performing as desired or not gaining selection isn't gut-wrenching, but rather that you should not allow it to define you.

Recovery, rest and sleep

Without adequate levels of recovery, rest and sleep, athletes will be vulnerable to a wide range of challenges, including injury, fatigue and emotional or mood challenges and fluctuations. Additionally, adequate sleep and rest facilitate alertness, capacity to absorb training loads and can help positive mood.

A comprehensive review of the sleep of athletes[14] outlined the importance of promoting positive sleep behaviour and avoiding situations that present risks to sleep. Some sport-related factors found to impact sleep include night competitions, high training loads and early morning training. Non-sport factors affecting sleep included social demands, lifestyle choices and work or study commitments that many athletes also have. Positive sleep hygiene includes avoiding meals close to bedtime, adequate exposure to natural morning light, not lying awake in bed for an extended time, a relaxing bedtime routine and a good sleep environment that contains a cool, dark space without electronic devices and with minimal noise or distraction.

When discussing sleep with athletes, a point I often suggest is a pre-bed routine. This involves allocating a generally consistent time to go to bed and a consistent routine for approximately 30 to 60 minutes prior to that time. The goal is to promote winding down and can include habits such as checking or confirming what is on the next day to feel organised, slowing down and relaxing, not eating and, at times, noting down anything that is on your mind so that once your head hits the pillow these thoughts do not surface and keep you awake. The aim is to reduce your worries and to avoid ruminating on them. When athletes are travelling, I also often discuss taking their own pillow and pillowcase. The familiar feel and scent can cue you into having a peaceful sleep.

Another challenge to falling asleep is worrying about not sleeping, as this can contribute to wakefulness. The original reason for not falling asleep or waking during the night can diminish in comparison to the anxiety about not sleeping. One way to counter this is to focus on the restorative capacity of deep rest. If you're not sleeping, then switching away from worrying and focussing on deep rest can have positive restoration benefits and enable a person to fall back asleep. Identifying a good sleep position, a relaxing breathing pattern and methods to clear your mind are possible strategies to adopt.

Using downtime to rest and learning how to switch off physically and mentally can assist recovery and build sleep habits. Naturally, we are discussing general sleep habits and not specifically your sleep the night before a major competition. As many athletes will attest to, prioritising and building skill in managing rest, recovery and sleep will aid wellbeing and performance.

Cognitive behaviour therapy and thinking traps

Cognitive behaviour therapy (CBT) has been described as a short-term, skills-focused approach to changing thoughts and behaviours. Over time, the term and the practice of CBT have emerged to represent the interaction between thoughts, emotions and behaviour.

Figure 6.1 is a model that is associated with cognitive behaviour therapy:

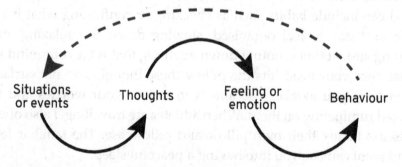

Situations or events — Thoughts — Feeling or emotion — Behaviour

Figure 6.1: cognitive behaviour therapy model

By applying certain strategies, managing situations, thoughts and behaviour can help wellbeing and performance. Feelings and emotions are more difficult to manage, but no less important to acknowledge. Certainly, emotions can provide clues that help people manage their thoughts, behaviours and circumstances.

From this model, to manage wellbeing or performance a person can look to managing the situation or their environment, as well as their thoughts or behaviour. I often begin conversations on this topic by considering triggers, situations or events that occur around people and the resulting thoughts that may dominate their thinking. Challenging worries or doubts, maximising positive self-talk and managing the overall narrative fall within the CBT model. Managing toxic negative self-talk is a part of this process.

Helping athletes to manage 'thinking traps' is a CBT strategy to help wellbeing. Catastrophising, generalising, all-or-nothing or personalising are only some thinking traps that are commonplace. How these thoughts are managed is important in life and sport.

Disputing irrational thinking, reducing self-consciousness and self-criticism can also be managed through CBT strategies.

> For a review of a wide range of thinking traps and strategies to manage them, a great resource is Sarah Edelman's *Change Your Thinking: positive and practical ways to overcome stress, negative emotions and self-defeating behaviour using CBT.*[15]

Environment, thinking and doing

In practical terms, I often consider managing wellbeing as managing the environment, thinking as well as actions or 'doing'. An environment perspective considers both personal and sporting environments.

Here are a few questions that can be checked to monitor environment:

Environment at training

- What are relationships in the environment like?
- Does the training load need to be managed?
- What time, how often and where is training?

Environment away from training

- What are living circumstances like?
- How are relationships away from training?
- Are friends helpful and supportive of a sporting lifestyle?
- What demands do they face outside of high performance sport?

Here are a few strategies to manage thinking:

Thinking

- Identify specific worries and challenge them.
- Manage thinking traps.
- Consider what you are proud of.
- Consider what you are focussing on. Use self-talk and neutral 'let's see' language when appropriate and be curious in your approach to situations, as discussed in step 3 on focus.
- Monitor and listen to warning signs, and be comfortable speaking about and being proactive in seeking support for in relation to wellbeing.
- Consider your SEAs — strengths, enjoyment and achievements. Record and reflect on these. Update the records routinely and get input from others to add to or confirm your own thoughts.

Here are a few questions to consider what you are doing:

Doing — non-sport

- Who am I connecting with?
- What nature place do I enjoy?
- When is my personal time?
- What could I read?
- What could I watch?

- What could I listen to (such as music or podcasts)?
- What movement could I do (outside your sport)?
- What food could I enjoy?
- What am I remembering?
- What am I looking forward to?
- What project or hobby am I working on?

Doing — sport

- Can I do anything more at or for training?
- Do I need to do less at training?
- Who am I communicating and connecting with?
- Do I have too much on?
- What do I need to do from a lifestyle perspective to help my sport?

Reflecting on these questions can assist you in gaining insight and control and contribute to your wellbeing and performance. Considering what you are thinking and doing to help yourself and your situation is also relevant.

Mindfulness and ACT

Herb Elliott described it back when he was racing some 60 years ago. When possible, his pre-race routine included just sitting under a tree to energise. This might have been an extension of his training base being conducted at Percy Cerutty's famed Portsea 'Spartan' camp. Portsea is a small town with a rugged ocean beach about 100 kilometres south of Melbourne. Back in 1960 it was an outpost of dirt roads, sand dunes and tea trees with myriad walking and running trails. To train there at that time would have meant an immersion in nature. Herb described that poetry, music, forests and solitude contributed to his spiritual strength. He emphasised that spirit, as much or more than physical conditioning, had to be stored up before a race — hence 'sitting under a tree' as part of his pre-race preparation. Whether knowingly or unwittingly, Herb was practising mindfulness.

Mindfulness has been defined in a variety of ways, but is predominantly identified as a present-moment, non-judgemental awareness. While you are aware of internal stimuli (thoughts, feelings or physical/body sensations) and external stimuli (your immediate environment), a mindful approach means not trying to control or change them. Mindfulness evolved as a practice to use in general day-to-day life. In recent years, its application in sport settings has gained momentum, including for both personal and performance benefit.

A fundamental concept of mindfulness is that in the moment both past and future become irrelevant. All attention is directed towards the here and now. Internal and external stimuli, including thoughts, are recognised without judgement. For this reason, mindfulness has been linked to a flow state or as a strategy to achieve a flow state.

Another concept athletes can use to benefit wellbeing and performance is Acceptance and Commitment Therapy (ACT). This concept combines mindfulness and acceptance skills to enhance psychological health by helping people develop a new relationship with challenging thoughts, feelings and emotions. Mindfulness-Acceptance-Commitment does not aim to change negative thoughts but to notice them and then allow them to pass, re-directing attention and keeping an athlete's focus in the present.

Mindfulness is often used interchangeably with meditation. Meditation is a practice to train attention and awareness and is typically understood as a deliberate, formal activity. There are, however, many formal and informal ways to become more mindful. 'Mindful eating', 'mindful walking', 'mindful breathing' or 'nature mindfulness' are just some mindful activities. In my workshops with athletes, I have conducted a range of mindfulness exercises, including mindful eating, nature mindfulness and diaphragmatic breathing (more on this soon).

Mindful eating includes becoming more fully conscious of the flavour, texture and even scent of the food we eat. Too often we eat quickly, distractedly, on the go. Mindful eating means appreciating fully what we are eating. It invites us to slow down, and pay attention to the act of preparing and cooking food, as well as eating, including the taste sensations and nourishment it offers, enhancing the experience of eating. Even where the food has come from.

Nature mindfulness involves a conscious focus on the sky, trees, wind, temperature and landscape, becoming fully aware of nature and what is happening around us without judgement. In this way, nature can assist us to be fully absorbed in the present. I have encouraged athletes to watch clouds or tree branches in the wind or feel the sensation of the earth under their feet.

The relevance to sport of such activities is that they can help athletes to anchor themselves in the present and create a sense of calm. Don't worry about who is in the race or the heats yesterday or the final tomorrow. Let go of worries or distractions, and be fully absorbed in what it is you're doing now. Embrace the competition, the challenge, the opportunity. It doesn't mean you don't care about the opposition or tactics. Rather, you are more fully absorbed in the task at this moment, without the distraction of negative emotion.

Research insights

Researchers investigated the impact of mindfulness traits on rumination and emotional regulation. The study included one group of 242 young elite athletes, and 65 elite adult athletes from various sports also took part in the study.

The researchers suggested that 'mindfulness in competitive athletes may lead to reduction in rumination, as well as an improved capacity to regulate negative emotions'.

They also determined that 'athletes who have trait-like (general) ability to be mindful in daily life tend to regulate their negative emotions effectively and not engage in excessive rumination, which may in turn improve their coping skills in relation to a variety of sport-related challenges'.[16]

Diaphragmatic breathing

Diaphragmatic breathing is one of the most effective exercises to assist people to manage their wellbeing and performance. It is a strategy that I teach regularly when working with athletes. It sounds so simple, but don't let the simplicity camouflage its significance or benefits.

Diaphragmatic breathing involves proactively engaging the diaphragm muscle that lies below the lungs and adjacent to the abdominal or stomach muscles. The diaphragm contracts and flattens on an inhale, creating a vacuum that helps pull air into the lungs. On an exhale, the diaphragm relaxes and assists in pushing air out of the lungs. In essence, on an inhale the diaphragm presses on the abdominal muscles, which can be observed to expand. On an exhale the abdominal muscles can be observed to contract inward towards the spine. Maintaining this pattern effectively when experiencing high demands for oxygen, fatigue and/or high levels of anxiety can be very challenging.

There are specific exercises to maintain effective diaphragm breathing, but the aim is for it to become almost instinctive. When done effectively, diaphragmatic breathing can be used away from an event to stimulate a calm or relaxed state, or in the lead-up to or during competition.

Supports and mentors

Speaking about his sporting journey, Dave Andersen declared, 'Support has been immense for me. I attribute my prolonged career to the support I've had. It helped me be a chameleon and adapt to the constant changes I experienced. And it wasn't just the people involved in the teams I was in but also my family, including my parents, brothers and sister. My wife Nerida has also been an enormous support. My first international contract was in Italy when I was 18. As a family we decided my brother Stewart would move over with me to help with the transition. It helped to have someone to talk to, and after crappy games to just chat and forget about it. We also did a lot of training together in extra sessions I did away from the team. A few years later, when I got a contract in Moscow, my other brother, Grant, came over and lived with me for a while.

'As well as family, I worked on building a support team of professionals around me. I'd consult with them about sport and life, and they were vital. They shared the journey too, which added another positive layer. I could pick up the phone from anywhere in the world and call them and they would be there for me. They were always checking in on me as well, sharing the highs and lows.'

The research on athlete mentoring is limited, but one review of the impact of peer mentoring (mentoring from a teammate) suggested that peer-mentored athletes were more satisfied with their sport experience personally and with their performance. These athletes were also more satisfied with team integration and ethics, and with training and instruction, compared with athletes who were not mentored. On this basis, the authors recommended that teams explore peer-mentoring programs.[17] In my own experience, athlete mentor programs have been enormously positive, both for mentees, and for the mentor.

Dave Andersen, of course, plays a traditional team sport, but Scott Draper also recognised the importance of supports on his journey in what is typically identified as an individual sport. 'What helped me in my tennis was realising it is not an individual sport. I had a personal and a professional support team. They were a huge part of it for me on many levels.' I put this question to many squads in sports such as swimming and athletics that are competed individually: 'Is it an individual or team sport?' *It's a team sport.* The benefits of a solid support network cannot be underestimated, and the earlier these are established in a sporting career, the better. While at times they evolve naturally, often they are created and managed carefully and deliberately. As Dave mentioned, they support and share the journey.

Wellbeing programs and data

With the increasing focus in recent years on athlete wellbeing and mental health, several recommendations and models have been put forward to maximise athlete wellbeing and minimise concerns. One such model recommends a four-tier framework for supporting athlete mental health and wellbeing.[18] The base of the model emphasises preventive components, including building mental health literacy, individual athlete development, and mental health and wellbeing screening and feedback.

It emphasises building cultures around acknowledging that to benefit both athlete wellbeing and performance, mental health needs are as important as physical needs. Such programs help athletes develop a range of self-management skills to deal with psychological distress.

In my work in professional sporting environments, I advocate strongly for such programs to be integrated into the organisation alongside performance development. As a part of this process, I have conducted both unidimensional mental health assessments and multidimensional wellbeing screening that have incorporated assessment of mental health symptoms. I prefer using holistic wellbeing data that is multidimensional. This type of assessment considers and collects information on a wide range of topics. One reason for this is because when associated with variables such as engagement, resilience and positivity, wellbeing is viewed in the context of specific relevant topics, which can be informative. These topics all inter-relate. Collecting data across a range of areas that impact wellbeing is also time-efficient in programs that are typically time-poor. This is one of the reasons I developed the Six-Star Wellbeing and Engagement survey that has three versions: one for students in schools, one for staff in different environments, including coaches, and administrators and one for athletes.

Utilising data collection in a sporting group creates opportunities for coaching wellbeing topics with groups of any size. Data also creates a layer of accountability to organisations on topics that are difficult to accurately determine objectively. The data also enables specific staff, such as psychologists within the sporting organisation, to monitor wellbeing over the athlete's sporting journey. I have also used wellbeing and mental health screening tools to collect data for the purpose of working with coaches.

A wide range of possible topics that can be incorporated in a wellbeing program for sports, includes (in no particular order):

- sleep and rest
- balance
- mood and mental health
- resilience
- engagement
- communication

- supports and mentors
- help-seeking
- relaxation
- mindfulness
- optimism and positivity.

Of course, such programs are more effective when supported by coaches and administrators. Coaches and support staff can be co-facilitators as well as recipients of these educational initiatives.

Wellbeing checklist

As outlined, when working with sporting teams and bodies, I advocate integrating wellbeing and mental health work into athlete programs, just as physical and mental skills performance training should be integrated.

I have created a 10-point checklist to guide this process:

1. Commit to the wellbeing of your sporting organisation by prioritising the wellbeing and mental health of its people — athletes, coaches and other staff. This includes selecting coaches and staff who embrace an athlete-centred approach. As part of this process, set wellbeing goals.

2. Allocate specific professional staff to monitoring and working on wellbeing of athletes and staff.

3. Screen all athletes and coaching/support staff on wellbeing, utilising a multidimensional tool at appropriate times in the year such as pre-season and in-season. If using daily or weekly apps that incorporate wellbeing factors, ensure that the data is used effectively and that appropriate staff are alerted when variations are detected. It can be very frustrating for athletes and staff when data is collected but not followed up on.

4. Provide whole-team or small-group feedback on de-identified wellbeing data. Proactively initiate wellbeing check-in meetings with individuals.

5. Look out for warning signs, and follow up with potentially vulnerable individuals.

6. Allocate time in the training program to discuss and coach wellbeing and mental health.

7. Refer to specific professionals or mental health service providers when appropriate. Commit funding to support this process and ensure that finances are not a barrier to obtaining support. Build relationships with these service providers to optimise internal and external referral opportunities.

8. Be flexible within the environment to enable personal emotional demands to be met, such as players having time away from training, if necessary. This may be as short as missing one or two sessions or half a day to longer breaks if needed.

9. Identify specific vulnerable times, such as at induction, exit or retirement, injury, form slumps, moving away from home, extended down time such as after major competition or surgery, transition away from sport, post non-selection phases or other specific circumstances.

10. Review organisation systems and practices as a whole and their impact on wellbeing of people across the organisation.

Building an environment of positive wellbeing, including good support structures, clear communication channels and prioritising the person above the athlete can have significant positive benefits on people and performance. Keep in mind that when done well, this can be done in a time-efficient manner and need not be a time consuming and laborious practice.

Summary

Coaches and staff working in teams and sporting organisations have a responsibility to prioritise proactive wellbeing education. An athlete-centred environment sees the athlete as a whole person. At the same time, athletes must take responsibility for their own wellbeing and be comfortable seeking help when needed. Recognising that wellbeing can sustain energy and motivation to drive performance also has to be considered.

There are many strategies to manage and maintain wellbeing. These should be understood and integrated into the thinking and practices of athletes, coaches and other staff. Data collection can help sporting organisations in a variety of ways. Most importantly, taking a preventive and proactive approach to wellbeing should be prioritised above all else. The person is always more important than the performance. In line with this philosophy, be sure that organisations, teams and individuals set wellbeing goals and do not sacrifice these for performance goals.

BUILD YOUR WELLBEING

- Prioritise wellbeing and the person over performance.
- Embrace the positives in your sport.
- Appreciate that no one is immune to wellbeing challenges, which are normal.
- Monitor and early-warning signs of threats to wellbeing.
- Embrace self-appreciation, self-permission, self-acceptance and self-compassion.
- Express gratitude and kindness.
- Consider keeping a journal or diary.
- Maintain a positive relationship with your sport and build an identity beyond sport.
- Be a help-seeker.
- Manage your narrative about your sport.
- Manage recovery, rest and sleep.
- Use CBT to manage worries and thinking traps.
- Engage in thinking and doing activities to balance lifestyle.
- Develop mindfulness skills.
- Use diaphragmatic breathing.
- Establish and maintain a support and mentor network.
- Identify and recognise your SEAs (Strengths, Enjoyment and Achievements).
- Focus on your overall journey and experience gained from sport involvement. Avoid basing your wellbeing solely on selection, winning or losing.

STEP 7

EXECUTE YOUR PERFORMANCE

Delivering a performance when it matters is a skill. Countless training sessions over years do not guarantee a great result on the day. In some sports there are limited opportunities to peak and qualify for a team. In other sports, competition performances must be sustained, week after week over a season, in varying conditions against different opponents. All athletes must not only strive to perform at their best at competition, but also contend with an opposition performance. In some sports, repeating an effort in heats and finals, managing tactics and dealing with a wide range of other variables can impact a performance. Tapering and peaking are specific skills as well, and they're not purely physical. Peaking is as much a mental skill as anything else. Accepting that peak performance also utilises mindset skills is the first step to ensuring that the work invested can be maximised when it counts.

Behind the scenes in Rome

Herb Elliott set a new world record for the mile in a time of 3.54.5 in Dublin in August 1958. Two years later, he set another when he took gold in the 1500 metres at the 1960 Rome Olympics in a time of 3.35.6. Over his short career, before retiring from racing at age 23, he was unbeaten over the 1500 metres and the mile.

Herb provided a unique insight into the lead-up to the final in Rome in his book with Alan Trengove, *The Golden Mile* (1960).[1] He shared his thoughts the night before the final as well as during the race. What they reveal is that his mindset was not what many would have anticipated, considering his dominance.

The night before: 'This is it. I think I'm ready. I'm the favourite, aren't I? Go to sleep. Forget the race and go to sleep. Everything will be alright…It's a bad race for the favourites. Oh nuts! That's not positive thinking. Relax. Think of Anne and James and go to sleep. Dear Anne! I've just got to win for her. And I will… Dammit, If only I'd come to Europe earlier. Listen, don't think like that. Be reasonable. OK. Think about good things. That run on the Hall Circuit, for instance [a sandy undulating loop at his training camp back in Portsea]. A run like that tomorrow will do just fine. I'm fit and well… If only I could get to sleep! It must be late. Let me see… half past twelve! I'll try counting sheep. One, two, three, four, five…'

The next day: 'My mind was composed and concentrating on what I was about to do… The gun was fired and sure enough I was boxed in…Well, this is it…Three laps to go. Three laps! I feel like I've run two already! I'm more tired than I should be. And I can hear the crowd. I'm not concentrating enough…We thundered down the back straight, then round the bend and I was breathing hard. The others in front looked strong and I had my worst moment of the race…this pace is killing me! Surely, I shouldn't feel as tired as this! Maybe I better not make my break where I thought I would. Maybe I ought to wait. *No, I won't. I'll give it a go and see what happens…* Surging down the finishing straight (having pushed to the lead) with one lap to go, it seemed somebody was on my tail. But the urge to look around had to be resisted. The bell sounded and I drove my strides even harder, panic squeezing some additional pace out of my body…half a lap from the tape, I made up my mind to sprint, but I was so swept with fatigue that it's doubtful whether the pace increased.' Ultimately, Herb crossed the line in first by a significant margin.

Herb's description of his swirling thoughts and feelings provides a unique insight into the mindset behind the outcome. He describes a balance of outcome and process thoughts that helped him on race day. He touches on one of his philosophies, 'do or die', and describes his training regime as 'very hard': he would regularly push himself to the limit in order to become mentally accustomed to sustaining effort when his body and lungs burned. He regularly did time trials over set courses to test himself. He used two other techniques in training to help sustain effort.

He would ring an imaginary bell in his mind, as if it was the bell for the last lap, and he'd use this as a trigger to surge. He would also imagine a competitor running just behind him trying to pass, and not letting him do so. These strategies, advocated by his coach, were a consistent part of his training. Mindset was at the forefront of his mind in training, enabling its transfer to competition. All of this helped when he was performing under the pressure of an Olympic final that he was expected to win.

In my work with athletes striving to enhance their performance I often discuss exploring their limits more in training. When the session is designed for this, it prevents going into protection mode. At times athletes can naturally tend to protect themselves from the experience to prevent disappointment, so exploring this realm without judgement or fear of slowing down has to be rehearsed. I have heard athletes discuss that it isn't like the pain of stepping on a nail. The discomfort goes away soon after the effort. To stay composed and continue encouraging oneself to sustain effort in this space is necessary. Herb had rehearsed this many times, which contributed to his performance in Rome.

Psychological characteristics and personality

Interest in what it takes to perform in high-level sport has captured the imagination of athletes, coaches and fans for as long as sport has existed. This is possibly in part because striving to achieve and perform is an almost universal interest at school, at work and in life in general. In turn, there is a growing interest in what psychological characteristics support performing at a high level.

Psychological characteristics are factors that are seen as readily changeable, such as concentration and relaxation. These can be influenced by psychological skills training, which has been defined as the 'systematic and consistent practice of mental or psychological skills for the purpose of enhancing performance, increasing enjoyment, or achieving greater sport and physical activity self-satisfaction'.[2]

There has been substantial debate over whether personality contributes to performance. Personality has been described as 'psychological qualities that contribute to an individual's enduring and distinctive patterns of feeling, thinking and behaving'.[3] Mark Allen has pointed to recent research supporting his conclusion that personality plays a role in sport performance. In his 2014 study he suggests that personality traits contribute to long-term sport success, interpersonal relationships, and athletes' psychological states before, during and after competition. He also points to 'evidence that physical activity contributes to personality change'.[4]

The way I see it, both what a person brings mentally and what they learn contribute to performance. Over time, however, what a person learns becomes more important than what they started out with. That's why you hear so many athletes say, 'I wish I knew what I know now when I was younger and starting my sporting career'.

Psychological skills training is a common ingredient for many sport and performance psychology professionals, as it has been for me. From casual weekend athletes wanting to compete in an event to professional athletes in team sports and Olympians striving for selection or medals, proactive athletes have sought help in building their mindset.

Mental skills of high performers

Daniel Gould has been involved in sport psychology for several decades and is widely recognised in the field. Some 20 years ago he investigated 'psychological characteristics and their development in Olympic champions', referred to in step 2 on resilience in relation to adaptive perfectionism.[5] The sample was very small and specific — just 10 athletes, but with 32 Olympic medals between them. From surveying and interviewing the athletes, their coaches and parents or significant others, the authors identified a range of characteristics that contributed to their performance, including:

- the ability to cope with and control anxiety
- resilience
- sport intelligence
- capacity to focus and block out distractions
- competitiveness
- confidence
- work ethic
- ability to set and achieve goals
- coachability
- high levels of hope and optimism
- adaptive perfectionism.

While some of the characteristics seem intuitive, what is noteworthy is that the skills were worked on to be developed for, and able to be recognised by, the athletes and those around them as contributing to their performances at the highest level.

Research insights

A review of studies investigating psychology skills for 'whole body endurance performance' provided some clues to mental skills used in these events. In this study, *endurance* was defined as 'performance during whole body, dynamic exercise that involves continuous effort and lasts for 75 seconds or longer'.

The authors found that imagery, self-talk and goal setting all improved performance. They also found that mental fatigue undermines endurance performance, while verbal encouragement and head-to-head competition can have a beneficial effect on performance.[6]

Research insights

To investigate capacity to sustain winning performances, 17 world champion athletes from seven sports and four different countries were studied.

The research identified that initial success on the world stage brought many additional demands and challenges. Only about one-third of the athletes were able to cope with these demands and continue to perform.

The authors concluded that high levels of success can lead to performance declines by creating additional demands, such as increased expectation from self and others, as well as increased external demands, such as media, public appearances and sponsors. To assist ongoing performance, control over these demands has to be managed to enable consistent quality training, rest and focus.[7]

This study showed how the skills needed to maintain performance go beyond sporting capacity. Dealing with the media, feelings of increased pressure and expectation to sustain performance, and increased time demands add to the difficulty of maintaining initial high performances. Athletes can be misjudged and treated harshly by the media and supporters. Coping with this requires a totally different skill than physical performance qualities. In addition, once a high benchmark is set, external (and sometimes internal) perception is that anything lower than a historical peak performance is deemed a failure. Mindset skills are relevant to all athletes, and while some of these skills may remain the same throughout an athlete's career, with greater success new ones must be developed. Hence mindset skills to perform often extend beyond mental skills directly related to performing in a sport. It is also about self-management.

Individual mindset plans

Many of the highest performing athletes I have worked with have invested heavily in their mental skill development. They have been very proactive, viewing mindset as an ongoing priority. It has contributed to both their development and eventually their performance when it counted. In this group of people, what I have noticed is that their attitude and commitment to mindset sets them above other athletes with similar aspirations I have worked with.

To investigate common characteristics of elite performance, research has been conducted with some of the highest achieving athletes from a variety of sports, as exemplified above. While it provides some clues to common mental skills, researchers and experienced practitioners recognise that there are many different mental skills required in different situations. This suggests that athletes generally need to build their own unique suite of mental skills and implementation styles. Hence, while there is some science to reflect on, individualising and applying mental skills is an art. Coaches and athletes will attest to this. The variety of approaches to training and competition will be influenced by the type of sport, the competition and the athlete themselves. Over time the same athlete may also use different methods to sustain their training and performance.

Using different approaches and mental skills in the lead-up to and during competition depending on the person is also standard practice. Before a competition, within any call room or warm-up area, some athletes are more charged, with looks that could kill, some still and some chatty. I have seen athletes reading performance notes and others reading newspapers; others use boxing to build energy. Some listen to music while some prefer quiet; some want to talk about the event while others will talk about anything other than the event.

During competition the variation is also wide — again depending on the sport, the event and the person. Some athletes use more self-talk, some try to clear their mind and others will focus on themselves while others will use their competitors to help focus or spur them on! Some athletes remain calm and composed while others benefit from being emotionally charged.

There's no set rule about the specific type of mindset required. Even within strategies that have been shown to assist performance, how they are applied varies. Knowing which mindset strategies may best suit a person, then how they can best apply them, combines the science and art of building a performance mindset.

Lifestyle

There is little doubt that in order to perform in sport at a high level, commitment to a certain lifestyle is required. This needs discipline. Constant training over many years is required to fine-tune skills, fitness and mindset to maximise talent. To sustain the level of training required necessitates early nights, eating well and often repetitious behaviour.

High performers embrace this truth. While the lifestyle may seem boring to some, high performers typically embrace it as the path towards a goal. Recognising that it is a 'choice' to embrace this lifestyle, as described in step 1 on motivation, assists commitment.

It's another reason why enjoyment and engagement are so important, because they enable commitment and discipline. I have heard people talk of the need to be obsessive. A degree of obsessiveness can help, but it can also become counterproductive.

In the book mentioned earlier, *Winning Attitudes*, one of the gold medal–winning rowers from the 'Oarsome Foursome' team, Mike McKay, describes how his obsessive desire to perform became counterproductive. He wrote, 'I cooked myself last year by thinking, righto, I really want to put the foot down and rev up for 1999. And I effectively put myself in hospital. I just did too much training ... burnt myself. I was challenging my immune system all the time, and then I just didn't give a shit. You reach a point where you are tired and run down.'[8]

Mike is describing the fine line between being determined and being overly-obsessive in training. It's a great strength to be able to commit to a disciplined lifestyle and to train hard day in, day out, but sometimes a person's greatest strength can also be their greatest weakness. Effective discipline includes knowing how to balance quantity and quality. It includes talking with a coach or other staff about getting the balance of their training program right. Lifestyle incorporates looking at the big picture but being able to do the small daily tasks that get them there. It's another reason why mindset is important in relation to work rate. Mindset helps people to do the work, but also to balance the work when necessary.

One reason why Sasa Ognenovski achieved his goal of playing soccer for Australia was that he and his family were prepared to travel and move to different parts of the world. After his selection to the Australian team, the travel continued. He moved to Qatar, then back to Sydney in the A-league, before eventually moving back to his home town of Melbourne when he retired at age 36. 'My family and I were prepared to move, first to strive for a career and then to keep it going. I was determined enough to accept low wages that other players were not prepared to move for. I made sure that everywhere I went I adapted to the level and then set a standard regardless of the constant change or being in a new and foreign country.' He embraced the lifestyle demands to achieve his goal.

Performance platform

It's very difficult to leap from a low performance to a high performance. Peak performances are generally achieved off a base of consistent training and competition performances. Exposure to low-key competitions, competition simulation or intense competition enables mindset practices to be rehearsed and refined. In his lead-up to Rome, Herb Elliott did time-trials on the track, some racing and a time-trial around a set course back in Portsea that he had punished himself on many times. He wasn't able to get to Europe and participate in lead-up races to the Olympics. Therefore, his goal was to push himself and rehearse mental skills so that once he had tapered and was physically fresher, he would have the mindset to maximise what he was physically capable of.

I often refer to the lead-up to a major event as seeking to create a *performance platform*. Most people don't know or discuss what happened in competition in the months or weeks leading up to a major event. What is relevant in this phase is the rehearsal of mindset and effort as much as physical training to maximise the chance of optimal performance at major competition.

When Sasa Ognenovski was selected to play his first game for Australia in Egypt, it was as if all his efforts and training were vindicated. 'I felt very comfortable at that level, because I had maintained my training standards in different environments for a long period of time. Most importantly, I also had the mentality that I didn't care who my opponent was on the world stage, because I had been thinking my "no one is superhuman" motto for a long time, so it was easy to apply that on any stage.'

Sasa had also developed a reputation for being super-competitive. 'My mentality of going into every game as if it was a battle was well entrenched by the time I played for Australia. My appetite to win on the field was known by others, but off the field I was very calm and had friends for life from many places,' he said. His story reflects the importance of building a mindset so ingrained it becomes a habit that can be applied under any conditions. *That's* a performance platform.

Confidence and competence

Confidence is often associated with performance. Some thinking on confidence has been based on the work of psychologist Albert Bandura, mentioned earlier. His work on self-efficacy — a person's judgement of their capacity to perform a particular task — has influenced research into confidence in sport. He has suggested that influences on self-efficacy include past performance, vicarious experiences, verbal persuasion, physiological state, emotional state and imagined experiences. The list highlights specific areas to emphasise to nurture confidence.

Vicarious experiences here are about seeing and relating to someone else's performance, and imagining yourself doing the same. I have worked with many people who have been inspired by others and thought, 'If they can do it, so can I'.

Research insights

In a 2007 research paper on 14 world-class athletes, Hays and colleagues noted a variety of sources that contributed to confidence. These included preparation, performance accomplishments, social support, experience and competitive advantage. In addition, different types of sport confidence were identified, including skill execution, tactical awareness and psychological factors.[9]

To assist athletes with confidence I have also asked them what they can be confident in. Is it effort? Is it execution? Is it the first part of a performance? Is it their strength? Is it communication? Is it positive thinking or focus? Finding something to specifically be confident in, rather than the whole or the outcome can assist to sustain confidence.

While confidence can be important, it can also be misleading. I have often seen athletes who expressed doubts, 'felt bad' and were low in confidence, yet performed very well. Of course, these doubts were within contained limits. At other times I have observed athletes brimming with confidence who 'felt great', but then underperformed. Feelings can be misleading. They can also distract from task focus that emphasises what is required to perform optimally.

Another interesting aspect of confidence is the *confidence–competence gap*. Some athletes have very high confidence that is not matched by their competence, while others have very high competence not matched by their confidence. Distinguishing between confidence and competence can assist athletes to focus on task and adopt appropriate mindset strategies. One way of enhancing confidence is to build competence, rather than simply the emotion of confidence. Performance will be maximised with high competence and matching confidence. This can best be achieved by a focus on both task- and confidence-building strategies. At times I have encouraged athletes to debate whether focus or confidence at competition is more important. This has yielded great discussion. Once at competition I prefer athletes to err towards sharpening their concentration.

When Brigitte Muir failed to reach the summit of Everest she might have interpreted it in various ways. Her approach was to go and climb a different 8000 metre peak without oxygen. In this way she reassured herself and her team, and reinforced her skills in order to sustain her goal of summiting Everest on another attempt, which she did. This is an example of building both competence and confidence.

Imagery and visualisation

Imagery or visualisation is a common and key skill utilised by many athletes to aid performance. Imagery can take many forms. Watching sport live, reviewing vision, day-dreaming, listening to commentary or engaging in a dedicated session of imagining a skill or performance being executed perfectly are all forms of imagery. Dedicated sessions may be as short as one or two minutes or much longer.

I encourage athletes at formal imagery sessions to imagine the scenery, the sound and even the atmosphere to try to make it as real as possible. When done well, the mind finds it difficult to distinguish between what is real and what is imagined. For athletes experienced in imagery techniques, a physical response can be elicited, as if they were preparing for or doing the event, including increased heart rate and other physiological responses. In imagery sessions with groups, some athletes report that they don't like to use these methods before bed for this reason. Some athletes dislike, while others embrace, using imagery at or during competition. The primary goal is for it to contribute to rather than distract or detract from performance.

When using imagery, some athletes step outside themselves, as though they're watching themselves on a screen, while others feel as though they're in the moment, performing the event. Still others visualise only parts of a performance or a specific skill, rather than the whole.

Imagery can also be used to assist with injuries and to relax. Imagining being on a beach or a favourite place is a common imagery technique for relaxing and calming down. I have created scripts with athletes to read and imagine a performance. It can also be used for a range of specific scenarios. Commentating a passage of play or event is another way for athletes to use imagery. This can be done in person or recorded and used at any time. It can also be fun to create a script about a future performance with a great outcome.

Debbie Flintoff-King explained in *Winning Attitudes*: 'I used to work a lot on imagery, to picture the race in my mind. I had a few faults in my race that I had to iron out and the way I would do it was to imagine that when I went out there I was doing it right. I could visualize myself running a race, but I couldn't visualize where I was in a race. I couldn't visualize people around me. And I could only see myself watching.'

Debbie's reflection illustrates just how individual imagery and visualising are. There is a significant amount of research in this space supporting a wide range of benefits from this mental skill. For this reason, and taking into account the above, it is a good idea to develop and use some form of imagery as part of your performance mindset build.

Mental skills programs

To maximise mental skills development, a mindset or mental skills program should be integrated into teams and sports. This should be continuous and incorporate the whole squad or team, small groups and individual athletes. Such programs should be proactive and not reactive, deficit based or only happen after disappointing performances. Coach support and involvement is pivotal. Coaches can have a shared voice with a sport psychologist, which helps to validate the importance of mental skills to a group. The sport psychologist is best placed to be the coordinator of these programs. Naturally, input from stakeholders, including coaches and athletes, in the development and execution of these programs is important.

To conduct education on leadership, culture, wellbeing or mental skills, 'chalk and talk' style presentations are common. Variation on this style, however, is useful. Involving athletes and coaches, making the information relevant to the group, and keeping it brief, can be beneficial. At times, ten minutes may be all that's needed for good impact. This encompasses follow-up with the group and individuals on the concepts presented. It can be frustrating for athletes to be presented with a topic that is not followed up or discussed further to assist them to understand and apply the concepts. Of course, at times, longer sessions are useful, depending on the age of the group and the number of sessions that can be conducted.

Practical examples and experience from the sport help engagement, relevance and, ultimately, the transfer of psycho-education skills into performance in the shortest possible time. Novel activities and varying the setting can sometimes be beneficial. Conducting sessions outdoors, using vision, internal or external guest speakers, and integrated into training can all be beneficial ways of conducting mental skills training.

Key components of a psychological skills training program might include:

- concentration development (including being in the present and distraction management, as well as routines and use of time)

- squad or team culture and values, and behavioural education

- maximising determination, effort and competitiveness (including using strengths)

- communication with and between athletes or coaches leading into, during or post competition

- lifestyle management

- nerve and anxiety management, including arousal management and self-regulation

- decision making

- embracing different competitive environments and scenario simulation

- a range of other specific mental skills topics, including self-talk, learning, resilience, confidence and imagery

- specific aspects to any sport, such as dealing with noise, managing time in a call-room or being in front or behind.

Note that it's important to keep as many of these components as specific as possible to the sport and application in the sport. For example, while there will be some common concentration skills across sports, there are specific strategies to enhance concentration for tennis compared with, say, football, triathlon or Formula One racing.

Specific skills relevant to the sport can be incorporated into these topics or as standalones. Examples include goal kicking and penalty shoot-outs, dealing with tapering, backing up for heats and finals, preparing for a final series or using time (including routines) between sessions. As noted, these are only some of the many topics that different sports may consider building into a dedicated mental skills program.

Mental skills for juniors

As I've mentioned already, developing mental skills at junior levels can have a positive contribution to enjoyment, positive experience, engagement and future performance in sport. It's important that coaches and sport programs are aware not to treat development of junior athletes and junior personal development or mental skills programs in the same way as senior adult athletes and programs. It's a mistake to take a senior program and adapt it to juniors without considering the group, the goals of the program and the athletes' age. This includes mental skills. Language, expectations and the topics discussed have to be modified when working with juniors.

In younger sport populations, an emphasis on enjoyment, variation and getting on with others (whether an individual or team sport) are all important. At the right time, providing junior athletes with an opportunity to offer input to their training, build friendships and share responsibilities can be very rewarding and enriching, in both sport and life beyond. In addition, involving juniors in unstructured training to embrace problem solving and unpredictability is worthwhile. Emphasising and coaching effort and determination, as well as skill development, over results can help build a foundation that drives future performances. All these experiences aim to increase engagement and mindset skills in an enjoyable way.

Learn competitiveness

As noted earlier, Scott Draper lost in the qualifiers of lowly tournaments in NSW three weeks in a row. At that stage he sat down with his sport psychologist and decided to reduce his scheduled travel and tournaments to work on his mindset. 'We made a plan to learn how to compete better. I set two goals. The first one was to learn to be the best competitor I could be. That included showing less negative emotion. I worked on it every single day. The second goal was related to the first. I envisaged my opponent as a candle and had the aim of observing when the candle was flickering.

'My specific goal was to blow the candle out by stepping up my actions when I sensed the candle flickering. That reduced my worrying about my own demons.' After shifting his mindset to being a competitor rather than winning, Scott started playing matches again and, as mentioned earlier, won 42 matches in a row, which led to a showdown with Andre Agassi in Japan. It was something he could not have imagined a year before.

What eventuated from the dedicated focus on becoming a better competitor was a shift in Scott's relationship with competition. 'I realised after a while that I played tennis to compete. I used to say to myself, you don't have to win, as long as you compete. It helped me fall in love with all the different emotions that come your way in competition. It helped me enjoy the problem solving. I would try to work out what to do with the emotions. It also helped me feel safer. In competition it's easy to feel a lack of safety and vulnerability.'

Scott's story illustrates how competing regularly at the highest level is a skill to be mastered. Just because a person is an athlete competing at the highest levels in their sport doesn't mean the capacity to compete or maintain a maximum effort is instinctive or at a high level. That's a myth. Competitiveness must be learned and rehearsed. Coaches, athletes and people in general are misguided if they think that an athlete will naturally be as competitive in one environment as in another. Multiple factors, both internal and external, impact capacity to compete and sustain maximal efforts.

Another myth is that competitiveness can be observed from physical behaviours such as aggression, jumping around, staring or fist pumping. Competitiveness is not necessarily any of those things. It's a capacity to maximise what one is physically capable of amid distractions. It includes maintaining determination.

Factors that impact capacity to compete include:

- an unhealthy level of nerves and anxiety or tension *in contrast to* physical and mental composure

- diluted concentration due to distraction, stress or confusion, or other variables *in contrast to* sharp focus on key factors

- worrying about the past or future *in contrast to* being in the present moment

- lack of mental preparation or readiness, *in contrast to* being prepared and ready for anything to enable adapting and adjusting quickly in the face of different circumstances

- capacity to deal with physical or mental discomfort and fatigue in the event *in contrast to* embracing and managing physical discomfort

- not sustaining a high level of determination for any reason *in contrast to* effort being consistent from start to finish regardless of circumstances

- lack of communication with teammates in team sports *in contrast to* clearly communicating, organising and supporting others

- under or overarousal for a specific situation *in contrast to* matching arousal levels based on demands

- personal factors that dilute capacity to direct energy on maximal performance *in contrast to* managing or blocking out personal factors until after competition.

Maximising effort: intrinsic and extrinsic strategies

Sometimes maximal effort is referred to as the 'hurt locker'. When striving to push oneself, new, unusual or challenging emotions and distractions can arise. Doubts creep or flood in and lower capacity to sustain effort. At the other end of the spectrum, willpower can override and assist to sustain maximum physical capacity. Vision of athletes staggering and collapsing towards finish lines are evidence of this. Australian 10 000 metres runner at the 2021 Tokyo Olympics Patrick Tiernan falling in the final lap of his race and stumbling to the finish line is one example. Australian marathoner Tani Ruckle, who staggered across the line of the 1990 Commonwealth Games marathon, legs buckling, is another.

Dealing with thoughts, worries and fear when feeling uncomfortable or in pain plays a part in maximal performances. From a mindset perspective, good self-talk and self-management can help coping. Interpreting physical discomfort not as uncomfortable but rather as a temporary state that leads to a desirable outcome is one way to manage discomfort. For experienced competitors, the burn and discomfort of maximal effort is a desirable space. It is a space that provides feedback and indicates they are where they need to be to perform to their utmost. Too comfortable indicates something may be left in the tank at the end, which equates to underperforming. Distinguishing between the two means striking a fine balance.

Being calm under such circumstances is essential, but not easy. Relaxation, composure and efficiency can help to sustain effort. An expression often voiced in pit lane among race-car drivers is 'to go faster, slow down'. I've used the line many times in different sports. It is possible to 'try too hard' and underperform.

To maximise effort, be clear about what you want to achieve. Link this to your goal, purpose or anything that consolidates your reason to perform. Once you've determined this, be clear on the physical and mental composure or arousal levels to draw out physical capacity. In the event itself, be clear where your attention needs to be directed. Fatigue and distractions take your focus away from what's important. When using triggers or self-talk be sure they aren't too complicated and are simple to draw on. The closer to competition, the simpler they should be. In line with mindfulness, being fully absorbed in the performance and in the present can block out distractions and physical discomfort too. Clarity is king.

At times comments from a teammate, an opponent, coach, referee or even supporter can stimulate another gear and enhance energy. Being forced into a demanding situation can also trigger an enhanced effort. Sometimes, with a certain amount of time left, effort increases — the carrot is visible. Knowing that specific environmental factors influence capacity to compete, these should be manipulated as much as possible. This demands that the athlete and coach know what will work for them.

These examples reflect some strategies to maximise effort. Whether an athlete uses one strategy more than another is quite individual and depends on a range of factors, as discussed. Overall, to maximise effort I believe athletes should rehearse and experience repeat maximal efforts under controlled, manipulated and varied conditions using intrinsic and extrinsic strategies. This helps to develop the skill of maximising performance.

Clutch and flow

Significant times in an event that can impact an outcome are often referred to as clutch moments. Serving for the match in tennis, kicking a goal to win the game or finishing a race strong are examples of clutch states. Flow states, as discussed in step 3 on focus, refer to performances that are more automatic.

A 2017 study investigated 'clutch' and 'flow' states. With a sample of 26 athletes around 30 years old across a range of sports, the researchers wanted to identify how clutch or excellent performances were achieved.[10] The athletes were from various European countries including Germany, England and Holland, and were at world-class level in their sports. Both team and individual sports were represented in the sample.

From interviews with the athletes in the days after a high-level performance, they concluded that 'flow occurred as a build-up of confidence, whereas clutch was a relatively sudden process of "switching on" in response to an appraisal of demands'. Different psychological skills were also used by the athletes. The paper presented an integrated model of flow and clutch states to achieve excellent performances in sport. They describe flow performances as including mindsets such as open goals, the absence of critical thoughts, and automatic or effortless styles of attention. Clutch states related to identifying fixed-style goals and using complete and deliberate focus with heightened awareness and intense effort to achieve excellent performance.

In summarising, the authors emphasised that from a practical perspective, rather than trying to prepare an athlete for one distinct or optimal state, to achieve optimal performance it was important to be aware of both distinct states. Good coaches and practitioners working in sport educate athletes to strive to achieve flow states and deal with clutch situations.

At the Tokyo Olympics, the men's decathlon captured the imaginations of the Australian public when Ash Moloney was vying for bronze. In the final event, the 1500 metres, he needed to run a certain time to secure his place and be the first Australian in the history of the event to medal. Fellow Aussie competitor Cedric Dubler, who was out of contention for a medal, decided to run beside and encourage his countryman to achieve his dream. After the goal was achieved Ash commented that he would not have been able to run the time without Cedric's encouragement. It was clearly a clutch moment and reflects how strong extrinsic forces can assist performance.

In one of the biggest pressure-cooker moments in Australian sport, Cathy Freeman used an intrinsic flow-like mindset to assist her victory in the 400 metres at the Sydney 2000 Olympics. 'I was like a lamb going into a lion's den,' she reported in the book *Cultivating Curiosity*.[11] 'I didn't want to get caught up in the chaos of the race. I knew if I did I may have gone out too hard and I would've stuffed it.' The phrase that came to her mind was 'just do what you know'. 'It was like a peace came over me,' she said. 'I can't even remember the noise. I tuned into my body and that's how I tuned out. It's a strange sensation. That's being fully present…in that split moment, as I was mid-air over the finish line, it was the first moment I had the chance to feel like I could let go…the light switch went on and it was like *"where am I?"* It's almost like I came out of a deep sleep…I felt totally disoriented and I had to sit down, just to get some stability under my body.'

Set up for sub-two-hour marathon speed

To illustrate the power of combining internal and external strategies on maximising performance, consider Eliud Kipchoge's sub-two-hour marathon. Before this amazing run, Eliud had already won an Olympic gold in the marathon. He also won the marathon at the Tokyo Olympics after this event. To put the performance into perspective, consider that a sub-two-hour marathon was even more unimaginable to past generations than the sub-four-minute mile had been. Eliud's time of 1.59.40 for the 42.195 kilometre distance broke his own official personal best time by about two minutes. In this 'unofficial' event, everything was primed to assist the feat.

It was October 12, 2019. A date that was chosen within a window of time as likely to have the best weather conditions to assist the goal. The run was on a course specifically created and designed to be fast. A car projecting a laser to reflect whether Eliud was in front, behind or right on pace provided perfect extrinsic feedback.

A cheering crowd extended along the course. His fluid intake during the race was measured by checking discarded bottles to ensure the next drink was adjusted to maintain optimal hydration. To assist relaxation and to create a draft, a bevy of rotating world-class runners ran around Eliud in a Y formation. Patrick Tiernan, mentioned earlier in this chapter, was one of them.

Interestingly, Eliud attempted this record in 2017 in Italy on the Monza Formula One racing track but missed his goal by 25 seconds. He and his team took lessons from that experience, however, to make another attempt in 2019. In a documentary portraying the assault on this remarkable feat titled *Kipchoge: the last milestone*, Eliud's strong mindset and capacity to withstand pain was frequently alluded to.[12] In the documentary he says, 'The way you think about pain is the way your life will be. In this world you need to undergo pain to be successful.' He adds that 'failure is part of the challenge ... if you understand what life is and what failure is, then it's easy to cope with. It's part of life.'

In this record-breaking performance Eliud also describes how he woke up at 2 am and didn't sleep properly again. He decided to get up at about 4 am. It shows that even one of the best performances in history didn't have the perfect lead-up. And while as many variables as possible were controlled, it wasn't possible to control them all.

Eliud has told reporters that he smiles to relax and work through pain. Now that he has physically experienced the exertion and pace, I would imagine that repeating the feat with fewer extrinsic variables would be simpler. That's part of the reward for being a trailblazer. The path becomes worn, and the mind finds it easier to traverse a trodden path. His first attempt in 2017 would have revealed to him what it felt like to work at that level for that long. His smile was another intrinsic strategy to help sustain rhythm at the pace he was running. He also describes running for a higher purpose: to inspire the human spirit. Of course the pain he describes is not an injury, but physical discomfort.

Eliud's performance is an example of combining extrinsic factors, such as chasing a line, having runners around him and an encouraging crowd, as well as intrinsic factors, such as smiling, staying relaxed and wanting to inspire to maximise his performance. All that enabled him to extract the training he had devoted his life to.

Create and execute a simple plan

In step 3 on focus we discuss chunking and race plans. Eliud achieving his sub-two-hour run is a perfect example of executing a plan. His calm demeanour assisted his execution. The calmness frees up headspace. The more stressed a person is leading into or during a big event, the less bandwidth they have for execution.

To maximise performance, having a clear and simple plan and remaining calm to direct energy into making it happen are extremely important. Many athletes I have worked with on performance have achieved this mindset. In this book, Jacqui Cooper keeping it simple pre-event and Garth Tander racing a lap at Bathurst are two examples that reinforce how vital this aspect of performance is. In addition, elements of the plan have to be rehearsed at training with a mindset that reflects a desired competition mindset.

Great performances

After reinventing herself following the disastrous injury the day before the 2002 Salt Lake City Olympics, Jacqui Cooper was again the favourite for gold at the 2006 Olympics at Turin in Italy. 'I saw it as an opportunity to unveil the new me,' she reflected. 'I hadn't performed the triple twisting, triple somersault on snow since 2002, but that is what I had planned for.' Using her trademark routine of 'not getting in her own way', in the semifinal she landed the jump. 'It was probably the greatest jump of my career,' Jacqui said. She broke world and Olympic records. Her competitors were in awe. Surely, this time she was on track to secure the gold.

After the semifinal, however, a heavy fog drifted across the mountain and the event was delayed by two days. Although the fog remained, it was eventually decided to proceed with the final. 'After perfect weather in the semi, I couldn't see a thing in the final,' she said. Jacqui didn't land either of her two jumps, crashing out of the competition.

That semifinal performance, however, inspired her to have another go, which meant another four years' wait. Her focus wasn't only on herself but was also on supporting her younger teammates and the sport itself. After a solid block of work, Jacqui did qualify for her fifth Olympic Games. It was Vancouver 2010, about 21 years since Geoff Lipshut spotted her jumping on a trampoline, and he had been on the journey the whole way. Ultimately she finished fifth. Having crashed out at three Olympics, it bettered the 16th place she had registered at her first games in 1994.

Having been world number one, winning world championships and world cups, Jacqui described the performance in Vancouver as the greatest of her career. 'The world record jump in the semifinal in Italy may have been my best jump, but Vancouver was the best performance of my career. The reason is because it was my greatest effort. You can't always win. I considered that if you put in your greatest effort, then that's your greatest performance. I'd take a high performance over a win any day,' she said. 'You can go to bed happy with that.' Who was the eventual winner in Vancouver? It was teammate Lydia Lassila, the young girl all those years ago who had asked Jacqui if she was 'the acrobatic moron'. No doubt part of the positive emotion from the competition was to see her teammate win. That's about the good culture she described earlier.

Jacqui's story raises an interesting question about performance. Is a personal best or a win necessarily an athlete's greatest performance, or might it rather be when they know they gave their all and did the best they could on the day, given the circumstances? I believe the latter. It's certainly what enabled Jacqui to sleep well.

Embracing new situations and challenges

Shelley Taylor-Smith is an athlete who valued the importance of mindset and self-talk. She told Simon Griffiths in *Outdoor Swimmer*,[13] 'It wasn't my physical condition that allowed me to win races but what went on between my ears — the most important six inches of your body.'

Shelley used her mindset to perfection at the world swimming championships in Perth in 1991. Her event was the challenging 25 kilometre ocean swim. She and the other competitors knew that unfortunate timing meant the water was infested with jellyfish. They couldn't be avoided. So Shelley came up with the plan of viewing the jellyfish as friends and supporters. 'If I head-butted into them, they were my supporters, cheering me on. The ones that stung were showing their affection,' she related. With that mindset she went on to win the race and gold. Shelley's example is one of using intrinsic strategies to deal with an external scenario that was totally unpredictable.

Shelley's story reflects a positive response to a new and unpredictable situation. This is something high performers do well. Even if the pitch is the same shape and size, the track or pool the same length or the opponent familiar, circumstances within an event change. People bring to events different emotions for different reasons. Adaptation is a constant requirement. That is why I sometimes refer to high performers as adventurers. There is always uncharted territory ahead. It is also why embracing problem solving is relevant; effective use of appropriate self-talk and self-encouragement at these times is warranted; and being prepared for and having to respond to a different situation is exactly what Shelley did to enable her performance.

Meaning contributes to performance

Another major consideration in striving for maximal performance is meaning. Why is the performance important? What does it mean to an individual or group? Being in touch with meaning can steel the heart and mind. Yousef Abdi's story in step 1 on motivation reflected this. Consider, for example, teams that have been narrowly defeated, only to return to another opportunity 12 months or more later. When managed effectively the loss can add meaning to future performances. Meaning could be derived from performing for oneself or for someone or something else. Meaning helps resilience and digging deep when the question *can I keep going?* is raised. It doesn't guarantee first place, but being in touch with meaning at the right moments contributes to maximising effort.

Another type of meaning derives from making a performance personal. It reflects the head-to-head battle referred to in the research mentioned earlier. This relates to individuals or teams. Many athletes would relate to this strategy. It can drive training as well as competitive efforts. Scott Draper used this strategy and challenged himself to achieve one of the best performances of his career. 'When I was in Rome in 1997 at the Italian Open that's played on clay, I was drawn to play Thomas Muster. Muster had a career high of number one in the world and was known as "The King of Clay". He had been undefeated on clay for a while. He was known as a warrior, as the benchmark. That appealed to me and for that match I had a different mindset. It was over 30 degrees and I thought to myself, "I'm going to show you." I decided I was going to be tough and not give an inch. It was a match of wills. I made it a match about who was mentally tougher, not about the score. It went for over three hours and eventually I won. I didn't give myself an out for that match and was stubborn about who I wanted to be more than anything.'

To be clear, this doesn't mean disliking an opponent. It may reflect respect for them as a competitor. Adding meaning by making a competitive experience personal is also not as simple as it seems. It requires a balance between why a high performance is wanted and a mindset about staying calm, clear and on task to execute what is required for this and your own performance.

Strengths win battles

On many occasions in different sports I have conducted strengths-based sessions. Focusing on strengths can be a powerful tool to assist performance.

Nicole Pratt explained how a focus on strengths helped her at a pivotal stage in her tennis career. 'Having clarity really helped my performance. It fed into my on-court identity. I was clear on my reputation on court. It was to be a little fox-terrier, nipping at opponents' heels. I didn't look to be the greatest player from a stroke perspective, but I knew what I had. When my ranking dropped it was influenced by different things, including a chronic plantar fascia foot injury. It meant I lost my greatest strength of movement, and I lost my identity. I started to try to play like a big dog and dominate. But it wasn't my identity or strength, and I went backwards. That also contributed to my goal setting to get back to 34 by 34. Making sure I got back to my identity and strengths.'

Everyone has their own unique strengths. They may be physical, mental, overt or subtle. Athletes may have blind spots about their own strengths and need others to identify them or even to convince them of their existence. However they appear, relative strengths need to be recognised, nurtured, developed and used more than relative weaknesses. Too often sports focus on developing weaknesses. Developing and using strengths should be a priority. Weaknesses will improve over time. Overemphasising weakness can deflect recognition and use of strengths. Being overly modest to ourselves can blind us to our strengths.

Strengths should be trained to become even more powerful. Some coaches move beyond strengths and use the term 'weapon' to reflect the importance of the assets an athlete has. A possible scenario is a golfer who becomes a professional with the skill and reputation of being a formidable putter, but on tour they focus on developing their driving at the expense of maintaining, let alone further developing, their putting. When it counts, they are vulnerable to both driving and putting letting them down. The key is, don't leave your strengths unattended.

To maximise strengths, they should be reviewed and recorded. Consider some activities I have conducted to maximise and use strengths:

- Record strengths in general or under different categories, such as personal, mental, technical or physical.
- Consider why something is a strength.
- Identify and record times when a strength was used.
- Record best performances, including when and what happened.
- Ask others to record your strengths and compare their thoughts with those others, including yourself.
- Post-performance, record what you did well and what contributed to the performance.

Sometimes I have asked individuals who find it difficult to identify their strengths to ask three or so nominated people to list their strengths for them. We then collate the responses to build a strengths sheet. At other times I have created sheets with images of athletes at the centre and had squad members or teammates write down strengths about that person on the sheet. It can produce an empowering collage that the athlete is able to keep and further add to as they progress through a season or career. Never underestimate your capacity to use your strengths. They can help fuel confidence and direct energy.

Managing performance anxiety and nerves

After his experience at the French Open, when his wife was ill and he lost the second round, Scott Draper's ranking fell. After some average performances and with Wimbledon looming, he was due to play at Queen's, which is one of the main tournaments leading up to Wimbledon. It's not a Grand Slam but it's certainly prestigious. 'I was there training with Tony Roach and woke up on the day of my first round with an allergy,' he recalled. 'I felt horrendous!

'I quickly went down a break in the first set, but rain interrupted play and we were delayed overnight. I said to myself, "You never know what might happen. If I can win this match, I might win the whole thing." I came out the next day and played some of the best tennis of my life. I won the match and went on to make the final. In the final I was performing well, leading 7–6, 4–3. All of a sudden, the past month hit me. I had a moment of "holy shit". I got caught only thinking outcome. It came on strong and fast in only 30 seconds. It was the most nervous I had ever been. I began thinking the worst. Thankfully it was a change of ends and I quickly realised I had to reframe my thinking. I distracted myself by reversing the score and imagining I was 3–4 down and not up. It meant I was serving to stay in touch, rather than being 4–3 up. The nerves also came on because I had never won a tournament on tour and the unfamiliarity gave me a jolt. But my strategy worked to settle me, and I went on to win 7–6, 6–4.' It was a clever strategy that Scott thought of in the moment to reduce his nerves and enabled him to go on and win the tournament.

Managing nerves through reframing

Scott's story shows that sometimes nerves can come out of seemingly nowhere and arise unexpectedly. On occasion, nerves manifest well before an event, such as in the weeks or days in the lead-up. Untamed, they can build to unmanageable levels, compromising performance and making functioning extremely difficult. If nerves impede performance, sometimes there will be another opportunity, sometimes not.

Competition nerves and anxiety undermine the performances of many athletes. Almost every athlete knows this from experience. There is significant research showing that physiological as well as mental factors are clearly impacted by nerves. Not all nerves are bad — they can reflect 'readiness'. How the symptoms are interpreted can influence their impact. A common strategy used by athletes is to reframe or reinterpret nerves as 'excitement'. You wouldn't be nervous if the event didn't mean anything, so seeing them as healthy can help control and reduce competition nerves.

Ideally, predetermined strategies need to be put in place to deal with nerves. A misconception is that nerves are purely mental. They may begin from a mental space, but they manifest physically, becoming a significant limiting factor. Many athletes could fight on if the nerves remained a cognitive experience, but when their heart rate escalates as if it's about to burst out of their chest and they feel desperately tired, and even at rest their hands and legs shake uncontrollably, it becomes extremely difficult to perform. There can even be a loss of motor control, feeling like or actually vomiting, a loss of coordination or blurred vision. The experience can be crippling and make optimal performance unlikely. From a thinking or cognitive perspective, inability to think clearly, being confused and forgetful, making poor decisions, going blank or feeling out of touch with reality are only some thought processes athletes describe when anxious. At times, the physical sensations, in-part, that occur from poor breathing lead to an imbalance of oxygen and carbon dioxide in the bloodstream.

When working with athletes, deciphering whether nerves are predominantly physiological or cognitive is a good starting point to narrow down which strategies may be most relevant and helpful. Often, a combination of physical and thinking strategies will be of most benefit to combat nerves.

Research insights

In one study, athletes who interpreted anxiety symptoms as 'facilitative' reported significantly more positive emotional states than athletes who interpreted feelings and thoughts as 'debilitative'.

The authors discuss how excitement and anxiety may be experienced concurrently preceding performance, which enables athletes to label their overall mental state as positive. It reinforces the earlier point that 'reframing' nerves as 'being ready' or 'excitement' can help to reduce them to a manageable level, so they don't compromise performance.[14]

Research insights

A team of researchers found that, along with other factors, underperformance from heightened anxiety can occur due to attention shifting away from task-relevant cues to task-irrelevant cues. This, in my experience, can also further heighten anxiety. It becomes a negative cycle.

The authors summarised a range of strategies to help athletes remain on task in pressure situations. These included using a pre-performance routine that incorporated deep breathing and using cue or trigger words to maintain task-relevant focus. Other strategies summarised included using music or humour to settle nerves.[15]

Taking control of nerves

A sporting competition environment is by its nature abnormal. Not many people have to do their job in front of thousands of observers, some applauding, some jeering, but all scrutinising them. At times, tension can build without a crowd due to the emphasis people place on the event. One strategy for managing nerves and anxiety is acceptance and embracing emotions that accompany these scenarios. Expecting and understanding that these emotions are part of the event can help them subside quicker. Worrying about them or fighting them can compound the negative experience. In my experience of being at AFL Grand Finals, Grand Slam tennis events, in Olympic stadiums and in the pit lane during Bathurst, I can report that the atmosphere is electric, typically very loud and a variety of coping behaviours by different people are very apparent.

Nerves, fears, worries or doubts are natural. Understanding where the nerves come from can be helpful in reducing and controlling them. Recognising that once a competition begins nerves often diminish or disappear can be established from experience. Some athletes describe driving or getting to the competition venue as the most nerve-racking part of the day. Or immediately before the competition. Once the event starts, a focus on the event can help muscle memory to take over and nerves to subside. The mind shifts away from worry to action.

The most common and effective strategy to manage nerves, anxiety and unwanted tension is diaphragmatic breathing, discussed in step 6 on wellbeing. Conscious breathing not only helps reduce unwanted physiological symptoms, but also provides a focus — something to consider and do other than giving way to nerves. It's a powerful technique that many athletes strive to master.

If appropriate and possible, the distraction of talking to others, teammates or coaches can help reduce nerves. Reassurance from others can distract from nerves and help them settle. One example is as simple as a fielder in cricket speaking to a bowler before the run-up or a batter speaking to their batting partner. Naturally there are countless examples. It can begin a chain of distraction from the anxiety, a sense of calm or positive self-talk. Reviewing strengths, focusing on plans, using triggers, and challenging worries and doubts also help to reduce nerves and their impact. These strategies are along the lines of the cognitive-behavioural method discussed in step 6 on wellbeing. The approach embraces challenging the anxiety head on. I have worked with athletes who have internally yelled at worries and nerves to go away, to positive effect. They have also been prepared to combat any anticipated doubts with pre-planned responses. This is relevant because when nerves take over, problem solving can become difficult. Self-encouragement can also go a long way to calming and focusing. Having these responses ready can even contribute to the nerves not arising in the first place.

Physically shaking muscles to keep them loose or rehearsing skills that are well drilled into your neuromuscular system can be effective ways of managing coordination. Physical triggers and routines also help manage nerves and enhance performance. You may, for example, tap your thigh to trigger an energising and positive thought, clap your hands to indicate your readiness, or drop your shoulders to control your rhythm and tension.

These are only some of the methods to manage nerves, anxiety and tension. Recognising that nerves are normal, reframing them, riding them out and using physical methods such as diaphragmatic breathing and grounding can limit their negative impact on performance.

Optimism and positivity

Some athletes fear that positivity and optimism may detract from focus, effort or motivation. Being positive does not mean being blind to negative consequences. Rather, it identifies opportunity and focuses on that to direct and sustain energy. But being positive in the lead-up to and during competition is easier said than done.

Of her doubles match at Wimbledon, Storm Sanders said, 'When I got to the big stage of the semifinal I embraced it. I thought about how I had dreamt of it ever since I was young. I was excited. I recalled the time not that long before when I was injured and couldn't lift my arm above my head. It helped me to focus on giving it everything, and if the result went the other way I could accept that. I knew you could perform the best you have ever done and still not walk away with the result. So my goal was to leave everything on court and have no regrets. I also wanted to savour the moment, because it was a great opportunity and time in my life.'

Positivity in realistic doses can enhance a healthy approach to training and competition, enabling appreciation and enjoyment, which in turn can fuel persistence. By contrast, a negative attitude and approach can be draining for oneself and others. A positive approach can enable maximisation of physical capabilities by keeping a person engaged in their sport and better able to deal with daily challenges.

I often ask athletes what they feel positive about. Positivity can be about past performances, training experiences, effort, plans or mindset. It doesn't have to be about the outcome. Simply appreciating and being grateful for the opportunity of being engaged in a sport can help maintain positivity. For example, being positive about working hard at the start of an event is much more realistic and achievable than being positive solely about winning.

Research insights

One research of slump-related coping sampled 213 athletes from a variety of individual and team sports such as hockey, football and triathlon. The researchers found that both 'optimism and sport-related confidence positively correlated with the use of problem-focused coping strategies and negatively correlated with emotional based coping strategies for dealing with performance slumps'.[16]

Research insights

A comparison of optimism levels and life-stress levels among NCAA Division 1 athletes and non-athletes attested to the benefits of optimism.

The study indicated that optimistic high-level athletes experience lower levels of life-stress than less optimistic athletes.[17]

Considering the daily commitment required in high-performance sport, negativity and negative emotional reactions can lead to a roller-coaster of emotions that are both mentally and physically draining. General positivity and optimism are certainly worth harnessing. As well as performance benefits, they can make a sporting journey for an athlete and those around them much more enjoyable. A question to ask is whether you see the negative among positives, or a positive among the negatives? This is different than paying attention to detail and repeatedly engaging in a task to improve.

Many paths to high performance

Here I have summarised some examples of performance mindsets, mental skills and approaches to training and competition to perform. They exemplify the many mindset variations to maximise performance. Individual personality, experience, the type of sport or event, and other circumstances are so varied that to perform consistently at a high level athletes need a wide array of mental strategies to draw upon.

Liz Watson told me: 'To help my performance I like to have a plan off the court. How to get to the start of the season. I focus on good relationships with the coach and staff. Trust in them helps me. Doing small extra things also helps. On court I don't want to overthink. I love the freedom of a game and playing. My default is to beat my opponent and I do whatever I can do for that. I also never want to plateau. Trying to get better all the time keeps me going and helps my performance.'

In his Paris–Roubaix winning performance, Mat Hayman was selected at the last minute as the last team member. He used his experience and self-talk to meet a challenge he encountered towards the end of the race that energised him to victory. 'How I managed that key moment was important in many ways,' he said.

Sasa Ognenovski described the competitiveness that he developed as a boy training with his older brother. He never forgot it and used those emotions when he was older. He adopted a 'siege mentality' to secure a contract and had a mindset to 'make the most of every opportunity' every time he played. This sat alongside his mantra of 'nobody is superhuman' that he used through his career.

'Investing in the mental side is key,' said Tayla Harris. 'I learned from boxing not to dwell on the past. In that sport, the only guarantee is you'll get hit again, sometimes in less than half a second. I have used that approach in my goal kicking in AFLW. If you get worked up, or you're worried and can't get over it, there's a higher chance you'll miss the next one. There's not enough time to stress about what's happened. You have to rectify any mistake in the next move you make and look forward.

'The key to performance is to always expect the best from yourself — that is, to give the best you can, whatever that is in the moment. You also have to be honest with yourself and understand your own ability on the day, based on circumstances and your performance. That's what you have to be comfortable with.

'In a team sport,' Tayla added, 'I've also learned that you play for your team, not just yourself. Relationships are so important. Small conversations help the relationship. All of those things help my performance mindset.'

Garth Tander reflected, 'My objectives have always been to win races and perform at the highest level I'm capable of. That never changed. When I was younger, though, it was only round by round and based on results or outcome. Then, when my career plateaued at about 24 or 25, I realised that there were 30 other drivers who were also very fast. I learned that some wins were not my best races. I realised how I measured my performance had to be a lot more self-analytical and detailed, and there was scope to improve in many ways, rather than just win. Part of it was recognising how much mindset and attitude could improve my general skills. My goals became about getting more out of myself, and that was a big part of my improvement. There's always scope to improve, outside of winning. There's no way I would have been as successful if I hadn't started focusing more on mindset.'

Sam Mitchell described what helped his performance: 'I spent 95 per cent of the time in the moment. I tried not to be too urgent on the field. I say *slow is smooth and smooth is fast*. Urgency is the enemy.

I tried to keep emotional control and think through things and was in constant problem-solving mode. I separated performance from talent, so if I missed a kick, I knew I was still good at footy. I used to be very obsessive, and preparation was everything. But when my wife had our first child, I spent the whole night before a game at the hospital. I focused on having the best preparation I could given the situation, rather than thinking I hadn't prepared. In my head I couldn't have had a better preparation given the circumstances. Thinking about what I could control helped me to perform.'

For Jacqui Cooper, 'Immediately pre-event, my routine involved not getting in my own way. I worked on having a clear mind and very few processes — *keep it clean and simple* immediately pre-event was a mantra.' She used this before the best jump of her career. But her best performance, she felt, was not that jump. Her best performance was another event that she described as her best mental effort. 'You can't always win. If I put in my greatest effort, that was my greatest performance. That's what you can go to bed happy with.'

For Dave Andersen, as outlined in step 2 on resilience, 'The most important part of performance is resilience. To be a high performer you always have to be ticking boxes. It helped me not to give in to injuries or distractions and keep motivated. Resilience enabled me to keep playing and performing at a high level for as long as I did. I also constantly set goals and if I wasn't able to achieve them, I re-set new ones.'

Towards the end of my conversation with Brigitte Muir, she said, 'There's one more thing. Performance is about the heart and the brain. You have to have a holistic picture.' It reminded me of something Herb Elliott told me: 'The best ingredients for success haven't changed in 50000 years. They are spirit, soul, body and mind. Mental toughness can be trained.'

Summary

There are clearly a wide variety of mental skills to use to maximise performance. These depend on the sport, circumstances and person. These should be used and rehearsed through training and not reserved for competition.

Some skills to assist performance are 'big picture', such as managing lifestyle and building a competition performance platform. Others are more specific, such as developing simple plans, using self-talk, rehearsing maximising effort, focussing on strengths and managing nerves or tension. All of these skills enable channelling energy into what is important at any given moment.

While some variations of mental skills are necessary to perform, the most important ingredient is ensuring to prioritise such skills as a part of training and strive to grow in this space.

BUILD YOUR PERFORMANCE

- Appreciate individuality in performance strategies and plans. Work out what is best for you.

- Work constantly on mental skills relevant to your sport and rehearse at training and competitions.

- Embrace the lifestyle required to achieve your goals.

- Build a performance platform.

- Manage confidence and competence.

- Maximise competitiveness and effort.

- Use simple plans for competition.

- Be prepared for new situations.

- Use meaning to maximise performance.

- Maximise strengths.

- Manage performance nerves and anxiety.

- Build optimism and positivity skills.

- Embrace a performance mindset over and above talent.

CONCLUSION

In *The Performance Mindset* I have introduced and explored a range of factors that I believe play a more important role than talent or work rate in achieving success in sport and in life. If you want to make the most of your sport, or any other aspect of your life, you need to build a performance mindset. Importantly, a performance mindset can be learned. Using multiple strategies to stay motivated, resilient and focused, managing wellbeing, embracing leadership, investing in and drawing from a culture, and performing when it counts — all involve skills developed through practice. Being proactive in building these skills is particularly relevant for athletes, as the window for a sporting career is typically small. Keep in mind this practice should be integrated into daily activities, not postponed for a major event.

With a performance mindset, an athlete not only engages in the hard work, but also better navigates the roller-coaster of experiences and emotions encountered enabling them to embrace their journey. Performance and enjoyment should not be viewed as mutually exclusive. Indeed, finding enjoyment and purpose in what one is doing and continually striving to perform go hand in glove.

The journey to peak performance in any field is rarely smooth sailing. It is about making good decisions at the right time and using mindset to capitalise on opportunities as they arise. Additionally, high-level performances are rarely achieved alone. A performance mindset recognises the value of support and of investing in oneself and others.

The stories shared by the athletes and coaches interviewed for this book attest to the value of a performance mindset. Their reflections and insights are only a small sampling of a myriad experiences that might be drawn upon. They illustrate how much goes on behind the scenes of a performance that is viewed live or on a screen. They also exemplify the heart and soul that are embedded in a performance mindset. Once these are engaged as part of a performance mindset, opportunities to achieve at high levels in sport and life are enhanced.

Use your mindset to learn and grow both in sport performance capacity and in experiences beyond sport. That is the promise of *The Performance Mindset*.

All the best with your endeavours and adventures.

Anthony J Klarica

REFERENCES

Introduction: Made not born

1   Coyle, D 2009, *The talent code*, Bantam Books, New York, NY.

2   *The Brady 6* 2011, television series episode in the year of the quarterback, TEN100, Los Angeles, CA. Produced by James Weiner and Mark Durand; directed by Chase Heavener and Shaun Silva.

3   O'Connor, I 2016, 'Tom Brady's greatest talent is his desire to be great', *ESPN*, 10 October, viewed 27 October 2021, www.espn.com

4   Hutchinson, A 2018, *Endure: mind, body, and the curiously elastic limits of human performance*, William Morrow, New York, NY, p. 3.

5   Hutchinson, A 2021, 'Testing whether fast kids make future champions', *Outside*, 29 January, viewed 27 October 2021, www.outsideonline.com

6   Baker, J, & Horton, S 2004, 'A review of primary and secondary influences on sport expertise', *High Ability Studies*, vol. 15, no. 2, pp. 211–28.

7   Holland, M, Woodcock, C, Cumming, J & Duda, J 2010, 'Mental qualities and employed mental techniques of young

elite team sport athletes', *Journal of Clinical Sport Psychology*, vol. 4, no. 1, pp. 19–38.

8   *In search of greatness* 2018, documentary film, Gabriel Polsky Productions, Los Angeles, CA. Produced and directed by Gabriel Polsky.

9   Gladwell, M 2008, *Outliers: the story of success*, Little, Brown and Company, Boston, MA.

10   Ericsson, K, Krampe, R, & Tesch-Römer, C 1993, 'The role of deliberate practice in the acquisition of expert performance', *Psychological Review*, vol. 100, no. 3, pp. 363–406.

11   Ericsson, A, & Pool, R 2016, *Peak: secrets from the new science of expertise*, Mariner Books, Boston, MA, pp. 110, 112, 122.

12   MacNamara, B, Moreau, D, & Hambrick, D 2016, 'The relationship between deliberate practice and performance in sports: a meta-analysis', *Perspectives on Psychological Science*, vol. 11, no. 3, pp. 333–50.

13   Collins, D, MacNamara, A, & McCarthy, N 2016, 'Super champions, champions, and almosts: important differences and commonalities on the rocky road', *Frontiers in Psychology*, vol. 6.

14   Syed, M 2011, *Bounce: the myth of talent and the power of practice*, Fourth Estate, London, UK, p. 8.

15   Yustres, I, Martin, R, Fernández, L, & González-Ravé, J 2017, 'Swimming championship finalist positions on success in international swimming competitions', *PloS One*, vol. 12, no. 11.

16   Mostaert, M, Vansteenkiste, P, Pion, J, Deconinck, F, & Lenoir, M 2021, 'The importance of performance in youth competitions as an indicator of future success in cycling', *European Journal of Sport Science*, pp. 1–10.

17   Forrester, N 2018, 'The secret formula for becoming an elite athlete', *The Conversation*, 13 August, viewed 27 October 2021, www.theconversation.com

18 Forrester, N 2013, 'Good to great in elite athletes: towards an understanding of why some athletes make the leap and others do not', PhD thesis, viewed 27 October 2021, Michigan State University Electronic Theses and Dissertations, https://d.lib.msu.edu.

19 Pearson, S 2021, Sally Pearson's LinkedIn profile page, viewed 10 November 2021.

20 Cerutty, P 1960, *Athletics: how to become a champion*, CreateSpace Independent Publishing Platform, CA, p. 99.

21 Klarica, A 1992, 'Finding the edge', *Australian Runner*, vol. 12, no. 2, p. 49.

Step 1: Harness your motivation

1 Cerutty, P 1960, *Athletics: how to become a champion*, CreateSpace Independent Publishing Platform, CA, p. 100.

2 Mallett, C, & Hanrahan, S 2004, 'Elite athletes: why does the "fire" burn so brightly?', *Psychology of Sport and Exercise*, vol. 5, no. 2, pp. 183–200.

3 Lenton, B, 1998, *Running Writings, interview with Herb Elliott*, no. 16, November, 1998.

4 Trengove, A, & Elliot, H 1961, *The golden mile: the Herb Elliott story as told to Alan Trengove*, Cassell, London, UK, pp. 172, 178.

5 Ryan, R, & Deci, E 2000. 'Self-determination theory and the facilitation of intrinsic motivation, social development, and well-being', *American Psychologist*, vol. 55, no. 1, pp. 68–78.

6 Podlog, L, Gustafsson, H, Skoog, T, Gao, Z, Westin, M, Werner, S, & Alricsson, M 2015, 'Need satisfaction, motivation, and engagement among high-performance youth athletes: a multiple mediation analysis', *International Journal of Sport and Exercise Psychology*, vol. 13, no. 4, pp. 415–33.

7   Elliott, H (introduction) 2000, *Winning attitudes: sports wisdom for achievement in life*, Hardie Grant Books, Melbourne, VIC.

8   Locke, E, & Latham, G 1985, 'The application of goal setting to sports', *Journal of Sport Psychology*, vol. 7, no. 3, pp. 205–22.

9   Colvin, G 2008, *Talent is overrated: what really separates world-class performers from everybody else*, Portfolio, New York.

10 Rosenthal, R, & Jacobson, L 1968, *Pygmalion in the classroom: teacher expectation and pupils' intellectual development*, Holt, Rinehart and Winston, New York, NY, p. 20.

11 Skinner, E, & Pitzer, J 2012, 'Developmental dynamics of student engagement, coping, and everyday resilience', in Christenson, S, Reschly, A, & Wylie, C (eds), *Handbook of Research on Student Engagement*, Springer US, Boston, MA.

12 Nicholls, A, Morley, D, & Perry, J 2015, 'The model of motivational dynamics in sport: resistance to peer influence, behavioral engagement and disaffection, dispositional coping, and resilience', *Frontiers in Psychology*, vol. 6.

13 Duda, J 2004. 'Goal setting and achievement motivation in sport', *Encyclopedia of Applied Psychology*, vol. 2, pp. 109–19.

14 Reilly, T, Williams, A, Nevill, A, & Franks, A 2000, 'A multidisciplinary approach to talent identification in soccer', *Journal of Sports Sciences*, vol. 18, no. 9, pp. 695–702.

15 Lochbaum, M, Zazo, R, Kazak Çetinkalp, Z, Wright, T, Graham, K-A, & Konttinen, N 2016, 'A meta-analytic review of achievement goal orientation correlates in competitive sport', *Kinesiology*, vol. 48, no. 2, pp. 159–73.

Step 2: Boost your resilience

1   *All for one* 2017, documentary film, Madman Production Company, Melbourne, VIC. Produced by Nick Batzias, Dan Jones and Virginia Whitwell; directed by Marcus Cobbledick.

2   Fletcher, D, & Sarkar, M 2013, 'Psychological resilience: a review and critique of definitions, concepts, and theory', *European Psychologist*, vol. 18, no. 1, pp. 12–23.

3   Fletcher, D, & Sarkar, M 2012, 'A grounded theory of psychological resilience in Olympic champions', *Psychology of Sport and Exercise*, vol. 13, no. 5, pp. 669–78.

4   Savage, J, Collins, D, & Cruickshank, A 2017, 'Exploring traumas in the development of talent: what are they, what do they do, and what do they require?', *Journal of Applied Sport Psychology*, vol. 29, no. 1, pp. 101–17.

5   Collins, D, MacNamara, Á, & McCarthy, N 2016, 'Super champions, champions, and almosts: important differences and commonalities on the rocky road', *Frontiers in Psychology*, vol. 6.

6   Nadal, F & Carlin, J 2012, *Rafa: my story*, Sphere, London, UK.

7   Seligman, M, Maier, S, & Geer, J 1968, 'Alleviation of learned helplessness in the dog', *Journal of Abnormal Psychology*, vol. 73, no. 3, pp. 256–62.

8   Seligman, M 1991, *Learned optimism*, Knopf, New York, NY.

9   Seligman, M, Nolen-Hoeksema, S, Thornton, N, & Thornton, K 1990, 'Explanatory style as a mechanism of disappointing athletic performance', *Psychological Science*, vol. 1, no. 2, pp. 143–6.

10 Schinke, R, & Jerome, W 2002. 'Understanding and refining the resilience of elite athletes: an intervention strategy', *Athletic Insight: The Online Journal of Sport Psychology*, vol. 4, no. 3.

11 Morgan P, Fletcher, D, & Sarkar M 2013, 'Defining and characterizing team resilience in elite sport', *Psychology of Sport and Exercise*, vol. 14, no. 4, pp. 549–59.

12 Gould, D, Dieffenbach, K, & Moffett, A 2002, 'Psychological characteristics and their development in Olympic champions', *Journal of Applied Sport Psychology*, vol. 14, no. 3, pp. 172–204, p. 190.

13 Hill, A, Mallinson-Howard, S, & Jowett, G 2018, 'Multidimensional perfectionism in sport: a meta-analytical review', *Sport, Exercise and Performance Psychology*, vol. 7, no. 3, pp. 235–70.

Step 3: Sharpen your focus

1 Van Raalte, J, Vincent, A, & Brewer, B 2016, 'Self-talk: review and sport-specific model', *Psychology of Sport and Exercise*, vol. 22, pp. 139–48.

2 Hardy, J 2006, 'Speaking clearly: a critical review of the self-talk literature', *Psychology of Sport and Exercise*, vol. 7, no. 1, pp. 81–97.

3 Hatzigeorgiadis, A, Galanis, E, Zourbanos, N, & Theodorakis, Y 2014, 'Self-talk and competitive sport performance', *Journal of Applied Sport Psychology*, vol. 26, no. 1, pp. 82–95.

4 Elliot, H (introduction) 2000, *Winning attitudes: sports wisdom for achievement in life*, Hardie Grant Books, Melbourne, VIC.

5 Albright, A 2021, *Update: if self-talk works for a grand slam champion, why not you?*, viewed 11 November 2021, andyalbright.com

6 Highlights Kingdom 2021, *'I told myself I can do it...'*, Novak Djokovic full press conference, Roland Garros 2021 [online video], YouTube, 14 June 2021, viewed 11 November 2021, youtube.com

7 Alcott, D 2018, *Able: gold medals, grand slams and smashing glass ceilings*, HarperCollins, Sydney, NSW, p. 178.

8   Jackson, R, & Baker, J 2001, 'Routines, rituals, and rugby: case study of a world class goal kicker', *The Sport Psychologist*, vol. 15, no. 1, pp. 48–65.

9   *Five Australian women across javelin, 1500m finals vie for medals at Tokyo Olympics*, 2021, televison program, AAP/7NEWS, 6 August 2021.

10 Flintoff-King, D 1992, 'The price of gold', *Australian Runner*, vol. 12, no. 2, pp. 50–1.

11 Masters, K, & Ogles, B 1998, 'Associative and dissociative cognitive strategies in exercise and running: 20 years later, what do we know?', *The Sport Psychologist*, vol. 12, no. 3, pp. 253–70.

12 Nideffer, R 1979, *The inner athlete: mind plus muscle for winning*, Ty Crowell Co, New York, NY.

13 Csikszentmihalyi, M 1992, *Flow: the psychology of happiness*, Rider Books, London, UK.

14 Swann, C 2016, 'Flow in sport', in Harmat, L, Orsted, F, Andersen, Ullen, F, Wright, J, & Sadlo, G (eds), *Flow experience: empirical research and applications*, Springer International Publishing, Switzerland, pp. 51–64.

15 Anderson, R, Hanrahan, S, & Mallett, C 2014, 'Investigating the optimal psychological state for peak performance in Australian elite athletes', *Journal of Applied Sport Psychology*, vol. 26, no. 3, pp. 318–33.

16 Alcott, D 2018, *Able: gold medals, grand slams and smashing glass ceilings*, HarperCollins, Sydney, NSW, p. 178.

17 Cricket views 2017, don bradman interview [online video], YouTube, 10 May 2017, viewed 11 November 2021, youtube .com

18 Furley, P, & Schweizer, G 2019, 'Body language in sport',
    in Tenenbaum, G, & Eklund, R (eds), *Handbook of sport
    psychology*, Wiley, Hoboken, NJ, pp. 1201–19.

19 Cohn, P 1990, 'Preperformance routines in sport: theoretical
    support and practical applications', *The Sport Psychologist*,
    vol. 4, no. 3, pp. 301–12.

Step 4: Champion your leadership

1   Leo, F, García-Calvo, T, González-Ponce, I, Pulido, J, & Fransen, K
    2019, 'How many leaders does it take to lead a sports team? The
    relationship between the number of leaders and the effectiveness
    of professional sports teams', *PloS One*, vol. 14, no. 6, p. 22.

2   Loughead, T, Hardy, J, & Eys, M 2006, 'The nature of athlete
    leadership', *Journal of Sport Behavior*, vol. 29, no. 2, pp. 142–58.

3   Crozier, A, Loughead, T, & Munroe-Chandler, K 2013,
    'Examining the benefits of athlete leaders in sport', *Journal of
    Sport Behavior*, vol. 36, no. 4, pp. 346–64.

4   Walker, S 2017, *The captain class: the hidden force that
    creates the world's greatest teams*, Penguin Random House,
    New York, NY.

Step 5: Foster your culture

1   Martens, R 1987, *Coaches guide to sport psychology*, Human
    Kinetics Publishers, Champaign, IL.

2   Schein, E 2004, *Organizational culture and leadership*, 3rd ed.,
    Jossey-Bass, San Francisco, CA.

3   Fletcher, D, & Streeter, A 2016, 'A case study analysis of a
    high-performance environment in elite swimming', *Journal of
    Change Management*, vol. 16, no. 2, pp. 123–41.

4   Schroeder, P 2010, 'Changing team culture: the perspectives
    of ten successful head coaches', *Journal of Sport Behavior*, vol.
    33, no. 1, pp. 63–88.

5   Bandura, A 1978, 'The self system in reciprocal determinism', *American Psychologist*, April, 1978.

6   Donoso-Morales, D, Bloom, G, & Caron, J 2017, 'Creating and sustaining a culture of excellence: insights from accomplished university team-sport coaches', *Research Quarterly for Exercise and Sport*, vol. 88, no. 4, pp. 503–12.

7   Edmondson, A 1999, 'Psychological safety and learning behavior in work teams', *Administrative Science Quarterly*, vol. 44, no. 2, pp. 350–83.

8   Fleming, N, Robson, G, & Smith, R 2005, *Sports coaching and learning: using learning preferences to enhance performance*, Fleming, Robson & Smith, New Zealand.

9   Edmondson, A 2008, 'The competitive imperative of learning', *Harvard Business Review*, vol. 86.

10 Edmondson, A 2019, *The fearless organization: creating psychological safety in the workplace for learning, innovation and growth*, John Wiley & Sons, New Jersey.

11 Kopp, A, & Jekauc, D 2018, 'The influence of emotional intelligence on performance in competitive sports: a meta-analytical investigation', *Sports*, vol. 6, p. 175.

12 Goleman, D 1996, *'Emotional intelligence: why it can matter more than IQ*, Bloomsbury Publishing, London, UK.

13 Harvard Business Review 2011, *HBR's 10 must reads on leadership*, Harvard Business Review Press, MA.

14 Fransen, K, McEwan, D, & Sarkar, M 2020, 'The impact of identity leadership on team functioning and well-being in team sport: is psychological safety the missing link?', *Psychology of Sport and Exercise*, vol. 51, p. 25.

15 Gosai, J, Jowett, S, & Nascimento-Júnior, J 2021, 'When leadership, relationships and psychological safety promote flourishing in sport and life', *Sports Coaching Review*.

16 Duda, J, Chi, L, 1992, 'The relationship of perceived motivational climate to intrinsic motivation and beliefs about success in basketball', *Journal of Sport & Exercise Psychology*, vol. 14, pp. 375–92.

17 Pensgaard, A, Roberts, G, 2002, 'Elite athletes' experiences of the motivational climate: the coach matters', *Scandinavian Journal of Medicine and Science in Sports*, vol. 12, pp. 54–59.

18 Curran, T, Hill, Andrew P, Hall, H, & Jowett, G 2015, 'Relationships between the coach-created motivational climate and athlete engagement in youth sport', *Journal of Sport & Exercise Psychology*, vol. 37, no. 2, pp. 193–98.

19 Kerr, J 2013, *Legacy*, Little Brown Book Group, London, UK.

20 Hodge, K, Henry, G, & Smith, W 2014, 'A case study of excellence in elite sport: motivational climate in a world champion team', *The Sport Psychologist*, vol. 28, no. 1, pp. 60–74.

21 *Chasing Great* 2016, documentary film, Southern Light Films, Auckland, NZ. Produced by Cass Avery; directed by Justin Pemberton and Michelle Walshe.

Step 6: Protect your wellbeing

1 Preston, C, Kerr, G, & Stirling, A 2015, 'Elite athletes' experiences of athlete centered coaching', *Journal of Athlete Centered Coaching*, vol. 1, no. 1.

2 World Health Organization 2018, *Mental health: strengthening our response*, World Health Organization, viewed 13 November 2021, www.who.int

3 Lundqvist, C 2011, 'Well-being in competitive sports — the feel-good factor? A review of conceptual considerations of well-being', *International Review of Sport and Exercise Psychology*, vol. 4, no. 2, pp. 109–27.

4   Lundqvist, C, & Andersson, G 2021, 'Let's talk about mental health and mental disorders in elite sports: a narrative review of theoretical perspectives', *Frontiers in Psychology*, vol. 12, pp. 1–3.

5   Keyes, C, 2002, 'The mental health continuum: from languishing to flourishing in life', Journal of Health and Social Behaviour, vol. 43, no. 2, pp. 207–222.

6   Australian Institute of Health and Welfare 2018, *Australia's health 2018*, Australian Institute of Health and Welfare, Canberra, ACT.

7   Rice, S, Purcell, R, De Silva, S, Mawren, D, McGorry, P, & Parker, A 2016. 'The mental health of elite athletes: a narrative systematic review', *Sports Medicine*, vol. 46, no. 9, pp. 1333–53.

8   Georgakaki, S, & Karakasidou, E 2017, 'The effects of motivational self-talk on competitive anxiety and self-compassion: a brief training program among competitive swimmers', *Psychology*, vol. 8, no. 5, pp. 677–99.

9   Hui, B, Ng, J, Berzaghi, E, Cunningham-Amos, L, & Kogan, A, 2020, 'Rewards of kindness? A meta-analysis of the link between prosociality and well-being', *Psychological Bulletin*, vol. 146, no. 12, pp. 1084–116.

10 Biles, S 2021, *the outpouring of love & support I've received.../* Twitter, 29 July, viewed 11 November 2021.

11 Campbell, C 2021, 'Olympian and lifelong swimmer Cate Campbell on what it means to press "pause" ', *Vogue*, viewed 29 October 2021, www.vogue.com.au

12 Campbell, C 2021, *In July 2020 I was diagnosed with depression.../* Instagram, 8 October, viewed 11 November 2021.

13 Gulliver, A, Griffiths, K, & Christensen, H 2012, 'Barriers and facilitators to mental health help-seeking for young elite athletes: a qualitative study', *BioMed Central Psychiatry*. vol. 12, no. 1.

14 Walsh, NP, Halson, SL, Sargent, C, et al., 2017, 'Sleep and the athlete: narrative review and 2021 expert consensus recommendations', British Journal of Sports Medicine, vol. 55, pp. 356–368.

15 Edelman, S 2003, *Change your thinking: positive and practical ways to overcome stress, negative emotions and self-defeating behavior using CBT*, ABC Books, Sydney, NSW.

16 Josefsson, T, Ivarsson, A, Lindwall, M, Gustafsson, H, Stenling, A, Böröy, J, Mattsson, E, Carnebratt, J, Sevholt, S, & Falkevik, E, 2017, 'Mindfulness mechanisms in sports: mediating effects of rumination and emotion regulation on sport-specific coping', *Mindfulness*, vol. 8, no. 5, pp. 1354–63.

17 Hoffmann, M, & Loughead, T 2016, 'A comparison of well-peer mentored and non-peer mentored athletes' perceptions of satisfaction', *Journal of Sports Sciences*, vol. 34, no. 5, pp. 450–58.

18 Purcell, R, Gwyther, K, & Rice, S 2019, 'Mental health in elite athletes: increased awareness requires an early intervention framework to respond to athlete needs', *Sports Medicine — Open*, vol. 5, no. 1, pp. 1–8.

Step 7: Execute your performance

1 Trengove, A, & Elliot, H 1961, *The golden mile: the Herb Elliott story as told to Alan Trengove*, Cassell, London, UK, pp. 172, 174.

2 Weinberg, R, & Gould, D 2006. *Foundations of Sport and Exercise Psychology*, 4th edn, Human Kinetics, Champaign, IL.

References

3   Cervone, D, & Pervin, L 2010, *Personality: theory and research*, 11th edn, Wiley, New York, NY.

4   Allen, M, Laborde, S, 2014, 'The role of personality in sport and physical activity', *Current directions in psychological science*, vol. 23, no. 6, pp. 460–65.

5   Gould, D, Dieffenbach, K, & Moffett, A 2002, 'Psychological characteristics and their development in Olympic champions', *Journal of Applied Sport Psychology*, vol. 14, no. 3, pp. 172–204.

6   McCormick A, Meijen C, & Marcora, S 2015, 'Psychological determinants of whole-body endurance performance', *Sports Medicine*, vol. 45, no. 7, pp. 997–1015.

7   Kreiner-Phillips, K, & Orlick, T 1993, 'Winning after winning: the psychology of ongoing excellence', *The Sport Psychologist*, vol. 7, no. 1, pp. 31–48.

8   Elliott, H (introduction) 2000, *Winning attitudes: sports wisdom for achievement in life*, Hardie Grant Books, Melbourne, VIC, p. 135.

9   Hays, K, Maynard, I, Thomas, O, Bawden, M 2007, 'Sources and types of confidence identified in world class performers', *Journal of Applied Sport Psychology*, vol. 19, pp. 434–56.

10 Swann, C, Crust, L, Jackman, P, Vella, S, Allen, M, & Keegan, R 2017, 'Psychological states underlying excellent performance in sport: toward an integrated model of flow and clutch states', *Journal of Applied Sport Psychology*, vol. 29, no. 4, pp. 375–401.

11 Cordy, E 2018, *Cultivating curiosity: how to unearth your most valuable problem to inspire growth*, Agents of Spring, Melbourne, VIC, p. 96.

12 *Kipchoge: the last milestone* 2021, documentary film, Universal Pictures, Universal City, CA. Produced by Ross Plummer; directed by Jake Scott.

13 Griffiths, S 2011, 'Shelley Taylor-Smith: dangerous when wet', *Outdoor Swimmer*, 4 November.

14 Mellalieu, S, Hanton, S, & Jones, G 2003, 'Emotional labeling and competitive anxiety in preparation and competition', *The Sport Psychologist*, vol. 17, no. 2, pp. 157–74.

15 Mesagno, C, Geukes, K, & Larkin, P 2015, 'Choking under pressure: a review of current debates, literature, and interventions', in Mellalieu, S, & Hanton, S (eds), *Contemporary advances in sport psychology: a review*, Routledge, UK, pp. 148–74.

16 Grove, J, & Heard, N 1997, 'Optimism and sport confidence as correlates of slump-related coping among athletes', *The Sport Psychologist*, vol. 11, no. 4, pp. 400–10.

17 Shearman, E, Czech, D, Burdette, T, McDaniel, T, Joyner, B, & Zwald, D 2011, 'A comparison of optimism levels and life stress levels among NCAA Division I athletes and non-athletes', *Journal of Issues in Intercollegiate Athletics*, vol. 4, pp. 190–206.

INDEX